"*The Anthropocene: Key Issues for the Humanities* provides an excellent survey of the debates surrounding the new geological 'Age of Humans' from the perspective of the humanities. It offers impressively precise and pointed summaries of essential arguments from philosophy, anthropology, history, politics, and the arts regarding human transformations of the global environment. Even the most complex ideas are presented in a clear and engaging fashion. A must-read for all readers with an interest in environmental issues!"

—*Ursula K. Heise, Marcia H. Howard Chair in Literary Studies at the Department of English and the Institute of Environment and Sustainability at UCLA, USA*

"Sometimes, timing is everything. Horn and Bergthaller intervene at an important moment in the debates about the Anthropocene. The idea that we are entering a new epoch of Earth time in which human beings are playing a key role is one that needs to be to be shaped and contested by the widest possible set of interlocutors. In order for that to happen, people beyond the 'core set' of those from various disciplines who have been debating the Anthropocene for the last two decades need to be given the tools to join this urgent collective task. This book, readable and clear without ducking the difficult questions, will help make that possible.

The authors are both accomplished and perceptive thinkers, but like the most generous of hosts they do not make themselves the centre of attention – instead, that place goes to their guests, the readers. Horn and Bergthaller provide a very balanced introduction to the terrain; but then, rather than offering yet another magical solution to all the political and epistemological tensions in the Anthropocene concept, and thereby simply adding to the cacophony of interpretations, they then give us a 'cartography of faultlines', gently guiding us through the task of coming to our own sense-making of this turbulent time in both Earth processes and human thought."

— *Bronislaw Szerszynski, Reader in Sociology, Lancaster University, UK*

"Over the past decade, the Anthropocene has become the paradigmatic object of inquiry in the emergent environmental humanities, but nowhere has it been explored so comprehensively or incisively as Horn and Bergthaller do here. 'Anthropocene' is also a vigorously contested term, for which they examine both predecessors and competitors, whilst making a persuasive case for its continued deployment in a nuanced manner that integrates pertinent critiques. As well as revisiting earlier theoretical paradigms, such as

Michel Foucault's notion of 'biopolitics', through the lens of the Anthropocene, they also introduce Anglophone readers to less well-known perspectives from German environmental theory, such as Rolf Peter Sieferle's eco-historical concept of the socio-metabolic regime. Underpinned by a careful consideration of the scientific research underlying the proposal that the planet has entered a new geological era marked by the largely ecologically disastrous impacts of globalising industrial society, Horn's and Bergthaller's brilliant analysis of the implications of this historically unprecedented, and extremely perilous, situation extends to questions of epistemology, religion, ethics, politics, aesthetics and poetics. Attending also to how the postulate of the Anthropocene is being taking up and reinterpreted in non-Western, especially Asian, contexts, this book has a valuably transnational as well as a profoundly transdisciplinary reach. As such, it is itself a fine exemplar of the project of the environmental humanities."

— Kate Rigby, Professor of Environmental Humanities, Bath Spa University, UK and Adjunct Professor of Literary Studies, Monash University, Australia

"The start of the Anthropocene marks a dangerous new phase in the life of the planet with profound and unsettling consequences to the human enterprise. For anyone in search of a lucid guide to these problems, Horn and Bergthaller have written an elegant and accessible survey, which introduces us to the intricacies of earth system science without ever losing sight of social and historical perspectives. In eleven succinct chapters, Horn and Bergthaller explore the key contributions of the Anthropocene framework to the humanities, including questions of agency, limits, justice, energy and scale. This is that rare kind of introductory text which will be of value to both newcomers and advanced students."

— Fredrik Albritton Jonsson, Associate Professor of British History, Conceptual and Historical Studies of Science, The University of Chicago, USA

"The Anthropocene – a proposed name for a new and human-dominated geological epoch - is both a scientific and a popular term, mired in debates and controversies that have deeply influenced humanist thought of our times. Readers will find in Horn and Bergthaller's book not only a lucid guide to these debates but also an intelligent and thoughtful framework through which to view them. A very welcome addition to the burgeoning literature in the humanities on the Anthropocene."

— Dipesh Chakrabarty, Lawrence A. Kimpton Distinguished Service Professor of History, South Asian Languages and Civilizations, The University of Chicago, USA

The Anthropocene

The Anthropocene is a concept which challenges the foundations of humanities scholarship as it is traditionally understood. It calls not only for closer engagement with the natural sciences but also for a synthetic approach bringing together insights from the various subdisciplines in the humanities and social sciences which have addressed themselves to ecological questions in the past. This book is an introduction to, and structured survey of, the attempts that have been made to take the measure of the Anthropocene, and explores some of the paradigmatic problems which it raises.

The difficulties of an introduction to the Anthropocene lie not only in the disciplinary breadth of the subject, but also in the rapid pace at which the surrounding debates have been, and still are, unfolding. This introduction proposes a conceptual map which, however provisionally, charts these ongoing discussions across a variety of scientific and humanistic disciplines.

This book will be essential reading for students and researchers in the environmental humanities, particularly in literary and cultural studies, history, philosophy, and environmental studies.

Eva Horn is a Professor at the Institute for German Studies at the University of Vienna, Austria.

Hannes Bergthaller is a Professor at the Department of Foreign Languages and Literatures at National Chung-Hsing University, Taichung, Taiwan.

Key Issues in Environment and Sustainability

This series provides comprehensive, original and accessible texts on the core topics in environment and sustainability. The texts take an interdisciplinary and international approach to the key issues in this field.

Sustainable Business: Key Issues
Helen Kopnina and John Blewitt

Sustainability: Key Issues
Helen Kopnina and Eleanor Shoreman-Ouimet

Ecomedia: Key Issues
Edited by Stephen Rust, Salma Monani and Sean Cubitt

Ecosystem Services: Key Issues
Mark Everard

Sustainability Science: Key Issues
Edited by Ariane König and Jerome Ravetz

Sustainable Business: Key Issues (2nd Ed)
Helen Kopnina and John Blewitt

Sustainable Consumption: Key Issues
Lucie Middlemiss

Human Rights and the Environment: Key Issues
Sumudu Atapattu and Andrea Schaper

The Anthropocene: Key Issues for the Humanities
Eva Horn and Hannes Bergthaller

The Anthropocene

Key Issues for the Humanities

Eva Horn and Hannes Bergthaller

Routledge
Taylor & Francis Group
LONDON AND NEW YORK

earthscan
from Routledge

First published 2020
by Routledge
2 Park Square, Milton Park, Abingdon, Oxon OX14 4RN

and by Routledge
52 Vanderbilt Avenue, New York, NY 10017

Routledge is an imprint of the Taylor & Francis Group, an informa business

© 2020 Eva Horn and Hannes Bergthaller

British Library Cataloguing in Publication Data
A catalogue record for this book is available from the British Library

Library of Congress Cataloging-in-Publication Data
Names: Horn, Eva, author. | Bergthaller, Hannes, author. | Routledge (Firm)
Title: The Anthropocene : key issues for the humanities / Eva Horn and Hannes Bergthaller.
Other titles: Key issues for the humanities | Key issues in environment and sustainability.
Description: First Edition. | New York : Routledge, 2020. |
Series: Key issues in environment and sustainability | Includes bibliographical references and index.
Identifiers: LCCN 2019029877 (print) | ISBN 9781138342460 (Hardback) | ISBN 9781138342477 (Paperback) | ISBN 9780429439735 (eBook)
Subjects: LCSH: Human ecology and the humanities. | Human ecology. | Nature (Aesthetics) | Environment (Aesthetics) | Biopolitics. | Sustainability.
Classification: LCC GF22 .H67 2020 (print) | LCC GF22 (ebook) | DDC 304.2--dc23
LC record available at https://lccn.loc.gov/2019029877
LC ebook record available at https://lccn.loc.gov/2019029878

ISBN: 978-1-138-34246-0 (hbk)
ISBN: 978-1-138-34247-7 (pbk)
ISBN: 978-0-429-43973-5 (ebk)

Typeset in Goudy
by Taylor & Francis Books

Contents

Figures

Acknowledgements

Every scholarly book is a collective endeavor. This is especially true of a volume such as this, in which we have strayed deep into unfamiliar territory far removed from our disciplinary home turf. That we didn't get lost, and returned sound in mind and body, we owe to the intellectual generosity and good fellowship of many more friends and colleagues than we can possibly acknowledge here. We are grateful to our home institutions, the University of Vienna and National Chung-Hsing University (NCHU), as well as to the German Research Association (DFG), The Rachel Carson Center Munich, the Vienna Anthropocene Network, Taiwan's Ministry of Science and Technology, the Research Center for the Humanities and Social Sciences, and the Innovation and Development Center of Sustainable Agriculture (which is supported by the Featured Areas Research Center Program within the framework of the Higher Education Sprout Project by Taiwan's Ministry of Education). Their funding enabled us to meet several times during the writing process, to organize a string of workshops and small conferences, as well as to present our work at other academic gatherings. A good share of the ideas which found their way into this book were hatched on these occasions, and we want to express our gratitude to the many people who made these events as fruitful as they have been for us, among them: Dipesh Chakrabarty, Chia-ju Chang, Shu-ching Chen, Huei-chu Chu, Jon Christensen, Gabriele Dürbeck, Catrin Gersdorf, Axel Goodbody, Hanna Hamel, Ursula Heise, Jean-Yves Heurtebise, Adeline Johns-Putra, Frederik Albritton Jonsson, Chi-she Li, Philip Lorenz, Bernhard Malkmus, Joe Masco, Franz Mauelshagen, Solvejg Nitzke, John Parham, Jürgen Renn, Kate Rigby, Chitra Sankaran, Adam Shih, Julia Adeney Thomas, Michael Wagreich, Susanne Weigelin-Schwiedrzik, and Verena Winiwarter. Special thanks are due to those of our colleagues and friends who were more closely involved with the manuscript, perceptively commenting on early drafts, helping us proof-read it in its more advanced stages, and all the other things it takes to usher a book into print: Luisa Drews, Ron S. Judy, Benjamin Robinson, Anastassiya Schacht, and Thomas C. Wall. Finally, there are those who are closest to us. They patiently endured our preoccupation with an often less than cheery subject and kept reminding us that the planetary scale is not the only one that matters. Thank you, Yufang Hsu and Meri Disoski.

1   Introduction

February 2000, Cuernavaca, Mexico. By the afternoon session of the annual meeting of the International Geosphere-Biosphere Programme, the vice-chairman has had it. All day long, the atmospheric chemist Paul Crutzen, who won a Nobel Prize in 1995 for his work on the ozone layer, has been listening to his colleagues lecturing on the profound changes that the Earth is currently undergoing. They keep referring to the present as the Holocene. Crutzen finally interrupts them: 'Stop using the word Holocene. We're not in the Holocene anymore. We're in the ... the ... the Anthropocene!' His outbreak is met with puzzled silence. But during the following coffee break, the scientists talk of nothing else. Shortly afterwards, Crutzen publishes a brief, programmatic paper with Eugene Stoermer, a freshwater biologist who has already been using the term informally for some time. Two years later, Crutzen publishes another much-quoted article in *Nature*. The two pieces not only describe the end of the Holocene; they also identify humans as a 'geological force' whose impact can be observed on a planetary scale (Crutzen and Stoermer 2000, Crutzen 2002).

Crutzen's intervention came at the right time and in the right place. The International Geosphere-Biosphere Programme (IGBP) had been established in 1987 to study the human impact on the biological, chemical and geophysical processes of the Earth system. It was the most important international forum for the development of the new and rapidly developing field of Earth system science, focused on what was then innocently called 'global change'. If the purpose of the program was to establish a whole new way of looking at the Earth, this had been achieved by the time it came to an end in 2015. But the discussion which started during that coffee break in 2000 is still going on, and drawing ever wider circles.

The propagation of the term 'Anthropocene' is not only the result of an interruption. It is *itself* an interruption. The concept encapsulates an ecological state of affairs which, in many of its fundamental aspects such as climate change, had been widely recognized for decades, but had been drowned out in the cacophony of bad news. It gives a name to the insight that humans are profoundly changing the ecology of the planet, and that they are doing so on a global scale. More than just a *crisis* which may come to an end at some point in the future, the Anthropocene—the 'new' (καινός) brought about by the 'human' (ἄνθρωπος)—designates an ecological *threshold.* It encompasses a vast number of different factors and locations, ranging from global climate change to disruptions in oceanic and atmospheric currents, the disturbance of the water cycle and of other important chemical cycles (e.g. of phosphorus and nitrogen), soil degradation, the rapid loss of biological diversity, pollution with toxic and non-degradable substances, all accompanying a continuous growth in the number of humans and their domesticates. Human activity moves more earth, sand, and stone worldwide than all natural processes together (Wilkinson 2005). Plastic has spread throughout the world, not just in the form of towering garbage dumps and plastic waste in the seas and rivers, but also in the form of microplastics which suffuse soil, water, and the entire food chain (Waters *et al.* 2016, Orb Media 2017). Since the Industrial Revolution, the carbon dioxide content of the atmosphere has increased by 44%, causing not only climate change but also the acidification of the oceans, profoundly transforming the living conditions of all marine organisms (Hönisch *et al.* 2012). Populations of wild fish, birds, reptiles, and mammals have shrunk by an average of 58% over the last 40 years (WWF 2016), and there is considerable evidence that the number of insects has also plummeted (Hoff 2018). Wildlife today accounts for only 3% of the biomass of terrestrial vertebrates, the rest being composed of humans (30%) and livestock (67%) (Smil 2012).

It has become more and more obvious that the Earth is entering a 'no-analogue state' (Moore *et al.* 2001)—a state for which there is no precedent in geological history. Many of the signs that we are crossing a geological threshold, however, are far from being recent discoveries. Since the 1960s, there have been frequent warnings that modern industrial societies were headed for ecological catastrophe. The public at large has known about climate change for more than 30 years. The ecological movement's mantra has long been that 'we cannot go on like this', but even if environmental politics has more or less successfully tackled some of the symptoms of the crisis, the last few decades have shown all too clearly that things *could* and *did* go on as before. Our present is the future that the environmental movement has been warning us against. And today there is no going back.

This is why the Anthropocene is more than just a crisis—it is a radical break: a break from the unusually stable ecological conditions that characterized the Holocene. The Holocene provided the environmental conditions for everything we have come to call human civilization: sedentariness, agriculture, cities, trade, complex social institutions, tools and machines, as well as all of the media that are used to store and disseminate human knowledge. The Holocene, in other words, was the well-tempered cradle of civilization. And this inevitably leads to the question: What will a departure from these conditions mean for human civilization—for human culture, social organization, and technology, and, in a more fundamental sense, for humankind's relation to the world? The Anthropocene heralds a future for humanity, the contours of which we are only just beginning to apprehend.

Ironically, although the Anthropocene concept was launched in the context of Earth systems science and is epistemically based on it (see Ch. 2: Definitions), the first discipline to take it on in systematic fashion was geology—a discipline that deals with the deep past of the Earth's history. If the Anthropocene is to be defined as a new geochronological epoch which follows the end of the Holocene, stratigraphic markers must be found to demonstrate the impact of human activity in a range of locations across the planet. In order to investigate these markers, the Anthropocene Working Group (AWG) was founded in 2009, under the direction of the renowned British geologist Jan Zalasiewicz. As a research group within the Subcommission of Quaternary Stratigraphy, the AWG's main goal is to examine the evidence for formalizing the Anthropocene as a geochronological epoch. In August 2016, it presented its recommendation in favor of a formalization of the Anthropocene to the International Commission on Stratigraphy (ICS). This was unique in the history of the discipline: never was an epochal threshold set *in the present*, rather than with a delay of at least a few millennia. Predictably, the AWG's recommendation (which is only a first step along the way to formal acceptance) was hotly debated among scientists in the field. Some geologists went so far as to argue that by formalizing the Anthropocene, geology would be giving up on its scientific standards and surrendering to politics or, worse yet, pop culture (Autin and Holbrook 2012, Finney and Edwards 2016).

Another unique characteristic of the AWG is its interdisciplinarity. The group includes not only geoscientists (in particular stratigraphers and sedimentologists), but also atmospheric chemists, oceanographers, biologists, archaeologists, historians of science, environmental geographers, environmental historians and lawyers. Clearly, it is not only the geochronological formalization of the Anthropocene that calls for an approach which transcends traditional geological practice; the concept as such demands a new form of transdisciplinary exchange. Even if the AWG's ongoing research is of paramount importance for a deeper understanding of the Anthropocene, its defining factors and starting dates, the relevance of the concept does not hinge solely or even primarily on whether it is adopted into official geological nomenclature. In the past ten years, the Anthropocene has become much more than just a specialized topic for scientists. The questions the term raises will not go away even if the geologists ultimately decide against its formalization. It has become a shorthand for some of the most pressing and most wickedly complex issues of our time.

That is why the term—despite its unwieldiness—rapidly entered popular usage. In 2011, *The Economist* dedicated its title page to the topic with the headline: 'Welcome to the Anthropocene.' *National Geographic* and *Nature* soon followed suit. *The Economist*'s editorial began: 'Humans have changed the way the world works. Now they have to change the way they think about it, too' (*The Economist*, 26 May 2011). This neatly encapsulates the challenge presented by the Anthropocene: it is about taking stock of the present and redefining our relationship to the world. Since the 2010s, a rising tide of popular and scholarly publications on the subject has swept across many different fields, encompassing the natural sciences, the social sciences and the humanities.

The humanities in particular have enthusiastically embraced the Anthropocene, along with the arts, film, and literature. The term not only attracts artists and curators, but also a growing lay audience. Exhibitions revolving around the concept have drawn huge crowds: the two-year *Anthropocene Project* at Haus der Kulturen der Welt in Berlin, the *Anthropocene* exhibition at Deutsches Museum in Munich 2014–16, Bruno Latour's curated 'thought exhibition' *Reset Modernity!* 2016 in Karlsruhe, *The Anthropocene Project* conference at Tate Modern, London, in 2015, Ed Burtynsky's *Anthropocene* exhibitions in Toronto and Ottawa, the *Museum of the Anthropocene* project in Indianapolis—to name just a few. Universities have started to include the topic in the curricula of diverse academic disciplines—not just in history and literary studies, but also in geography, law, architecture, and economics. They are also forming their own networks and research groups on the Anthropocene. While in the art world the term Anthropocene has become a buzzword signaling topicality and political relevance (see Ch. 7: Aesthetics), in academia it has not only opened up new perspectives within individual disciplines, but has been received as a call for a new, transdisciplinary order of knowledge. Tellingly, it was financial support from a cultural institution, the Haus der Kulturen der Welt in Berlin, as well as from the Max-Planck-Institut in Mainz, which provided the initial funding for the stratigraphic work of the AWG.

What the arts, academia and politics share in common in their engagement with the Anthropocene is the awareness of 'living on a damaged planet' (Tsing *et al.* 2017). This entails a consciousness of the present as the moment of crossing a boundary or facing a common danger. The historian Dipesh Chakrabarty, one of the first scholars to open up the Anthropocene debate for the humanities (Chakrabarty 2009), set out to capture the specificity of this consciousness in his 2015 Tanner Lectures. Drawing on the term 'epochal consciousness' coined by the German philosopher Karl Jaspers, Chakrabarty sought to develop 'a shared perspectival position that can inform—but not determine—competitive and conflicted actions by humans when faced with the unequal and uneven perils of dangerous climate change' (Chakrabarty 2015, p. 143). An epochal consciousness for the Anthropocene is the consciousness of a threat common to all humans, or, more precisely, a communality that derives from a global threat affecting all humankind. By definition, it precedes all cultural, political, and economic differences. Such an epochal consciousness does not offer solutions but rather tries to articulate their preconditions. It indicates a shared destiny, an ethical challenge which defines our situation and sets the stage for political action: 'it is what sustains our horizon of action' (ibid., p. 146).

An essential part of this epochal consciousness is the realization that many of the categories used to grasp the relationship between humans and nature have become obsolete. 'Sustainability' or 'environmental conservation' have long been seen as political issues among many other, seemingly more pressing, concerns, such as social welfare and economic or political stability. The Anthropocene requires us to rethink these priorities, along with the terminology we use in order to articulate them. A 'politics of nature' (as Bruno Latour puts it) is not just one political issue among others but deals with the very foundations on which any political community can exist. What is nature when it is fundamentally transformed by human impact? What is culture when it can no longer be understood as a human-made and locally circumscribed environment but has to be seen instead as something that interferes with the forces of nature at a planetary scale? What is humankind, if it is understood as a dominant species whose behavior profoundly affects the Earth system? What is human consciousness if it has endowed humans with a power that eludes conscious control? And what is politics if it must deal with these problems not on a national but on a global level? This book maps out some of the most important questions and ongoing debates revolving around the Anthropocene. But mapping an object that is changing so rapidly is like surveying an avalanche in full fall. What we offer, therefore, can be little more than a snapshot—albeit one that highlights structural elements and thus provides a guide for readers trying to find their way into Anthropocene thought.

In contrast to many recent books authored by members of the AWG (Zalasiewicz 2008, 2019, Ellis 2018, Lewis and Maslin 2018), this book does not come from a natural science perspective but addresses the Anthropocene from the point of view of the humanities. We nonetheless start from the assumption that the insights of the natural sciences form an indispensable basis for an adequate understanding of the Anthropocene. Quite a few contributions from the humanities tend to either ignore the scientific debates or even reject the sciences as inherently technocratic and hegemonic. Yet without some models and concepts from the sciences, neither 'nature', nor 'history', nor the human impact on the planet can be adequately grasped. Nature, for instance, can today no longer be conceived of as 'wilderness' or as being in a 'natural balance'; it must be understood as a *self-regulating* system in a *dynamic* (and therefore fragile and ever-changing) equilibrium, as first outlined in Lovelock and Margulis's Gaia Hypothesis and further elaborated by Earth system science. Likewise, a historical approach to the Anthropocene as an epochal threshold needs to take into account geostratigraphic data and debates about the starting date of the epoch which, in turn, draw heavily on environmental and colonial history (see Ch. 2: Definitions). Without models from Earth system science such as 'planetary boundaries' (Rockström 2009), or a basic understanding of scale problems in biology, ecology, and physics, some of the essential difficulties of thinking the Anthropocene must remain incomprehensible.

The Anthropocene therefore also challenges the traditional separation between the 'sciences' and 'humanities', famously encapsulated in the catch-phrase of 'the two cultures' (Snow 1959). It calls for a new cooperation between academic fields, be it in the form of a mutual exchange of data, concepts and hypotheses, or in the form of complementary approaches to shared problems. As Jürgen Renn has argued, we need a new 'knowledge economy' which would be able to integrate heterogeneous forms of knowledge beyond disciplinary boundaries (Renn 2018). In this regard, the Anthropocene Working Group, although dominated by geologists, provides a model with its inclusion of historical and legal perspectives, and by being explicitly open to cooperation with the humanities. (As we write this, for example, the geologist Jan Zalasiewicz is co-authoring a book with the historian and Japanologist Julia Adeney Thomas.)

In the humanities, a similar move towards more interdisciplinary perspectives is underway under the banner of the 'environmental humanities'. The ascendancy of the term runs almost exactly parallel to that of the Anthropocene: the publication of a manifesto on the 'ecological humanities' by a group of Australian researchers in 2001 marks a point of origin, but only over the last decade has the concept begun to spread at a rapidly accelerating pace, such that today many of the most prestigious universities around the world host research programs which bring together scholars from history, literature, philosophy, art history, anthropology and geography who study the cultural dimensions of ecological change (Bergthaller *et al.* 2014). Underlying these efforts is the fundamental insight that in order to grapple with the ecological effects of human behavior, one must also understand the systems of belief and the social structures which condition that behavior, and which play a decisive role in how societies react—or fail to react—to developments in the sciences. Much more than traditional forms of humanities scholarship, the environmental humanities are also oriented towards a general public, because they recognize that the 'global environmental crisis demands new ways of thinking and new communities that produce environmental solutions as a form of civic knowledge' (Emmett and Nye 2017, p. 7).

So the Anthropocene is forcing both the natural sciences and the humanities out of their comfort zones. While the natural sciences traditionally define themselves by an apolitical production of 'matters of fact', those in the arts and humanities see their task as addressing 'matters of concern'. While scientists tend to be blind to the political impact of their findings, the humanities tend to view their objects as mere 'discourse' or contingent 'social constructions', thereby entrenching themselves in cultural relativism, as Bruno Latour has famously pointed out (Latour 2004). Today, both attitudes have become untenable. The sciences have to accept and embrace the fact that their findings—as in the case of climate science—can become eminently contentious, and thus political. The humanities, meanwhile, need to acknowledge the ecological and material foundations of cultures, societies and cultural artifacts. They need to see their work within the larger framework of the Earth's history, i.e. the long-term history of humankind and its cultures, its energy sources and forms of biological coexistence. The Anthropocene thus opens up new research possibilities both for the sciences and for the humanities by compelling the 'two cultures' to talk to each other.

This book focuses on the epistemological challenges of the Anthropocene for the humanities. While we aim to provide basic orientation for readers new to the debate in our early chapters, in the later chapters we expound some of the more complicated issues at work in thinking about the Anthropocene. As a guiding structure for this endeavor, we borrow three concepts from geology: *stratigraphy*, the investigation of historical sediments; *metamorphism*, the transformation of older rocks under the pressure of tectonic forces; and *fault lines*, the fractures and discontinuities produced by movement of tectonic plates. The first part, *Stratigraphies*, deals with the historical layers of the concept. Chapter 2: Definitions not only introduces the fundamental models that have been crucial in defining the Anthropocene, but also presents the various theories and narratives put forward to explain its causes and to demarcate a starting point. These range from theories of an 'Early Anthropocene', to the 'Columbian Exchange' or the Industrial Revolution, to the 'Great Acceleration' of the 1950s (which is the starting date suggested by the AWG). As the Anthropocene, since its introduction to a wider audience, has been subjected to strong criticism, we also review alternative terms which have been proposed such as 'Capitalocene', 'Plantationocene', 'Anglocene'—and many more. Each of these terms accentuates a different narrative about the causes and pathways that have led to the current situation. Basically, these alternative propositions (mis)understand the concept as one which names a culprit, in this case a generalized humanity. As they reject the generalizing of human responsibility implied in the 'Age of Humans', they propose alternative culprits, such as capitalism, colonial plantation economics, or the type of industrialization that originated in England.

No less contentious than the term itself is the question of its intellectual history or genealogy which we outline in Chapter 3: Genealogies. A genealogy of the Anthropocene concept must not only review predecessors such as, for example, Antonio Stoppani's *era anthropozoica*, it also has to present, as Christophe Bonneuil and Jean-Baptiste Fressoz have argued, a history of 'environmental reflexivity'. It must be an intellectual history of an understanding of the *Earth as a system*, but also a history of the many debates revolving around environmental degradation. Yet such a genealogy is itself controversial: historicization can, on the one hand, show that the Anthropocene is the result of contingent decisions that were violently contested in their time and could have turned out differently (Bonneuil and Fressoz 2016); on the other hand, such a search for 'antecedents' of the Anthropocene concept could deflate its radical novelty and thereby vitiate its political impact (Hamilton and Grinevald 2015).

The second part of the book, *Metamorphisms*, deals with the way in which thinking about the Anthropocene involves taking up, but also fundamentally transforming, concepts and questions which have always been central to the humanities. Just as tectonic processes imprint a new structure on geologically older rocks, the debate about the Anthropocene forces us to rethink traditional topics, such as the distinction between culture and nature, the exceptionality of the human species, the foundations of political order, or the aesthetics of nature. As nature is transformed by human action on a planetary scale, the relationship between nature and culture has to be rethought, as we show in Chapter 4: Nature and culture. The new model of the planet as a complex system of self-regulating processes suggests that humans must be understood as an integral part of that system. But this raises a host of questions: Who exactly is this '*anthropos*' from whom the Anthropocene takes its name? Who is the 'human' who is now to be conceived of as a 'geological force' (Crutzen and Stoermer 2000)? And what are the distinctive qualities which enabled our species to attain such a dominant position on the planet? This is the topic of Chapter 5: The *anthropos*. As Chakrabarty has pointed out, such questions are caught up in the tension between two very different conceptions of the human: humans as culturally differentiated beings, on the one hand, and, on the other, humans as a biological species among other forms of life, albeit with a metabolism impacting the entire planet. Current debates about humankind as the eponymous author of the Anthropocene tend to often focus either on one or the other conception. We argue that the paradoxical quality of human agency in the Anthropocene—the combination of an immense power with a frightening loss of control—can only be explained in the light of this tension.

This dual conception of the human is also fundamental to the political problems the Anthropocene raises, discussed in Chapter 6: Politics. The geological force of humanity is a cumulative effect of innumerable uncoordinated individual actions across the globe. Collective human action, in contrast, is only possible in culturally and politically differentiated groups. However, this differentiation of humanity into groups with conflicting interests also constitutes the chief obstacle to the measures which are necessary in order to limit human impact on the Earth system. The Earth thus threatens to fall victim to what Garrett Hardin has described as 'the tragedy of the commons' (Hardin 1968). The core problem of a politics of the Anthropocene is to develop forms of cooperation that escape this self-destructive logic. Last, but not least, a central concern of a humanities approach to the Anthropocene is that of aesthetics. Beyond the inflationary use of the term 'Anthropocene' in the art world, Chapter 7: Aesthetics is devoted to possible aesthetic strategies attuned to a post-natural word. We believe that an 'Anthropocene aesthetics' must address the problem of aesthetic *form*. The question to be asked is how new (and old) forms can represent what Thomas Friedman has aptly called the 'global weirding' of our life world (Friedman 2010).

While *Metamorphisms* emphasizes the continuities between traditional humanities scholarship and Anthropocene thought by tracing the transformation of long-established problems, the chapters in the third part of the book focus on *Fault lines*, areas in which the Anthropocene forces us to break with established terminology because they pose entirely new epistemic challenges. Here, we present new perspectives for research, but also point to some of the epistemic difficulties of thinking about the Anthropocene. Chapter 8: Biopolitics addresses an aspect of the Anthropocene that is often excluded from polite conversation: population growth had been a central concern of the early environmentalist movement, but has since been declared taboo. The Anthropocene requires a new take on this issue which focuses not only on human populations but on questions of coexistence and symbiosis with non-human species. Another perspective that has rapidly been gaining ground in the humanities is addressed in Chapter 9: Energy. It considers the energy regimes at the foundation of human cultures. The replacement of the solar-agrarian energy regime by fossil fuels in the course of the Industrial Revolution not only enabled new forms of technology, but also propelled changes in social structures, ethical values and subject formation. 'The mansion of modern freedoms', notes Chakrabarty, 'stands on an ever-expanding base of fossil-fuel use' (Chakrabarty 2009, p. 208). Cultural history, but also literary and art history, ought to take this base into account in order to be able to grasp the historical path that led us into the Anthropocene. It will also help us to understand the social and individual resistances we face in the restructuring of our energy systems.

The two final chapters in the section *Fault Lines* deal with a fundamental epistemological difficulty in thinking about the Anthropocene: the collision of different quantitative, spatial, and temporal magnitudes. Indeed, Timothy Clark has argued that the 'Anthropocene is itself an emergent scale effect' (Clark 2015, p. 71). This problem, we argue, presents itself in two different ways. Firstly, as a question of quantitative and spatial scales, to which Chapter 10: Scales I: The planetary is devoted. Such problems arise in the disjunction between the individual and the cumulative consequences of human action. The notion of the planetary, often invoked in relation to the Anthropocene, implies a tension between spatial scales: the singularity of the local and abstractness of the global. A second, and separate, question is that of the temporal magnitudes invoked by the collision of Earth history and human history. While the former involves the 'deep time' of very long, relatively event-less time periods, human history is based on the 'shallow time' of human generations. How can a historiography attuned to the Anthropocene fold these scales into each other? In Chapter 11: Scales II—Deep time, we deal not only with the challenges large temporal scales pose for historiography, but also those of a 'deep future' that radically exceeds the horizons of modern strategies for managing the future.

In our concluding outlook we ask how 'Western' the Anthropocene concept really is. The relative lack of interest in the term in regions such as Asia or Africa does not mean that these regions are not affected by it. On the contrary: the shape of the new geological age will depend crucially on developments outside the 'West', and particularly on the economic and technological dynamism of Asia. In the final chapter, we examine how the different ways in which modernity was experienced outside the old industrial nations shape different responses to the Anthropocene, and what these responses might bode for the future.

This book joins an already very large body of publications on the Anthropocene, many of which take wildly divergent positions. Needless to say, the approach we have followed in this survey is not the only one possible. There are, however, a few basic conceptual decisions that have guided our considerations.

(1) First, we consider the historicization of the Anthropocene—both as a phenomenon and as a concept—to be indispensable. While cataloging the competing 'narratives' of the Anthropocene is a useful exercise insofar as it helps to understand some of the concept's crucial implications (Bonneuil 2015, Dürbeck 2018), it cannot be more than a starting point. Rather, current debates must be understood as the culmination of a long history of ecological reflexivity, as Bonneuil and Fressoz (2016) have argued. Such a history includes, on the one hand, the conceptual forerunners of modern Earth system science, from Buffon's *Epochs of Nature* ([1778] 2018), to George Perkins Marsh's *Man and Nature* (1864), to the *Limits to Growth* (Meadows *et al.* 1972) and the Gaia theory (Lovelock 1979). On the other hand, it traces the continuing struggle to understand the practical significance of this knowledge. To historicize the Anthropocene also means to create a new perspective on the cultural and species history of humanity—from the paleoanthropological 'deep history' of *homo sapiens* to the energy sources and inter-species relations on which cultural evolution is based. Rather than reject any historicization of the Anthropocene (Hamilton 2015), we are concerned with unfolding the historical implications of the term. This involves new forms of historiography which are able to make sense of the rapid ascendancy of our species from a mid-sized, omnivorous primate into a geological force.

(2) Secondly, we are not convinced that thinking about the Anthropocene necessarily calls for a new 'flat' *ontology* (Bryant 2011). Theorists such as Timothy Morton, Graham Harman, Bruno Latour, Donna Haraway, Jane Bennett, Anna Tsing and others have argued that the Anthropocene is first and foremost to be understood as an *ontological* shock—'a quake in being' (Morton 2013, p. 1). According to Morton, the idea of 'the world' as a stage or container of human existence and experience can no longer be maintained in the Anthropocene: 'the world as such—not a specific idea of world but "world" in its entirety—has evaporated' (ibid., p. 101). Such a position means abandoning the classical distinction between subject and object, as

well as the epistemic dichotomy between a human observer and an observed world of things which Latour views as the core of the 'modern' mode of being-in-the-world (Latour 2017). The ontological approach to the Anthropocene also calls for the attribution of 'agency' not only to humans but also to things: non-human forms of life, the Earth system, or the material world in the broadest sense. Such a conception of agency erases the distinction between purposive, intentional action and causal efficacy (see Ch. 5: The *anthropos*). As a consequence, it also downplays the distinction between beings endowed with consciousness and cognition, and beings which lack these faculties. The traditional 'anthropocentrism' of Western metaphysics is countered with a 'strategic anthropomorphism' (Bennett 2010, pp. 98–9), and the issue of coexistence with non-human beings moves to the center of ethical and political debates (Haraway 2003).

There is no doubt that a modern epistemology that sees 'nature' or the 'world' merely as the passive and stable background of human action has become untenable in the Anthropocene. It is equally clear that the human power to affect the Earth system cannot be understood merely in terms of the intentional actions of conscious agents. Nonetheless, we do not believe that one can do justice to the epistemological, political and ethical challenges of the Anthropocene by leveling out human and non-human qualities and capacities. The focus on ontology, in our opinion, distracts from more urgent problems, such as *ethical* questions regarding human responsibility and *political* questions of collective action (see Ch. 5: The *anthropos*, and Ch. 6: Politics), *epistemological* questions regarding incommensurate scales (see Ch. 10: Scales I, and Ch. 11: Scales II), or the question of *aesthetics* in times of an unnatural nature (Ch. 7: Aesthetics). The indiscriminate use of the term 'agency' has a tendency to obscure or even negate human responsibility for past and future actions.

(3) This brings us to the third point. The calls for a new ontology for the Anthropocene usually locate the 'original sin' of modernity in an anthropocentric ontology which elevated the human to the center of creation, or, in the more secular versions of this narrative, to the position of a privileged external observer and demiurgic transformer of nature. The arrogant belief in human exceptionalism is supposed to be the wellspring of ecological destruction. In order for the Earth to have a future, this belief must therefore be rooted out. Yet the sympathetic image of a different, 'non-anthropocentric' human being as it is sketched in some of the new ontologies—one who is symbiotically entangled and striving for respectful coexistence with non-human beings (Haraway 2016)—ultimately cannot be anything other than precisely that: an *image* which is addressed to humans themselves, appealing to their unique capacity to regulate their behavior in accordance with ethical norms. Anthropocentrism is not so easily overcome. But thinking about what makes humans 'special' in comparison with other living beings does not automatically imply a normative claim to human superiority (Hamilton 2017, p. 43). On the contrary, the question of what enabled

humans to become a dominant species and geological force points to the indefinite, ambivalent nature of humans. Humans thus are *at once* natural *and* cultural beings. On the one hand, they are one biological species among others, a product of evolutionary history, entangled in mutual dependencies, with needs, behaviors, and a genetic code that differ only marginally from those of other living organisms. On the other hand, they are capable of, and condemned to, self-reflection. Lacking instincts and adaptations which would fit them to a particular ecological environment, humans are perpetually compelled to secure their own being through images, stories and social institutions that tell them what it means to be who they are—men or women, rich or poor, citizens of this or that country, rational beings, bearers of universal rights, and, finally, merely one biological species among others.

In several of his writings, Dipesh Chakrabarty has emphasized the tensions integral to the Anthropocene: a humanity that is *at the same time* culturally and economically differentiated *and* a unitary species; a history that is *at once* a history of the Earth *and* a history of human societies; an active power that is *both* a blind geological force *and* a consciously exercised capacity. We share Chakrabarty's perspective. In ancient philosophy, the 'epoche' referred to a suspension of judgment, a holding-out in uncertainty. To think about the Anthropocene as an epoch in this sense means not to resolve but rather to recognize and work through the tensions, the contradictions and aporias of the present. We are less interested in naming culprits—be they 'capitalism', 'modernity', or 'Western thought'—than in tracing these fault lines of the Anthropocene. They have served us as points of orientation in negotiating this difficult terrain.

Ever since Crutzen's intervention at the turn of the millennium, the Anthropocene has been a disruption. It is also—as we became painfully aware in the course of writing this book—a disruption of the intellectual routines of the humanities. It involves dealing with unfamiliar bodies of knowledge and with scientific data that can no longer simply be analyzed as 'discourse' and filed alongside other discourses. It requires that we familiarize ourselves with problems that are alien to established traditions of humanistic inquiry, such as the non-negotiable ecological and energetic foundations of culture. It also means that subject matter which stood at the center of the humanistic enterprise—local, relatively homogeneous cultural traditions and short, hyper-differentiated historical periods—is cast in a strange and unfamiliar light, perhaps sometimes even consigned to irrelevancy. In all academic disciplines, as well as in politics and the arts, the Anthropocene demands that we look at 'the bigger picture'. It calls for the development of a different, systemic perspective, and the rethinking of the relations between the particular and the universal; between the 'shallow' history of culture and the 'deep' history of life; and between local, individual practices and their cumulative impact on the planet. While the natural sciences work towards a description of a world whose complexity always remains elusive, the humanities are tasked with the formulation of an epochal consciousness. In the face of a multitude of life forms, divergent world-views and conflicting interests, they must articulate communality. More than ever, the epochal consciousness of the Anthropocene is pervaded by fractures, tensions and contradictions. The challenge is not to resolve them, but to account for them as precisely as we can. This book is a cartography of these fault lines.

EH

References

Autin, W.J., and Holbrook, J.M., 2012. Is the Anthropocene an issue of stratigraphy or pop culture? *Geological Society of America Today*, 22(7), 60–61.

Bennett, J., 2010. *Vibrant Matter. A Political Ecology of Things*. Durham/London: Duke University Press.

Bergthaller, H., *et al.*, 2014. Mapping Common Ground: Ecocriticism, Environmental History, and the Environmental Humanities. *Environmental Humanities*, 5, 261–276.

Bonneuil, C., 2015. The Geological Turn. Narratives of the Anthropocene. In: C. Hamilton, F. Gemenne and C. Bonneuil, ed. *The Anthropocene and the Global Environmental Crisis. Rethinking modernity in a new epoch*. New York/London: Routledge, 17–31.

Bonneuil, C., and Fressoz, J.-B., 2016. *The Shock of the Anthropocene. The Earth, History and Us*. London/New York: Verso.

Bryant, L.R., 2011. *The Democracy of objects*. Michigan: Open Humanities Press Imprint.

Buffon, G.-L., [1778] 2018. *The Epochs of Nature*. Trans. and ed. J. Zalasiewicz, A.-S. Milon, M. Zalasiewicz. Chicago and London: The University of Chicago Press.

Chakrabarty, D., 2009. The Climate of History. Four Theses. *Critical Inquiry*, 35(2), 197–222.

Chakrabarty, D., 18–19 February2015. *The Human Condition in the Anthropocene, The Tanner Lectures in Human Values* [online], New Haven, Yale University. Available from: https://tannerlectures.utah.edu/Chakrabarty%20manuscript.pdf [Accessed 14 April 2019].

Clark, T., 2015. *Ecocriticism at the Edge. The Anthropocene as a Threshold Concept*. London and New York: Bloomsbury.

Crutzen, P.J., 2002. The Geology of Mankind. *Nature*, 415(6867), 23.

Crutzen, P.J., and Stoermer, E.F., 2000. The 'Anthropocene'. *Global Change Newsletter* [online], IGBP 41, Mai 2000, 17–18. Available from: www.igbp.net/publica tions/globalchangemagazine/globalchangemagazine/globalchangenewslettersno4159. 5.5831d9ad13275d51c098000309.html [Accessed 14 February 2019].

Dürbeck, G., 2018. Narrative des Anthropozäns. Systematisierung eines interdisziplinären Diskurses. *Kulturwissenschaftliche Zeitschrift*, 3(1), 1–20.

The Economist, 2011. Welcome to the Anthropocene. *The Economist* [online], 26 May. Available from: www.economist.com/leaders/2011/05/26/welcome-to-the-anthrop ocene [Accessed 15 June 2019].

Ellis, E.C., 2018. *The Anthropocene. A very short introduction*. Oxford: Oxford University Press.

Emmett, R.S., and Nye, D.E. 2017. *The Environmental Humanities: A Critical Introduction*. Cambridge, MA: MIT Press.

Finney, S.C., and Edwards, L.E., 2016. The 'Anthropocene' epoch: scientific decision or political statement? *Geological Society of America Today*, 26(3–4), 4–10.

Friedman, T., 2010. Global Weirding is Here. *The New York Times*, 17 February.

Hamilton, C., 2015. Getting the Anthropocene so Wrong. *The Anthropocene Review*, 2(2), 102–107.

Hamilton, C., 2017. *Defiant Earth. The Fate of Humans in the Anthropocene*. London: Polity Press.

Hamilton, C., and Grinevald, J., 2015. Was the Anthropocene anticipated? *The Anthropocene Review*, 2(1), 59–72.

Haraway, D., 2003. *The Companion Species Manifesto. Dogs, people, and significant otherness*. Chicago and Bristol: Prickly Paradigm and University Presses Marketing.

Haraway, D., 2016. *Staying with the Trouble. Making Kin in the Chthulucene*. Durham: Duke University Press.

Hardin, G., 1968. The Tragedy of the Commons. *Science*, 162(3859), 1243–1248.

Hoff, M., 2018. As Insect Populations Decline, Scientists Are Trying to Understand Why. *Scientific American* [online], 1 November. Available from: www.scientificam erican.com/article/as-insect-populations-decline-scientists-are-trying-to-understa nd-why/ [Accessed 2 March 2019].

Hönisch, B., *et al.*, 2012. The geological record of ocean acidification. *Science*, 335 (6072), 1058–1063.

Latour, B., 2004. Why Has Critique Run out of Steam? From Matters of Fact to Matters of Concern. *Critical Inquiry*, 30(2), 225–248.

Latour, B., 2017. *Facing Gaia. Eight Lectures on the New Climate Regime*. Trans. C. Porter. London: Polity.

Lewis, S.L., and Maslin, M.A., 2018. Welcome to the Anthropocene. *IPPR Progressive Review*, 25(2), 214–219.

Lovelock, J.E., 1979. *Gaia. A new look at life on Earth*. Oxford: Oxford University Press.

Lovelock, J., and Margulis, L., 1974. Atmospheric Homeostasis by and for the Biosphere: The Gaia Hypothesis. *Tellus*, 26(1–2), 2–9.

Marsh, G.P., 1864. *Man and Nature, or: Physical Geography as modified by human action*. New York: John F. Trow.

Meadows, D., *et al.*, 1972. *The Limits to Growth. A report for The Club of Rome's project on the predicament of mankind*. New York: New American Library.

Moore, B., *et al.*, 2001. Amsterdam Declaration on Earth Systems Sciences 2001. Global Change: International Geosphere-Biosphere Programme [online]. Available from: www.igbp.net/about/history/2001amsterdamdeclarationonearthsystemscience.4.1b8ae 20512db692f2a680001312.html [Accessed 13 April 2019].

Morton, T., 2013. *Hyperobjects, Philosophy and Ecology after the End of the World*. Minneapolis: University of Minnesota Press.

Orb Media, 2017. *Invisibles. The plastic inside us. An investigative report by Chris Tyree and Dan Morrison* [online]. Available from: https://orbmedia.org/stories/invisi bles_plastics [Accessed 12 March 2019].

Renn, J., 2018. The Evolution of Knowledge. Rethinking Science in the Anthropocene. *Journal of History of Science and Technology*, 12(1), 1–22.

Rockström, J., *et al.*, 2009. Planetary boundaries. Exploring the safe operating space for humanity. *Ecology and Society*, 14(2), 32.

Smil, V., 2012. *Harvesting the Biosphere. What we have taken from nature*. Boston: MIT Press.

Snow, C.P., 1959. *The two cultures and the scientific revolution. The Rede Lecture 1959*. Cambridge: Cambridge University Press.

Tsing, A.L., *et al.*, eds., 2017. *Arts of Living on a Damaged Planet. Ghosts and Monsters of the Anthropocene.* Minneapolis: Minnesota University Press.

Waters, C., *et al.*, 2016. The Anthropocene is functionally and stratigraphically distinct from the Holocene. *Science*, 351(6269), 137,aad2622–2621–aad2522–2510.

Wilkinson, B.-H., 2005. Humans as geologic agents: A deep-time perspective. *Geology*, 33(3), 161–164.

WWF, 2016. *Living Planet Report 2016: Risk and resilience in a new era* [online]. Available from: https://wwf.panda.org/wwf_news/?282370/Living-Planet-Report-2016 [Accessed 12 March 2019].

Zalasiewicz, J., 2008. *The Earth After Us. What legacy will humans leave in the rocks?* Oxford: Oxford University Press.

Zalasiewicz, J., *et al.*, 2019. *The Anthropocene as a Geological Time Unit. A Guide to the Scientific Evidence and Current Debate.* Cambridge: Cambridge University Press.

Part I
Stratigraphies

2 Definitions

The Anthropocene is a concept that derives its extraordinary power from the countless controversies and criticisms it has provoked—not only in the humanities, but just as much in the natural sciences, albeit for different reasons. Indeed, the environmental historians Christophe Bonneuil and Jean-Baptiste Fressoz have argued that the Anthropocene should be understood as an 'event', or turning point—hence the original French title of their book, *L'événement Anthropocène* (Bonneuil and Fressoz 2016). The Anthropocene marks a turning point in two senses: on the one hand—as a geochronological epoch—it names a rupture between the Holocene and the present day; on the other—as a concept—it represents an intellectual break or new beginning which requires us to recast such venerable ideas as 'the human being', 'nature', 'culture' and 'history' (Chakrabarty 2009). For this reason, Timothy Clark has suggested that the term 'Anthropocene' may best be understood as a 'threshold-concept' (Clark 2015). It radically alters our perspective on the object of investigation, puts previous knowledge into a new constellation, and thus opens up a new epistemological field.

In the humanities and social sciences, as well as in the arts, the concept of the Anthropocene owes its remarkable proliferation to two qualities. First, it situates the present state of affairs in a much broader historical context than such designations as 'the modern age' or 'the contemporary'. Often, the title 'xyz in the Anthropocene' therefore simply has replaced the phrase 'xyz today' (Davies 2016, p. 51). As the most 'current' term to describe the present, it thus runs the danger of being used simply as a fashionable marker of topicality and political relevance, as can be seen most clearly in its omnipresence in the art world. Properly understood, however, it does not designate mere contemporaneity, but serves rather to historically locate the present. In this respect, the Anthropocene can be compared to the badly weathered concept of 'post-modernism', which in the 1980s gave a name to the departure from the cultural climate of twentieth-century modernism. Both 'post-modernism' and 'the Anthropocene' denote a rupture; yet, in the case of the Anthropocene, this rupture is not with frames of thought that prevailed for a few decades, but with the living conditions of the past 12,000 years. For if the present is understood as a distinct geochronological epoch, it marks a break from the Holocene, which encompasses the entire history of what we are used to calling civilization. In order to understand the present from the vantage point of the Anthropocene, we therefore not only have to reappraise the current state of affairs, but we also have to revise and rewrite the history of the Holocene.

Second, the term serves as a convenient shorthand for the multiple and complex aspects of the global ecological crisis (Ellis 2018, p. 130). It sums up such different phenomena as climate change, loss of biodiversity, air pollution, the hole in the atmospheric ozone layer, the proliferation of toxins and microparticles (e.g., microplastics), ocean acidification, changes in the water cycle, and so on. But the Anthropocene is more than a catchphrase for the many symptoms of ecological crisis. It also shifts these problems onto a different conceptual plane where many of the familiar antagonisms of environmental politics—e.g. between economic development and ecological stability, between present-day social imperatives and long-term sustainability—appear in a new light. Radicalizing or even displacing the concept of sustainability, the Anthropocene reorders political priorities. It not only draws attention to the material foundations of all communal life (such as the quality of water, air and soil, the stability of the climate, and security against natural disasters), but also calls into question the conceptual foundations on which our understanding of these issues has rested, above all the distinction between nature and culture (Latour 1993). The Anthropocene does not only require more environmental awareness or a firmer commitment to sustainability; it is about nothing less than a new way of *being-in-the-world* (Horn 2017, p. 9).

Despite the concept's success in the humanities, and the many historical and philosophical lines of inquiry it opens up, it is important not to lose sight of the fact that it originated in the natural sciences, and specifically in Earth system science. The perspective of Earth system science forms the epistemic foundation to any adequate understanding of the Anthropocene. As the name of this young field suggests, it seeks to offer a systemic and holistic view of the planet which emphasizes the interplay of the various spheres of the Earth system (atmosphere, lithosphere, pedosphere, biosphere, hydrosphere and cryosphere). The Earth system is marked by planetary feedback processes that form a self-regulating system, as argued in the famous Amsterdam Declaration on Earth System Science of 2001:

> The Earth system behaves as a single, self-regulating system comprised of physical, chemical, biological and human components. The interactions and feedbacks between the component parts are complex and exhibit multi-scale temporal and spatial variability. [...] Human activities are significantly influencing Earth's environment in many ways in addition to greenhouse gas emissions and climate change. Anthropogenic changes to Earth's land surface, oceans, coasts and atmosphere and to biological diversity, the water cycle and biogeochemical cycles are clearly identifiable beyond natural variability. They are equal to some of the

great forces of nature in their extent and impact. Many are accelerating. Global change is real and is happening now.

(Moore *et al.* 2001)

This planetary view regards humankind as a new and potentially destabilizing influence in the Earth system. It does not concern individual biotopes or regions, but an all-encompassing perspective on the Earth as a whole. Yet this whole contains, as one of its increasingly unruly elements, humans. ⟵

This view of human interference on a planetary scale is expressed in two famous diagrams that have become the defining illustrations of the dimensions of the Anthropocene. The first (Fig. 2.1) is taken from an influential 2011 article by Will Steffen, Jacques Grinevald, Paul Crutzen and John McNeill, who are all members of the Anthropocene Working Group

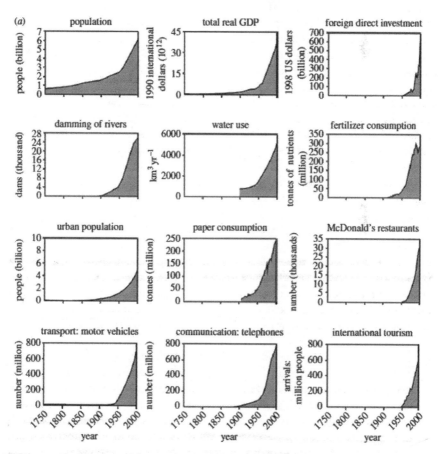

Figure 2.1 Steffen, W., Grinevald, J., Crutzen, P., McNeill, J., 2011. Tʰ pocene. Conceptual and historical perspectives. Philoˀ tions of the Royal Society A, 369(1938), 842–67.

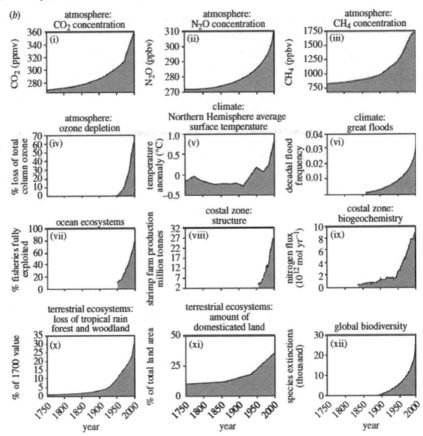

Figure 2.1 (Cont.)

(AWG). It shows 'the increasing rates of change in human activity since the beginning of the Industrial Revolution' in 24 simple graphs.

These graphs illustrate various 'indicators of human activity' between 1750 and 2000. They show (a) socioeconomic trends, such as population growth and urbanization, the average gross national product, and the use of exemplary consumer goods like paper or tourism; and (b) indicators of global ecological effects, such as the concentration of the greenhouse gases carbon dioxide, methane, and nitrous oxide, surface temperatures, and the loss of tropical rainforests and biodiversity. While many other parameters could be added, the figure's intention is clear: the authors describe the Anthropocene as a meta-crisis composed of a variety of coalescing indicators. These range from the rapid rise of industrialization, transportation, urbanization and globalization to a sharp climb in consumerism (first in the industrialized nations, and from the 1970s onward in major emerging economies), combined with massive population growth.

The crucial point, however, is the temporal convergence of these indicators shown by the graphs. Some factors, such as land use and population growth, have risen at a relatively steady pace since the eighteenth century and then surged sharply after the Second World War. Other factors become measurable only after the World War, but then promptly skyrocket. The graphs consistently show a steep rise following 1950—a convergence which Steffen *et al.* have termed the 'Great Acceleration'. In 2016, in line with these findings, the AWG proposed the Great Acceleration as the actual starting point of the Anthropocene. While this choice is backed by historical developments of the sort shown in the graphs, the AWG bases this suggestion for a formalization of the Anthropocene as a geochronological epoch primarily on geostratigraphic markers such as 'plastics, fly ash, radionuclides, metals, pesticides, reactive nitrogen' (Waters 2016, p. 137, Zalasiewicz 2017).

The second figure (Fig. 2.2) that has become famous for visualizing the Anthropocene comes from the research group around the Swedish scholar Johan Rockström. In 2009, Rockström *et al.* published an article arguing that some of the fundamental ecological parameters of the Earth system are currently in the process of exiting the 'safe operating space for humanity' based on the state of these parameters in the pre-industrial Holocene (i.e. the ecological state of the Earth around 1700). Rockström *et al.* identify nine fundamental factors in the Earth system, some of which are already transgressing what could potentially be an ecological breaking point of the planet.

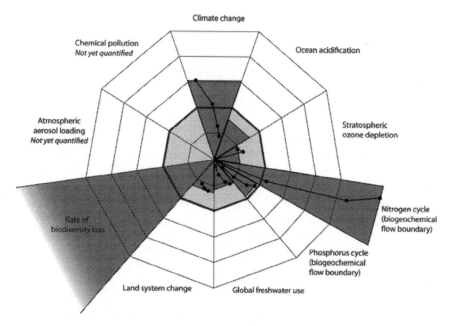

Figure 2.2 Rockström, J., *et al.*, 2009. Planetary Boundaries. Exploring the Safe Operating Space for the Humanity. *Ecology and Society*, 14(2), Art. 32.

While three of these factors—climate crisis, ozone depletion, and ocean acidification—are globally operative and have known thresholds, the other six—biodiversity loss, atmospheric pollution, chemical pollution, the disruption of important biochemical cycles (nitrogen and phosphorous), freshwater use, and land use—have regional impacts and are only partially calculable at a global level (which led to criticism of Rockström's model, see Ellis 2018, pp. 125–7, and Barry and Maslin 2016). Three of these thresholds (biodiversity, nitrogen cycle, and climate change) have already been exceeded with potentially dire consequences for the future.

In a recent update to this figure (Fig. 2.3), it is noteworthy that the factor 'chemical pollution (not yet sufficiently quantified)' has been changed to 'novel entities'. This new version takes into account the possibility that there may be other factors and thresholds for ecological stability that we are not even aware of yet. Like the graphs presented by Steffen *et al.* (2011), Rockström's figures signal a paradigm shift from the current mainstream of environmental thought, which tends to fixate on climate change. The Anthropocene is presented in the Rockström diagram as a multi-focal crisis, one that is furthermore open to a vast field of epistemological uncertainty, ranging from problems of quantification, unknown thresholds and tipping points, to 'novel entities'. The Anthropocene is alarmingly rife with 'unknown unknowns'.

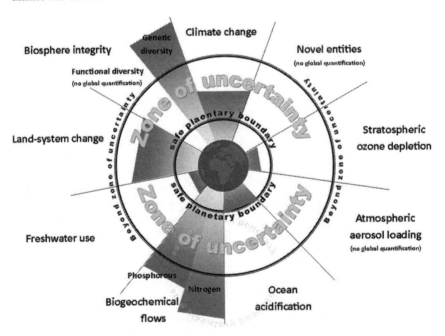

Figure 2.3 Revised planetary boundaries according to Steffen, W., Richardson, K., Rockström, J., *et al.* 2015. Source: Stockholm Resilience Centre. Credit: J. Lokrantz/Azote Images.

One of the central problems for a historical definition of the Anthropocene is the question of its starting dates. In this debate, various disciplinary approaches collide. On the one hand, geologists and stratigraphers are concerned with the possibility of formalizing the Anthropocene as a geochronological epoch within the established geological nomenclature. This is the task of the AWG, founded in 2009 under the direction of British stratigrapher Jan Zalasiewicz. On the other hand, scholars in the humanities and social sciences are less interested in sediment layers than in providing a plausible narrative of the causes and drivers leading up to the current ecological situation.

Consequently, very different disciplines working with very different types of narrative clash in the discussions over the starting dates of the Anthropocene: geology and historiography, environmental and intellectual history, technological and colonial history, pre- and ancient history, and paleoclimatology. What represents a global turning point from the perspective of technological or industrial history, such as the Industrial Revolution, may not leave the sort of distinct stratigraphical marker necessary for recognition in geology. Important thresholds in the deep time of human history, such as the utilization of fire (1.8 million years ago) or the so-called Neolithic Revolution (10,000 years ago), the transition to sedentary forms of life and the development of agriculture, are proof of humankind's age-old transformations of the environment. But taking these as starting dates of the Anthropocene would blur the specifics of the current situation. Each proposal for a starting date gives a different historical account, pointing to different criteria and kinds of causality. The most important positions are briefly outlined in the following.

The Great Acceleration

The graphs in Steffen *et al.* (2011) clearly demonstrate how certain socioeconomic trends and their ecological effects increase dramatically around the middle of the twentieth century (Fig. 2.1). Industrialization, consumption, traffic and many other factors started in the nineteenth century and then rose sharply after the Second World War in Europe and the US. Today, the economies of countries such as China and India are swiftly catching up with these trends. From 1950 to 2010, the world's population more than tripled. In this regard, the mid-twentieth century is a very plausible starting date for the Anthropocene, as Steffen *et al.* argue:

> Only beyond the mid-20th century is there clear evidence for fundamental shifts in the state and functioning of the Earth System that are beyond the range of variability of the Holocene and driven by human activities. Thus, of all the candidates for a start date for the Anthropocene, the beginning of the Great Acceleration is by far the most convincing from an Earth System science perspective.
>
> (Steffen *et al.* 2015a, p. 81)

Inspired by the title of Karl Polanyi's work on the emergence of modern industrialized societies, *The Great Transformation* (1944), the Great Acceleration offers a holistic view on the technological, economic and social transformation from 1950 onward and its impact on the Earth's system (Steffen *et al.* 2015a, p. 82). For the AWG, the starting date around 1950 has the further advantage of offering a distinct (albeit ephemeral) geological marker: the fallout from nuclear bombs and atomic testing since 1945. The Great Acceleration as starting date thus fulfils the geological requirement for formalizing the term as a geochronological epoch. It offers, in stratigraphic terminology, a clear GSSP (Global Boundary Stratotype Section and Point, also known as a 'golden spike') in principle detectable in sediment worldwide. Traces of radioactive isotopes left by nuclear bomb tests between 1950 and 1963, but also substances such as plastic, elemental aluminum, and concrete form a layer distinct and global enough to be considered a 'golden spike'. In August 2016, the AWG gave its formal recommendation to the Subcommission on Quaternary Stratigraphy in favor of formalizing the Anthropocene, suggesting a starting date with the Great Acceleration (Waters *et al.* 2016, for a comprehensive appraisal of the Great Acceleration, see McNeill and Engelke 2016).

The Industrial Revolution

Basically, this starting date suggests that the Anthropocene begins with modernity. In their early articles, Paul Crutzen and Eugene Stoermer, neither of whom is a geologist by training, proposed that the Anthropocene started not with the Great Acceleration but in the latter half of the eighteenth century with the Industrial Revolution (Crutzen and Stoermer 2000, pp. 17–8, Crutzen 2002, p. 23). They singled out the year 1784, in which 'James Watt invented the steam engine'. (In fact, in 1784 Watt patented 'Watt's linkage', which significantly improved the effectiveness of the steam engine developed by Thomas Newcomb and patented in 1769.) Crutzen and Stoermer's proposal, however, is not based on the details of technological history, but on the rise of coal as a source of energy, which (especially in England) starts much earlier, but was greatly accelerated by the development of the steam engine. In terms of climate history, too, a slow increase in atmospheric carbon dioxide can be observed in the last decades of the eighteenth century, but a significant rise only occurs after 1850. From the perspective of the humanities, the Industrial Revolution is especially plausible as a starting date because it coincides with the ideological and social-historical origins of modernity. It suggests that the Anthropocene emerged alongside the Enlightenment and secularization, the emancipation of the bourgeoisie, the beginning of modern industrial capitalism, and the formation of an urban working class. The time around 1800 also sees the rise of a hitherto unknown form of 'environmental reflexivity' in Europe, but also among settlers in the New World (Bonneuil and Fressoz 2016, Locher and Fressoz

2012): concern about anthropogenic change in landscapes, climates and water cycles. Deforestation, river siltation, soot from coal burning and the changing of local climates became not only subjects of political debate, but also of painting and literary production.

The convergence of the Anthropocene and modernity therefore provides one of the historically most convincing arguments. Even if it cannot be backed by a stratigraphic 'golden spike', it is supported by countless studies in environmental history on the social and economic revolutions which accompanied the use of coal and the steam engine (Malm 2016, Jonsson 2012). Linking the Anthropocene to modernity also means, conversely, that the history of modernity—often understood as an era of liberation from religious dogma and feudal hierarchy—must be rewritten as a history of energy regimes and ecological transformations (see Ch. 9: Energy). If modernity is understood as the beginning of the Anthropocene, its history would have to be written not only as one of emancipation and technological progress, but more importantly as that of a new relationship to the ecological environment in which nature is reduced to a 'raw material' or 'resource' to be used, processed, traded and exploited. With the transition to fossil fuels, the process of industrialization taps into a gigantic yet finite reservoir of cheap, high-density energy. Such an ecological history of modernity and modernization is not just the dark side of technological and social revolution. It is also a history of the massive production of inequality: while a swift social, environmental and economic transformation took place in industrialized countries, other parts of the world did not partake in the prosperity generated by industrialization, the social and environmental costs of which were increasingly 'outsourced' to more impoverished parts of the world (Nixon 2011). While ecological transformation occurred at a global level, the affluent lifestyles afforded by industrialization were for a long time concentrated in Europe and North America.

The Columbian Exchange 1492 – Columbus to new americas

This proposal shifts the focus away from Europe to the colonial history of the early modern period (Lewis and Maslin 2015a, 2018). The term itself was coined by the environmental historian Alfred Crosby, whose work on the ecological consequences of the European 'discovery' of the Americas focuses on the exchange of biological species (Crosby 1972). Within the first 100 years, global trade networks were formed that enabled a worldwide traffic in plants, animals, and human beings (most notably in the form of slavery), as well as the spread of diseases. As a result, local agricultures and habitats changed both in the Old and in the New World. While the Old World thrived under the influence of more efficient crops and the early modern agricultural revolution, the New World suffered tremendously. The transfer of pathogenic germs to which the indigenous population of the Americas did not have sufficient immunity led to massive epidemics, alongside the ruin brought on by colonial war and enslavement. These plagues alone led to at least 50 million deaths during the first 100 years of colonization, probably over 90% of the original population (Lewis and Maslin 2018, p. 157). This is not a new insight but a fact long known to colonial historians (McNeill 1976, Crosby 1986). Lewis and Maslin, however, give it a new spin by suggesting that the Columbian Exchange is also attestable in climate history: the regrowth of plants following the massive decrease in the indigenous population led to a short but pronounced dip in atmospheric carbon dioxide around 1610 which they call the 'Orbis spike' (Lewis and Maslin 2015a, 2015b, 2018). The Orbis spike, however, has been criticized by the AWG as insufficient for a GSSP (Zalasiewicz *et al.* 2015, Brooke and Otter 2016). Lewis and Maslin have also faced criticism for misconceiving the Anthropocene in terms of changes in specific regional ecosystems, rather than a state of the Earth (Hamilton 2015, for a response see Lewis and Maslin 2015b).

Yet the proposal that the Anthropocene begins in the early modern era, too, is compelling from a strictly historical perspective. It is also methodologically fruitful insofar as it brings with it a new criterion for the framing of the Anthropocene: the exchange and migration of organisms. Considering this the 'organic Anthropocene' (Brooke and Otter 2016) involves introducing a genuinely ecological perspective into the pre-history of the Anthropocene, shifting from chemical changes in the soil and the atmosphere to changes in the biota. From this point of view, not only the colonial exchange of humans, animals, plants and germs, but also the changes to cultivation and breeding methods in the course of the agricultural revolution in the early modern period (Clutton-Brock 1999, Olmstead and Rhode 2008) come into consideration as criteria for assessing the anthropogenic transformation of the environment. It is also no coincidence that the enormous wave of species extinctions known as the 'sixth extinction' begins in the seventeenth century (Kolbert 2014). Focusing on the early modern era highlights the early history of globalization as not just a history of conquest, global trade networks, enslavement and genocide, but also—in terms of environmental history—as a history of the opening up of new lands to cultivation and the introduction of new species. The Columbian Exchange foregrounds colonialism as the central factor of global environmental history. Because it entailed massive clearings of forests, the introduction of 'cash crops', the establishment of plantations, and economic exploitation, colonialism can be seen as one of the significant factors leading up to the Anthropocene. The sociologist Jason Moore has analyzed this process as the production of what he calls the 'four cheaps' on which capitalism is founded: labor, energy, food, and raw materials. The 'four cheaps' are cheap in the sense that their market costs are kept low because the environmental and social cost of their extraction and use are not factored in, but instead outsourced to the countries of their origin, to society or to nature (Moore 2016a, pp. 1–12).

Early Anthropocene

The thesis of an Early Anthropocene comes in several variations. One suggestion is that, long before the beginning of the Holocene and sedentary civilization, humans had already profoundly reshaped ecosystems through the use of fire and the hunting of large game. It can be objected, however, that by reducing the number of herbivores, humans would have promoted the growth of plants and reduced greenhouse gases in the atmosphere (Glikson 2013, Stuart 2015). Another variant situates the beginning of the Anthropocene in the early Holocene. According to the paleoclimatologist William Ruddiman, the fluctuations of warm and very cold periods characteristic of the Pleistocene would have been interrupted by the greenhouse gases produced by early forms of agriculture. According to Ruddiman, methane from rice paddies and increased levels of atmospheric carbon dioxide as a result of deforestation, desertification, and nascent agriculture staved off the next ice age cycle and thereby brought about the unusually stable and comparatively warm period that we know as the Holocene (Ruddiman 2003, 2013).

By this logic, the very beginning of civilization with sedentism and agriculture also marks the beginning of the Anthropocene (Ellis *et al.* 2013). The Anthropocene would then be just another name for the Holocene. The Early Anthropocene proposals declare any kind of human transformation of local biotopes to be 'anthropocenic'. Their arguments pertain primarily to the (paleontological) question of what defines *homo sapiens* as opposed to other species, rather than to contingent thresholds in subsequent cultural history. Changing the environment would then just be part of 'human nature' (Smith and Zeder 2013). This anthropological perspective focuses on the exceptionality of human beings, who, through social and cultural cooperation, create their own ecological niches (Ellis 2016). The proposals for an Early Anthropocene suggest that it is simply 'human nature' to alter and, eventually, degrade environments—a tendency that needs to be kept in check through better technology and greater political control (Davies 2016, p. 46). That Chinese contributions to the Anthropocene debate mainly emphasize the Early Anthropocene thesis (Weigelin-Schwiedrzik 2018) can thus also be seen as reflecting a preference for approaches that tackle the environmental challenges of the present through improved technology and greater social control (see Ch. 12: Conclusion).

From the historical perspective of the humanities, these different proposals for the start date of the Anthropocene should not be viewed as mutually exclusive alternatives, but rather as presenting successive stages of the Anthropocene (Ruddiman 2013, McNeill 2016, Kunnas 2017, Ellis 2018, pp. 161–2). A group led by the archaeologist Matt Edgeworth has proposed the concept of a 'diachronic Anthropocene' not determined by any single stratigraphic marker (Edgeworth 2015). Except for the very early Anthropocene (Smith and Zeder 2013, Glikson 2013), all propositions point to irreversible, yet contingent thresholds, from the turn to agriculture and the transformation of landscapes to colonialism and the use of fossil fuels. Even if these thresholds have become, in hindsight, points of no return, there were always alternatives that would have allowed for entirely different trajectories. Everything hinges on the narratives by which one gives form to these events: whether a 'Promethean' narrative of human emancipation and progress, or a narrative of exploitation and extinction, or a story of asynchronous developments and the externalization of environmental costs (Moore 2016a, Crist 2013).

This is where the criticisms of the Anthropocene concept come in. The very idea of an 'Age of Humans', it is often argued, reflects and reinforces the 'human exceptionalism' or 'anthropocentrism' at the basis of Western thought. Instead of understanding humans as living beings dependent on a network of other species and nonhuman actors, the term is said to reaffirm an instrumental, dominating stance towards nature (Haraway 2008, 2016).

Many positions criticize the concept for presenting a deeply ideological narrative which reduces the complexities of environmental, economic and colonial history to an inevitable, unilineal process (Bonneuil 2015, Kunnas 2017). They see the term as a continuation of an anthropocentric narrative of human power over nature—even if it is now recast as a story of catastrophe rather than success. Scientists, it is often suggested, have a troubling tendency to speak of 'humankind' as if it were a single, homogeneous actor. By identifying the abstraction 'humankind' as culprit, differences of wealth and lifestyle, economic systems, and ecological impact are obscured (Malm and Hornborg 2014, Bonneuil 2015, Bonneuil and Fressoz 2016, Roelvink 2013). Such narratives thus obfuscate the actual causes of ecological destruction: industrialized capitalism, the uneven distribution of prosperity and power, globalization, and the production of 'cheap nature' (Moore 2016b). By attributing the Anthropocene to the species *homo sapiens* rather than to specific groups and social formations, the critics argue, environmental destruction is 'naturalized', turning it into an inevitable consequence of 'human nature' (Malm and Hornborg 2014, p. 65) (see Ch. 5: The *anthropos*).

As a consequence, the term has been said to motivate calls—especially in the 'eco-modernist' projects for a 'good Anthropocene'—not for less, but more technological interventions into nature through 'green technology' or 'geo-engineering'. In this line of critique, the concept of the Anthropocene is seen as entailing an idea of environmental politics as driven by technocratic elites, rather than by social movements and public consciousness (Bonneuil 2015, Bonneuil and Fressoz 2016). According to Bonneuil and Fressoz, it implies a 'geocratic grand narrative' that all but erases the history of ecological awareness (Bonneuil and Fressoz 2016). The long litany of complaints adds up to a devastating indictment of the Anthropocene concept: it is unacceptably universalistic, oblivious to history, technocratic, and economically naïve.

Out of this unease regarding both the term and the narratives it entails, countless alternative concepts have emerged (for an overview see Davies

2016, pp. 52–4). What they all have in common is that they imitate the term, yet propose entirely different narratives and causal pathways: 'Capitalocene' (Moore 2016a, 2016b), 'Econocene' (Norgaard 2015), 'Homogenocene' (Samways 1999), 'Plantationocene' (Haraway 2015, Bubandt *et al.* 2016), 'Chthulucene' (Haraway 2015, 2016), 'Anglocene' (Bonneuil and Fressoz 2016). Indeed, some are already calling for a 'Post-Anthropocene' (Colebrook 2017). In many instances, the proposals are little more than a polemic dressed up in an awkward pun—e.g. the 'Misanthropocene' (www.themisanthropocene.com) or the 'Anthrobscene' (Parikka 2014). Their reference to the Anthropocene is ironic or, as it were, parasitical. The most substantial alternative concept is undeniably the 'Capitalocene', originally proposed by Andreas Malm and developed further by Jason Moore (2013, 2016a). While Moore understands his concept as a 'counterpoint' to the Anthropocene, he construes it in a fashion similar to the original term (Moore 2016b). For Moore, capitalism, by treating nature as a commodity and resource, is the actual cause of the current crisis—not the abstract, universalistic, composite called 'humanity'. While many of Moore's concrete analyses are very convincing and have produced valuable arguments and case studies for an understanding of the Anthropocene, one can reasonably ask whether the reference to 'capitalism' is really any less abstract and generalizing than the terms it is meant to supplant.

In our view, these alternative concepts should be understood not as antitheses or refutations, but rather as different interpretations of what is at stake in the conceptualization of the Anthropocene. Moore has emphasized the dialectic nature of what he calls the 'Capitalocene': 'dialectical reasoning moves through, not despite variations' (Moore 2016b). This also holds true for the Anthropocene. It does not imply a fixed narrative but rather has become the site of important and novel arguments, narratives, and even practices and policies revolving around the massive ecological transformation of the planet. The best way to understand the Anthropocene is thus not as a concept but as a problem, not as an accomplished theory but an open question, a research program rather than a research result. Instead of providing a 'grand narrative', the Anthropocene derives its conceptual and intellectual productivity from the array of competing narratives and hypotheses it produces (Dürbeck 2018).

EH

References

Barry, A., and Maslin, M., 2016. The politics of the Anthropocene: A dialogue. *Geo: Geography and Environment*, 3(2), no pages.

Bonneuil, C., 2015. The geological turn. Narratives of the Anthropocene. In: C. Hamilton, F. Gemenne and C. Bonneuil, eds. *The Anthropocene and the Global Environmental Crisis. Rethinking modernity in a new epoch*. London: Routledge, 15–31.

Bonneuil, C., and Fressoz, J.-B., 2016. *The Shock of the Anthropocene: The Earth, History and Us*. Trans. D. Fernbach. London and New York: Verso.

Brooke, J.L., and Otter, C., 2016. Concluding Remarks: The Organic Anthropocene. *Eighteenth-Century Studies*, 49(2), 281–302.

Bubandt, N., *et al.*, 2016. Anthropologists Are Talking—About the Anthropocene. *Ethnos*, 81(3), 535–564.

Chakrabarty, D., 2009. The Climate of History. Four Theses. *Critical Inquiry*, 35(2), 197–222.

Clark, T., 2015. *Ecocriticism at the Edge. The Anthropocene as a Threshold Concept*. London and New York: Bloomsbury.

Clutton-Brock, J., 1999. *A Natural History of Domesticated Mammals*. 2nd edition. Cambridge: Cambridge University Press.

Colebrook, C., 2017. We Have Always Been Post-Anthropocene: The Anthropocene Counterfactual. In: R. Grusin, ed. *Anthropocene Feminism*. Minneapolis: University of Minnesota Press, 1–20.

Crist, E., 2013. On the Poverty of our Nomenclature. *Environmental Humanities*, 3, 129–147.

Crosby, A., 1972. *The Columbian Exchange. Biological and Cultural Consequences of 1492*. Westport: Greenwood Press.

Crosby, A., 1986. *Ecological Imperialism. The Biological Expansion of Europe, 900–1900*. New York: Cambridge University Press.

Crutzen, P.J., 2002. The Geology of Mankind. *Nature*, 415(6867), 23.

Crutzen, P.J., and Stoermer, E.F., 2000. The 'Anthropocene'. *Global Change Newsletter* [online], IGBP 41, Mai 2000, 17–18. Available from: www.igbp.net/publications/globalchangemagazine/globalchangemagazine/globalchangenewslettersno4159.5.5831d9ad13275d51c098000309.html [Accessed 13 February 2019].

Davies, J., 2016. *The Birth of the Anthropocene*. Oakland: University of California Press.

Dürbeck, G., 2018. Narrative des Anthropozäns. Systematisierung eines interdisziplinären Diskurses. *Kulturwissenschaftliche Zeitschrift*, 3(1), 1–20.

Edgeworth, M., *et al.*, 2015. Diachronous beginnings of the Anthropocene: The lower bounding surface of anthropogenic deposits. *The Anthropocene Review*, 2(1), 33–58.

Ellis, E.C., 2016. Why Is Human Niche Construction Transforming Planet Earth? *RCC Perspectives 5: Molding The Planet: Human Niche Construction at Work*, 63–70.

Ellis, E.C., 2018. *The Anthropocene. A very short introduction*. Oxford: Oxford University Press.

Ellis, E.C., *et al.*, 2013. Used Planet: A Global History. *Proceedings of the National Academy of Sciences*, 110(20), 7978–7985.

Glikson, A., 2013. Fire and Human Evolution: The Deep-Time Blueprints of the Anthropocene. *Anthropocene*, 3, 89–92.

Hamilton, C., 2015. Getting the Anthropocene so Wrong. *The Anthropocene Review*, 2(2), 102–107.

Haraway, D., 2008. *When Species Meet*. Minnesota and London: University of Minnesota Press.

Haraway, D., 2015. Anthropocene, Capitalocene, Plantationocene, Chthulucene: Making Kin. *Environmental Humanities*, 6(1), 159–165.

Haraway, D., 2016. *Staying with the Trouble: Making Kin in the Chthulucene*. Durham and London: Duke University Press.

Horn, E., 2017. Jenseits der Kindeskinder: Nachhaltigkeit im Anthropozän. *Merkur*, 71(814), 5–17. Available from: www.merkur-zeitschrift.de/2017/02/23/jenseits-der-kindeskinder-nachhaltigkeit-im-anthropozaen/ [Accessed 8 January 2019].

Jonsson, F.A., 2012. The Industrial Revolution in the Anthropocene. *Journal of Modern History*, 84(3), 679–696.

Kolbert, E., 2014. *The Sixth Extinction. An Unnatural History*. New York: Henry Holt & Company.

Kunnas, J., 2017. Storytelling: From the early Anthropocene to the good or the bad Anthropocene. *The Anthropocene Review*, 4(2), 136–150.

Latour, B., 1993. *We have never been modern*. Trans. C. Porter. Cambridge, Mass.: Harvard University Press.

Lewis, S.L., and Maslin, M.A., 2015a. Defining the Anthropocene. *Nature*, 519(7542), 171–180.

Lewis, S.L., and Maslin, M.A., 2015b. Anthropocene: Earth System, geological, philosophical and political paradigm shifts. *The Anthropocene Review*, 2(2), 108–116.

Lewis, S.L., and Maslin, M.A., 2018. *The Human Planet: How We Created the Anthropocene*. London: Penguin.

Locher, F., and Fressoz, J.-B., 2012. Modernity's Frail Climate: A Climate History of Environmental Reflexivity. *Critical Inquiry*, 38(3), 579–598.

Malm, A., 2016. *Fossil Capital. The Rise of Steam Power and the Roots of Global Warming*. London and New York: Verso.

Malm, A., and Hornborg, A., 2014. The geology of mankind? A critique of the Anthropocene narrative. *The Anthropocene Review*, 1(1), 62–69.

McNeill, J.R., 2016. Introductory Remarks: The Anthropocene and the Eighteenth Century. *Eighteenth-Century Studies*, 49(2), 117–128.

McNeill, J.R., and Engelke, P., 2016. *The Great Acceleration. An Environmental History of the Anthropocene since 1945*. Boston: Harvard University Press.

McNeill, W., 1976. *Plagues and Peoples*. Garden City, NJ: Anchor.

Moore, B., et al., 2001. *Amsterdam Declaration on Earth Systems Sciences 2001*. Global Change: International Geosphere-Biosphere Programme [online]. Available from: www.igbp.net/about/history/2001amsterdamdeclarationonearthsystemscience.4.1b8ae20512db692f2a680001312.html [Accessed 13 February 2019].

Moore, J.W., 2013. *Anthropocene, Capitalocene, and the Myth of Industrialization. Part I-III* [online]. Available from: https://jasonwmoore.wordpress.com [Accessed 13 February 2019].

Moore, J.W., ed., 2016a. *Anthropocene or Capitalocene? Nature, History, and the Crisis of Capitalism*. Oakland: PM.

Moore, J.W., 2016b. *Name the System! Anthropocenes & the Capitalocene Alternative*. Blog 9 October [online]. Available from: https://jasonwmoore.wordpress.com/2016/10/09/name-the-system-anthropocenes-the-capitalocene-alternative/#_ftnref1 [Accessed 13 February 2019].

Nixon, R., 2011. *Slow Violence and the Environmentalism of the Poor*. Cambridge: Harvard University Press.

Norgaard, R., 2015. The Church of Economism and Its Discontents. *Great Transition Initiative*, December 2015. Available from: www.greattransition.org/publication/the-church-of-economism-and-its-discontents [Accessed 13 February 2019].

Olmstead, A.L., and Rhode, P.W., 2008. *Creating Abundance. Biological Innovation and American Agricultural Development*. Cambridge: Cambridge University Press.

Parikka, J., 2014. *The Anthrobscene*. Minneapolis: University of Minnesota Press.

Rockström, J., *et al.*, 2009. Planetary boundaries. Exploring the safe operating space for humanity. *Ecology and Society*, 14(2), 32.

Roelvink, G., 2013. Rethinking species-being in the Anthropocene. *Rethinking Marxism*, 25(1), 52–69.

Ruddiman, W., 2003. The Anthropogenic Greenhouse Era Began Thousands of Years Ago. *Climatic Change*, 61(3), 261–293.

Ruddiman, W., 2013. The Anthropocene. *Annual Review of Earth and Planetary Sciences*, 41, 45–68.

Samways, M., 1999. Translocating fauna to foreign lands: Here comes the Homogenocene. *Journal of Insect Conservation*, 3(2), 65–66.

Smith, B.D., and Zeder, M.A., 2013. The onset of the Anthropocene. *Anthropocene*, 4, 8–13.

Steffen, W., *et al.*, 2011. The Anthropocene. Conceptual and historical perspectives. *Philosophical Transactions of the Royal Society A*, 369(1938), 842–867.

Steffen, W., *et al.*, 2015a. The Trajectory of the Anthropocene: The Great Acceleration. *The Anthropocene Review*, 2(1), 81–98.

Steffen, W., *et al.*, 2015b. Planetary boundaries: Guiding human development on a changing planet. *Science*, 347(6223), no pages.

Stuart, A.J., 2015. Late Quaternary Megafaunal Extinctions on the Continents: A Short Review. *Geological Journal*, 50(3), 338–363.

Waters, C., *et al.*, 2016. The Anthropocene is functionally and stratigraphically distinct from the Holocene. *Science*, 351(6269), no pages.

Weigelin-Schwiedrzik, S., 2018. Doing Things With Numbers: Chinese Approaches to the Anthropocene. *International Communication of Chinese Culture*, 5(1), 17–37.

Zalasiewicz, J., 2017. The Working Group on the Anthropocene: Summary of evidence and interim recommendations. *Anthropocene*, 19, 55–60.

Zalasiewicz, J., *et al.* (=AWG), 2015. Colonization of the Americas, 'Little Ice Age' climate, and bomb-produced carbon: Their role in defining the Anthropocene. *The Anthropocene Review*, 2(2), 117–127.

3 Genealogies

The earliest publications introducing the Anthropocene usually included short genealogies of its conceptual 'antecedents' (Crutzen 2002, Steffen et al. 2011, pp. 843–5). A genealogy of the Anthropocene is not, however, limited to identifying possible precursors that sound similar, such as the 'anthropozoic era' proposed by the Italian geologist Antonio Stoppani as early as 1873, or the more recent term 'Anthrocene' coined by the science journalist Andrew Revkin (Stoppani 1873, Revkin 1992). Rather, a genealogical investigation must bring the most important implications of the Anthropocene into focus. Devising a conceptual history of the Anthropocene therefore is not just an academic exercise intended to lend the new concept the dignity of a tradition. On the contrary, it concerns both the theoretical implications and the political impact of the term. Precisely for that reason, any effort to write a history of the concept will be a highly contentious undertaking. On the one hand, there have been calls to historicize the Anthropocene in order to reconstruct a long tradition of 'ecological reflexivity', a tradition that is obscured when the Anthropocene is hailed as a recent discovery (Bonneuil and Fressoz 2016, Locher and Fressoz 2012). On the other hand, it has been argued that such a historicization of the concept 'deflates' it theoretically and robs it of its political urgency (Hamilton and Grinevald 2015, Hamilton 2016, pp. 60–2). Both of these lines of argument are at once political and epistemological.

The environmental historians Christophe Bonneuil and Jean-Baptiste Fressoz have to date been the most vocal and prolific proponents of a conceptual history of the Anthropocene. Their work demonstrates that 'environmental reflexivity'—simply put, a critical awareness of the environmental consequences of human action—has been around for centuries, as evidenced by the heated debates on forest clearance, water pollution, waste management and the change of local climates, for example (Bonneuil and Fressoz 2016, Locher and Fressoz 2012). Because they purposefully ignore this long history, Bonneuil and Fressoz argue, the seminal narratives of the Anthropocene—predominantly provided by natural scientists such as Crutzen (2002) or Steffen et al. (2011)—are politically debilitating: 'Rather than suppressing the environmental reflexivity of the past, we must understand how we entered the Anthropocene despite very consistent warnings, knowledge and opposition, and forge a new and more credible narrative of what has happened to us' (Bonneuil and Fressoz 2016, p. 79). Even though they share the environmental diagnosis, they are highly critical of Anthropocene discourse, which they see as marked by a naïve faith in technology and scientific expertise. This attitude ultimately advocates such quick fixes as geo-engineering rather than calling for a more profound social transformation. While this critique is in many ways justified, we do not think that it warrants giving up on the concept altogether. On the contrary, historicizing the Anthropocene can also lend it more conceptual and political heft. Against the background of the historical controversies that Bonneuil and Fressoz, along with many others, have reconstructed, the Anthropocene may actually become politically effective in contesting the ecological and economic regime of the present.

The philosopher Clive Hamilton, by contrast, has vehemently argued against historicizing the concept of the Anthropocene. In 2015, he published a paper together with the historian of science Jacques Grinevald which criticized any search for 'antecedents' as a misunderstanding of the Anthropocene's epistemological implications. For Jacques Grinevald, who as a co-author of Steffen *et al.* (2011) is most likely the author of the pages discussing 'antecedent' terms (Steffen *et al.* 2011, pp. 843–5), this marks a strange about-face: from sketching a genealogy of the Anthropocene to rejecting the very idea of such a genealogy. Hamilton and Grinevald write:

> In referring to precursors, perhaps to bolster the credibility of the new concept by locating it within a respected tradition ('on the shoulders of giants'), the original proponents of the Anthropocene unwittingly undermined the radical novelty of the concept and the actuality of the proposed new geological epoch.
>
> (Hamilton and Grinevald 2015, p. 60)

As the Anthropocene concept can only be correctly understood within the framework of Earth system science, Hamilton and Grinevald argue, any resemblance to earlier terms prior to the establishment of this scientific field should be seen as inessential. A history of knowledge about the Anthropocene can thus only be a history of this relatively recent discipline. At the same time, they criticize any historicization as 'deflationary', depriving the term of its political clout:

> It 'gradualizes' the new epoch so that it is no longer a rupture due principally to the burning of fossil fuels but a creeping phenomenon due to the incremental spread of human influence over the landscape. This

misconstrues the suddenness, severity, duration and irreversibility of the Anthropocene [...]

(Hamilton and Grinevald 2015, pp. 66–7)

This position insists not only on the Anthropocene as a relatively recent rupture in the Earth system but also on the radical novelty of the Anthropocene concept. Only with the paradigm shift from a locally anchored, and therefore limited, awareness of environments to a systemic view of the planet as a whole can one properly speak of the Anthropocene (see Ch. 10: Scales I). It is, Hamilton writes, about 'the Earth that evolves as a totality, as a unified, complex system comprised of the tightly linked atmosphere, hydrosphere, geosphere and biosphere. It is not about ecosystems' (Hamilton 2014). In terms of the intellectual history of the Anthropocene, this is an extreme self-limitation; it reduces the pre-history of the concept to sources that exactly correspond to the current definition. Hamilton measures past forms of knowledge against an epistemic standard which is set by the present and exclusively determined by the natural sciences.

The debate between a historicizing and a presentist understanding of the Anthropocene echoes similar debates about the starting date of the Anthropocene (see Ch. 2: Definitions). While Hamilton's presentist understanding insists on a narrow conceptualization taking its cues from Earth system science, the historicizing approaches are concerned with conceiving of a different history of the present, a different understanding of the history of humans and the Earth. Seen in this light, the two points of view are, once again, not so much contradictory as complementary. While the presentist position focuses primarily on the effects of human action and an understanding of these effects on a planetary level, the historicizing approach asks about the causes of anthropogenic changes, that is, those human practices and technologies that have brought about the global change in question. To historicize the term Anthropocene means to ask how humans have caused these changes. Yet, instead of postulating a generalized 'human nature', it takes the cultural, historical, and economic diversity of human forms of life as the starting point for understanding the trajectory which led to the Anthropocene. It involves writing a history of contentious and contingent cultural practices. It also requires that we recognize historical, 'obsolete' knowledge as an element of a heterogeneous pre-history of the Anthropocene *avant la lettre*. By contrast, the presentist perspective constructs an extremely lean, epistemically homogeneous narrative ex post by excluding any discourses that do not feed into the current paradigm. In many ways this divide reflects the tradition of 'two cultures' (Snow 1959) insofar as it sharply separates the approach of the humanities from that of the natural sciences. Seen from this perspective, the historical approach to the Anthropocene looks like the incursion of the 'soft' humanities into the domain of the natural sciences. Hamilton's criticism, however, is by no means shared by all advocates of the Anthropocene in the natural sciences. On the contrary, many scientists welcome the contributions of the humanities (in particular environmental or colonial history and archaeology) and see them as providing important foundations for their own theses. A prime example would be the Columbian Exchange hypothesis proposed by the plant ecologist Simon Lewis and the climatologist Mark Maslin (2015, 2018), which is based on colonial and environmental history as well as on paleoclimatic data (see Ch. 2: Definitions).

The question of precursors was already taken up in some of the very first publications proposing the Anthropocene as a concept (Crutzen and Stoermer 2000, Crutzen 2002, Steffen *et al.* 2011). Providing a genealogy conveyed historical dignity on the 'neologism' (Steffen *et al.* 2011, p. 843). The criterion for inclusion in the list of precursors was the conception of human intervention in the geology of the Earth. Crutzen and Stoermer mention George Perkins Marsh, an important forerunner of the conservation movement in the US who gave the second edition of his book *Man and Nature* (1864) the new title *The Earth as Modified by Human Action* (1874), and the Italian geologist Antonio Stoppani, who used the term 'anthropozoic era' in his *Corso de Geologia* and described humans as a 'telluric force' (Stoppani 1873, p. 732). They also refer to the Russian geochemist Vladimir Vernadsky and his Paris colleagues Edouard Le Roy and Pierre Teilhard de Chardin. Vernadsky's concept of the 'biosphere', a term he first coined in 1929, has been crucial for the conception of the Earth system (Vernadsky 1929). Building on Vernadsky's work, Teilhard de Chardin proposed the term 'noosphere' to designate the domain of human consciousness as emerging from and supervening on the biosphere (Teilhard de Chardin [1955] 1960). This list was expanded by Steffen *et al.* (2011) to highlight in particular the role of Vernadsky's fundamental work on biogeochemistry (Vernadsky 1924, 1929) and that of his predecessor, the Austrian geologist Eduard Suess (Suess 1875, 1883–1909). Steffen and his co-authors also include more recent positions that highlight, above all, the global dimension of human change, such as Fairfield Osborn's *Our Plundered Planet* (1948) and Robert Lionel Sherlock's *Man as a Geological Agent* (1922). With the Club of Rome's report *Limits to Growth* (Meadows *et al.* 1972) and the Gaia hypothesis (Lovelock and Margulis 1974a, Lovelock 1979), the genealogy of Anthropocene thought arrives on the threshold of the Earth system paradigm. The inclusion of some of the figures in this genealogy has since been criticized, in particular that of Stoppani and Teilhard de Chardin, whose work is strongly informed by Christian theology, and who deviate from a secular understanding of the Anthropocene (Hamilton and Grinevald 2015, p. 66).

In the meantime, a number of other precursors have been proposed, while new research has further highlighted the pivotal role of Vernadsky as a pioneer of Earth system science (Grinevald and Rispoli 2018). In light of the above, two primary strands can be identified: (1) a cultural history of the Anthropocene which studies the forms in which the human transformation of nature has been recognized and theorized; (2) an ecological history which focuses on precursors to the planetary understanding of nature as a system. Let us now take a closer look at each of these two strands.

(1) A genealogy of the awareness of human interference with nature is epistemologically extremely heterogeneous. It brings together early evidence of ecological reflexivity focusing on the relationship between humans and nature in practices, discourses and, not least, in the many controversies that were sparked by environmental change. The relevant documents are diverse and include such disparate subjects as deforestation, water use, the shift from water to coal as an energy source, and European colonization (see esp. Bonneuil and Fressoz 2016, Locher and Fressoz 2012, Malm 2016). A history of ecological reflexivity also includes early observations of anthropogenic changes in landscapes, climates, bodies of water, or fauna and flora. Impressive examples of this kind of reflexivity are the early descriptions of local climate change due to industrialization or the extensive cultivation of soils in Europe (Rauch 1818, Fourier 1847) and in the colonies (Williamson 1770).

Early on, ecological reflexivity is triggered by the observation of local changes in the climate. As the most important environmental factor influencing cultures, religions, and social institutions, climate had been a central subject of European cultural theories for centuries. In the eighteenth century it became an explanatory model for the differences between cultures, from their customs and mindsets to the style of their national literature (see, for example, Du Bos 1719, Montesquieu [1742] 1989). As the biblical account of the history of the Earth was abandoned, historical changes of climate attracted the attention of early geologists such as Georges-Louis Buffon. Buffon's *Epochs of Nature* (1778) may count as a first—albeit entirely speculative—document of Anthropocene thought. Buffon presupposes a continuously cooling planet. He sees human beings, who effectively warm the climate through deforestation and the draining of marshes, as an important—positive—factor that 'assisted the power of nature' in forestalling the lethal cooling of the Earth (Buffon [1778] 2018, p. 7, also see Heringman 2015).

The German philosopher Johann Gottfried Herder took up this idea of the human being as an active shaper of climate. He developed a cultural anthropology based on the reciprocal influence of cultures and local climates. Against the prevailing idea that cultures are inevitably determined by their climate, Herder argues that 'the climate does not force, but inclines' (Herder [1784–1791] 1966, p. 176). He points to the fact that cultures gain their particular character not least through the techniques by which they change their local climates and environments. Whatever humans are in the diversity of their bodies and lifestyles, they are in equal measure passively influenced by nature and actively engaged in transforming it (Horn 2016). Herder's cultural anthropology of climate is based on a reciprocal feedback between nature and culture. Herder's theory is remarkable as an alternative to Kantian anthropology insofar as it avoids a categorical separation between the animal and moral nature of the human, between subjugation to nature and freedom from it (Kant [1798] 1996, p. 3, see also Chakrabarty 2016).

Theories of the origins of culture point to the reciprocal transformation of nature and culture. Already in Jean-Jacques Rousseau's *Discourse on the Origin of Inequality* (1755), it is clear that the genesis of society brings with it a profound transformation of the landscape (Rousseau [1755] 1923, Trachtenberg 2015). The French social theorist Charles Fourier further developed this idea into the vision of a utopian future which would be marked by anthropogenic global warming, heating up the entire globe to pleasant Mediterranean temperatures (Fourier [1808/1841] 1996). In contrast to Fourier, who viewed the parallel reorganization of nature and society as a way of bringing the two into a lasting harmony, the French lawyer and author Eugène Huzar saw technological progress as a source of grave danger. According to Huzar, humankind's unfettered pursuit of technological advancement was driving towards the 'end of the world' (Huzar 1857, p. 103). His work thus presents an early 'progressive critique of progress' (Fressoz 2010, p. 97), a criticism of the unchecked development of science and technology that also informs certain strands of contemporary Anthropocene thought. Already in the middle of the nineteenth century, the idea of a nature completely conquered and transformed by humankind was a topic of popular scientific literature, even if such voices remained isolated. As early as 1867, the German zoologist and philosopher Ernst Haeckel, most famous today for coining the term 'ecology', described his own time as 'the era of Man, the anthropolithic or anthropozoic period' in his lectures (Haeckel [1870] 1876, p. 17).

A genealogy of Anthropocene thought must also include anthropological theories addressing the ecological and cognitive distinctiveness of the human being as a transformer of its natural environment. Particularly relevant in this regard, although little known in the Anglophone world, is the discourse of philosophical anthropology. Emerging as a distinctive school of thought in the 1920s, philosophical anthropology took its point of departure from Jakob von Uexküll's revolutionary conception of 'environment' (*Umwelt*) as relative to the perceptual and behavioral capacities of each species (Uexküll 1909). The ability of humans to technically and cognitively construct their own environments was singled out as the defining feature of the species. According to Arnold Gehlen, one of the movement's key figures, humans are distinctive insofar as they are physically and instinctually feeble and thus not optimally adapted to their natural environments (Gehlen [1940] 1988). Humans are, according to Gehlen, 'deficient beings' (*Mängelwesen*). For this reason, they need technologies and social institutions in order to create and reproduce the stable environments in which they are able to flourish (see Ch. 5: The *anthropos*). Such a theory can begin to explain how an apparently weak and ill-adapted creature such as *homo sapiens* could develop into a being capable of transforming not just local environments but eventually the entire planet. Anthropological reflections on the history of the species were first comprehensively brought into relation with ecological, political, and economic approaches at the conference of the Wenner-Gren Foundation for

Anthropological Research in Princeton in 1955. The proceedings from this famous multi-disciplinary conference bear a programmatic title: *Man's Role in Changing the Face of the Earth* (Thomas 1956). The collaborative research group composed of anthropologists, historians, environmental scientists, economists, biologists, geographers, physicists, and zoologists undertook the first explicitly global review of 'what man has done, and is doing, to change its physical-biological environment on the Earth' (Thomas 1956, p. iix).

A cultural-historical genealogy of the Anthropocene focuses on the human as a geological force. It investigates the human faculties and cultural practices that would explain this force. While the anthropological approach focuses on the distinctiveness of humans as a biological species among others, a genealogy of environmental reflexivity seeks out the documents in which a critical awareness of this force manifests itself. What they share is a common focus on humans as the cause of environmental transformation.

(2) The second, ecological, strand of a genealogy of the Anthropocene focuses not on the human being but on the development of planetary ecological thinking, its basic concepts and models. Its sources can be found in the history of geology, biology, and climate science; it essentially amounts to a pre-history of Earth system science and therefore is epistemologically much more homogeneous. An important early source for any systemic understanding of nature as a whole is Alexander von Humboldt's influential but unfinished *Cosmos* project, which had a lasting impact on the natural sciences in the nineteenth century (Humboldt [1845–1862] 1847–1870), but fell into obscurity in the twentieth century as scientific disciplines became more and more compartmentalized. A more direct precursor of Earth system science can be found in the work of Vladimir Vernadsky. When Vernadsky was developing his concept of the biosphere, he traced the notion back to the French biologist Jean-Baptiste de Lamarck and the Austrian geologist Eduard Suess (Lamarck [1802] 1964, Suess 1875, see Grinevald 1996). In his only geological publication, *Hydrogeology*, Lamarck introduced the category of a global sphere of living organisms to explain how life alters the surface of the Earth (Lamarck [1802] 1964). Suess, whom Vernadsky had met in Vienna in 1911, introduced the term 'biosphere' in his book *The Origin of the Alps* to refer to the entirety of all living beings and related it to the 'atmosphere', the 'lithosphere', and the 'hydrosphere', in order to describe the interpenetration of these planetary dimensions in the emergence of geological forms (Suess 1875, pp. 158–60; later also Suess 1883, Teilhard de Chardin 1921). However, Suess conceived of the biosphere as static and spatially fixed. Vernadsky took up but decisively changed Suess's concept in *Geochemistry* ([1924] 2006) and *Biosphere* ([1929] 2006). While both books are today recognized as pioneering in the conceptualization of the Earth as a system, they were at first neglected. Unlike Suess, Vernadsky understands the biosphere as a subsystem of a more comprehensive biogeochemical system which is constantly evolving (Grinevald 1996, Guillaume 2014). Vernadsky thus historicizes the biosphere. In dialogue with the

philosopher and mathematician Edouard Le Roy and the paleontologist and theologian Pierre Teilhard de Chardin, but also referring to the Russian geologist A.P. Pavlov, Vernadsky subsequently shifted his attention to the role of humans in this system. He writes:

> In the twentieth century, man, for the first time in the history of the Earth, knew and embraced the whole biosphere, completed the geographic map of the planet Earth, and colonized its whole surface. Mankind became a single totality in the life of the Earth. [...] All this is the result of 'cephalization,' the growth of man's brain and the work directed by his brain. [...] Thus the whole of mankind put together represents an insignificant mass of the planet's matter. Its strength is derived not from its matter, but from its brain. If man understands this, and does not use his brain and his work for self-destruction, an immense future is open before him in the geological history of the biosphere.
>
> (Vernadsky 1945, p. 8)

For Vernadsky, the technological and material efficacy of the human intellect marks a new phase in which the biosphere itself enters modernity. Le Roy referred to this new phase as the 'noosphere' (drawing on the Greek word for spirit: νοῦς), a term which Vernadsky adopted (Le Roy 1928, pp. 37–57, Vernadsky 1945, see Grinevald and Rispoli 2018). The term was later popularized by Teilhard de Chardin's book *The Phenomenon of Man* ([1955] 1960). However, while Vernadsky valued him as a friend and colleague, Teilhard gave the concept a theological and anthropocentric twist that is very different from Vernadsky's understanding (Grinevald 1996, pp. 40–1, Grinevald and Rispoli 2018).

Whereas Vernadsky's work has only recently been rediscovered, planetary scientist James Lovelock and microbiologist Lynn Margulis have long been recognized as trailblazers of a genuinely systems-theoretical conception of the planet. Their Gaia hypothesis is widely seen as a ground-breaking step towards a model of the Earth system as we understand it today (Lovelock and Margulis 1974a, Margulis and Lovelock 1974b). The hypothesis is based on the insight that the Earth's atmosphere is a product of the biosphere. Lovelock and Margulis proposed that the organic and inorganic subsystems of the Earth must be understood as a single, self-regulating system to which they gave the name of the Greek goddess of the Earth, Gaia. While this name caused a fair amount of misunderstanding, as it seemed to suggest an anthropomorphic, all-controlling 'higher consciousness', Lovelock always emphasized that the Gaia hypothesis is based on a cybernetic model of spontaneous, undirected self-organization and self-regulation. In recent decades, Lovelock has not tired of warning that human interventions in this system could lead to the self-annihilation of our species:

> Gaia is an evolutionary system in which any species, including humans, that persists with changes to the environment that lessen the survival of

its progeny is doomed to extinction. By massively taking land to feed people and by fouling the air and water we are hampering Gaia's ability to regulate the Earth's climate and chemistry, and if we continue to do it we are in danger of extinction.

(Lovelock 2006, p. 109)

This model of the Earth system implies what Lovelock calls 'discontinuities' (Lovelock 2006, pp. 50–1). These are tipping points which are difficult to anticipate. Passing them will have long-term and possibly catastrophic global consequences. Lovelock's cybernetic perspective on the Earth thus introduces a new kind of catastrophism into ecological thought, which sees nature as characterized by discontinuities, sudden leaps, and dangerous escalations. Even though many factors in the Earth system are linear and thus easily predictable, there are also numerous non-linear factors (and complex relationships between them) which can lead to sudden change once a particular threshold is crossed. The thawing of the permafrost and the melting of the polar ice caps are perhaps the best-known examples of this, but it also applies to the desertification of landscapes, and it underlies scenarios involving a change in the monsoon or the collapse of the Gulf Stream (Lenton 2016, pp. 100–6). Non-linear dynamics are a hallmark of the Anthropocene, not least in the exponential increases of consumption, population, environmental pollution, and many other indicators as they manifest themselves in the period of the Great Acceleration (see Ch. 2: Definitions).

Following this ecological strand, a genealogy of the Anthropocene cannot avoid also tracing a tradition of thinking about discontinuities and tipping points. Such a tradition can only be very briefly outlined here. One important waymark is Thomas Malthus's infamous *Essay on the Principle of Population* (1798) (see Ch. 8: Biopolitics). Dealing with the relation between population growth and food production, the essay presents one of the earliest attempts to mathematically model population dynamics and to use such models as a basis for political arguments. On the supposition that increases in food production proceed in a linear fashion, whereas population grows exponentially, Malthus argued that if the human drive to procreate were left unchecked, it would inevitably lead to famine and a catastrophic decline of the population. While Malthus's predictions were not borne out by subsequent developments, his theorem played a key role in the development of ecological and, more particularly, biopolitical thought. In *The Origin of Species*, Charles Darwin conceived of the 'principle of population' as the motive force of natural selection, as organisms must compete for finite resources (Darwin 1859). In animal ecology, this formed the basis of the concept of 'carrying capacity', which in turn became central to the emergence of Neomalthusian thought after the Second World War. It found its most famous expression in the report of the Club of Rome, *Limits to Growth* (Meadows *et al.* 1972), which warned that the growth of the human population and consumption was outstripping the ability of the planet to support it. In the report, the scientists focused on five factors—world population, industrialization, pollution, food production, and resource depletion—to model different scenarios for the world's future. Two out of the three scenarios anticipated social and ecological collapse. Even though these prognoses turned out to be wrong, the report helped to popularize an idea that remains fundamental not only to an ecology, but also to an economy of the Anthropocene: the idea that growth has limits and that the planet's carrying capacity is finite (see Ch. 9: Energy). More recently, Jared Diamond has dramatized these limits for a popular audience. Tracing the historical development of various past societies, he argues that their failure to take ecological limits into account led them to collapse—and that contemporary world society is heading the same way (Diamond 2005). This tradition of thinking about disruptions, tipping points and escalations is one of the definitive elements of all serious efforts to think the Anthropocene, its ecology and economy. From the Great Acceleration to the Planetary Boundaries (see Ch. 2: Definitions), understanding the Anthropocene means reckoning with radical discontinuities.

Investigating the genealogy of the Anthropocene thus sheds light on several implications of the concept that are of crucial importance. Such a genealogical approach, as we have shown, draws on wide-ranging and heterogeneous sources. We believe that a cultural-historical tradition of environmental reflexivity and an ecological pre-history of Earth system thought do not exclude, but rather complement one another. Far from diluting the concept, as Hamilton believes, an intellectual history of Anthropocene thought *avant la lettre* allows us to better understand its anthropological, ecological, economic and epistemological implications. It furthermore underlines the fact that, despite the paradigm shift marked by the emergence of Earth system science and the vast increase in knowledge about our planet, ecological reflexivity is by no means an achievement of the last 30 years. Perhaps most importantly, it shows that the long history of thinking about the human impact on nature is also a story of misjudgments and myopia, of willful ignorance and failures to translate knowledge into action.

EH

References

Bonneuil, C., and Fressoz, J.-B., 2016. *The Shock of the Anthropocene. The Earth, History and Us.* London and New York: Verso.

Buffon, G.-L., [1778] 2018. *The Epochs of Nature.* Trans. and ed. J. Zalasiewicz, A.-S. Milon, M. Zalasiewicz. Chicago and London: The University of Chicago Press.

Chakrabarty, D., 2016. Humanities in the Anthropocene: The Crisis of an Enduring Kantian Fable. *New Literary History*, 47(2–3), 377–397.

Crutzen, P.J., 2002. The Geology of Mankind. *Nature*, 415(6867), 23.

Crutzen, P.J., and Stoermer, E.F., 2000. The 'Anthropocene'. *Global Change Newsletter* [online], IGBP 41, May 2000, 17–18. Available from: www.igbp.net/publica

tions/globalchangemagazine/globalchangemagazine/globalchangenewslettersno4159.
5.5831d9ad13275d51c098000309.html [Accessed 13 February 2019].

Darwin, C., 1859. *On the Origin of Species*. London: John Murray.

Diamond, J., 2005. *Collapse. How Societies Choose to Fail or Succeed*. New York: Viking Press.

Du Bos, A.J.-B., 1719. *Réflexions critiques sur la poesie et sur la peinture*. 2 Vol. Paris: Jean Mariette.

Fourier, C., 1847. Détérioration matérielle de la planète. *La Phalange*, 16(6), 401–440, 497–536.

Fourier, C., [1808/1841] 1996. *The Theory of the Four Movements*. Ed. G. Stedman Jones and I. Patterson. Cambridge: Cambridge University Press.

Fressoz, J.-B., 2010. Eugène Huzar et l'invention du catastrophisme technologique. *Romantisme*, 150(4), 97–103.

Gehlen, A., [1940] 1988. *Man. His Nature and Place in the World*. New York: Columbia University Press.

Grinevald, J., 1996. Sketch for a History of the Idea of the Biosphere. In: P. Bunyard, ed. *Gaia in Action, Science of the Living Earth*. Edinburgh: Floris Books, 34–53.

Grinevald, J., and Rispoli, G., 2018. Vladimir Vernadsky and the co-evolution of the biosphere, the noosphere, and the technosphere. *Technosphere Magazine* [online], 1–9. Available from: https://technosphere-magazine.hkw.de/p/Vladimir-Verna dsky-and-the-Co-evolution-of-the-Biosphere-the-Noosphere-and-the-Technosphere-nuJGbW9KPxrREPxXxz95hr [Accessed 14 April 2019].

Guillaume, B., 2014. Vernadsky's philosophical legacy: A perspective from the Anthropocene. *The Anthropocene Review*, 1(2), 137–146.

Haeckel, E., [1870] 1876. *The history of creation: On the development of the Earth and its inhabitants by the action of natural causes. A popular exposition of the doctrine of evolution in general, and of that of Darwin, Goethe, and Lamarck in particular*. 2 Vol. Trans. E.R. Lankester. London: Henry S. King.

Hamilton, C., 18 August2014. Ecologists butt out: You are not entitled to redefine the Anthropocene. Blog. *The Anthropocene Review* [online]. Available from: www. theanthropocenereview.com/2014/08/ecologists-butt-out-you-are-not.html [Accessed 8 January 2019].

Hamilton, C., 2016. The Anthropocene as rupture. *The Anthropocene Review*, 3(2), 93–106.

Hamilton, C., and Grinevald, J., 2015. Was the Anthropocene anticipated? *The Anthropocene Review*, 2(1), 59–72.

Herder, J.G., [1784–1791] 1966. *Outlines of a Philosophy of the History of Man*. Trans. T. Churchill. New York: Bergmann.

Heringman, N., 2015. Deep Time at the dawn of the Anthropocene. *Representations*, 129(1), 56–85.

Horn, E., 2016. Klimatologie um 1800. Zur Genealogie des Anthropozäns. *Zeitschrift für Kulturwissenschaften*, 1, 87–102.

Humboldt, A.v. [1845–1862] 1847–1870. *Cosmos. A sketch of a physical description of the universe*. Trans. E.C. Otté. 5 Vol. London: Henry G. Bohn.

Huzar, E., 1857. *L'Arbre de la science*. Paris: Éditions Dentu.

Kant, I., [1798] 1996. *Anthropology from a pragmatic pint of view*. Trans. V.L. Dowell. Carbondale: Southern Illinois University Press.

Lamarck, J.-B., [1802] 1964. *Hydrogeology*. Urbana: University of Illinois Press.

Lenton, T., 2016. *Earth System Science. A Very Short Introduction*. Oxford: Oxford University Press.

Le Roy, E., 1928. *Les origines humaines et l'evolution de l'intelligence*. Paris: Boivin et Cie.

Lewis, S.L., and Maslin, M.A., 2015. Defining the Anthropocene. *Nature*, 519(7542), 171–180.

Lewis, S.L., and Maslin, M.A., 2018. *The Human Planet: How We Created the Anthropocene*. London: Penguin.

Locher, F., and Fressoz, J.-B., 2012. Modernity's Frail Climate: A Climate History of Environmental Reflexivity. *Critical Inquiry*, 38(3), 579–598.

Lovelock, J.E., 1979. *Gaia. A new look at life on Earth*. Oxford: Oxford University Press.

Lovelock, J.E., 2006. *The Revenge of Gaia*. London: Penguin.

Lovelock, J.E., and Margulis, L., 1974a. Atmospheric Homeostasis by and for the Biosphere: The Gaia Hypothesis. *Tellus*, 26(1–2), 2–10.

Malm, A., 2016. *Fossil Capital. The Rise of Steam Power and the Roots of Global Warming*. New York and London: Verso.

Malthus, T.R., 1798. *Essay on the Principle of Population*. London: J. Johnson.

Margulis, L., and Lovelock, J.E., 1974b. Biological Modulation of the Earth's Atmosphere. *Icarus*, 21(4), 471–489.

Marsh, G.P., 1874. *The Earth as modified by human action. A new edition of 'Man and Nature'*. New York: Scribner, Armstrong & Co.

Meadows, D., *et al.*, 1972. *The Limits to Growth. A report for The Club of Rome's project on the predicament of mankind*. New York: New American Library.

Montesquieu, C.L.S.d., [1742] 1989. *The Spirit of the Laws*. Trans. A.M. Cohler, B.C. Miller, and H.S. Stone. Cambridge: Cambridge University Press.

Osborn, F., 1948. *Our Plundered Planet*. New York: Little, Brown and Company.

Rauch, F.-A., 1818. *Régénération de la nature végétale*. 2 Vol. Paris: L'Imprimerie de P. Didot L'aîné.

Revkin, A., 1992. *Global Warming. Understanding the Forecast*. New York: Abbeville Press.

Rousseau, J.-J., [1755] 1923. A Discourse on the Origin of Inequality. In: J.-J. Rousseau. *The Social Contract and Discourses*. Trans. G.D.H. Cole. London and Toronto: J. M. Dent and Sons, 155–239.

Sherlock, R.L., 1922. *Man as a Geological Agent, An account of his action on inanimate nature*. London: H. F. & G. Witherby.

Snow, C.P., 1959. *The two cultures and the scientific revolution. The Rede lecture 1959*. Cambridge: Cambridge University Press.

Steffen, W., *et al.*, 2011. The Anthropocene. Conceptual and historical perspectives. *Philosophical Transactions of the Royal Society A*, 369(1938), 842–867.

Stoppani, A., 1873. *Corso di geología*. 2 Vol. Mailand: G. Bernardoni & G. Brigola.

Suess, E., 1875. *Entstehung der Alpen*. Wien: Wilhelm Braumüller.

Suess, E., 1883–1909. *Das Antlitz der Erde*. 3 Vol. Wien, Leipzig and Prag: Freytag.

Teilhard de Chardin, P., 1921. La face de la terre. *Études*, 169, 585–602.

Teilhard de Chardin, P., [1955] 1960. *The Phenomenon of Man*. 4th ed. London: Collins.

Thomas, W.L., 1956. *Man's Role in Changing the Face of the Earth*. Chicago: The University of Chicago Press.

Trachtenberg, Z., 2015. Anticipating the Anthropocene. *Earth's Future*, 3(9), 313–316.

Uexküll, J.v., 1909. *Umwelt und Innenwelt der Tiere*. Berlin: Julius Springer.

Vernadsky, V., 1945. The Biosphere and the Noosphere. *American Scientist*, 33, 1–12.

Vernadsky, V., [1924, 1929] 2006. *Essays on Geochemistry and the Biosphere*. Trans. O. Barash. Sante Fe: Synergetic Press.

Williamson, H., 1770. An Attempt to Account for the Change of Climate, Which has been Observed in the Middle Colonies in North-America. *Transactions of the American Philosophical Society*, 1, 272–280.

Part II
Metamorphisms

4   Nature and culture

In ordinary terms, the question of what nature and culture really are poses no problems. The tree in front of my window and the bird nesting in its branches—that's nature. The window through which I look at the tree, or the book which tells me what it is that I am seeing—those are not part of nature, but belong to the domain of the artificial, the man-made, in short: culture. The binary distinction between nature and culture is a matter of course which shapes everyday life (e.g. with regard to consumer preferences: twinkies or whole-grain muffins?; a visit to the museum, or a holiday in the mountains?), but it also structures our knowledge. The sciences, which deal with the world of things, are opposed to the humanities, which are concerned with the products of the human mind, with history, ideas, art, etc. This distinction rests on the assumption that nature and culture are essentially different: the two terms denote different ontological categories, ways of being or modes of existence which require distinctive forms of knowledge.

A recurring theme in discussions about the Anthropocene is the idea that it puts an end to this distinction between nature and culture. If humankind has itself become a force of nature and is changing the Earth system in its entirety, then the distinction between nature and culture no longer makes sense. The Anthropocene, it is said, marks the 'end of nature'. This idea is not new, however. For more than 30 years, scholars in the humanities and social sciences have been talking about the present as an age 'after nature'. In *The End of Nature*, published in 1989, US environmentalist Bill McKibben lamented that climate change had destroyed the very idea of a nature that exists apart from human interference (McKibben 1989, pp. 58–60). Around the same time, German sociologist Ulrich Beck announced that the nature which the environmental movement purported to save had already ceased to exist (Beck 1988, p. 62). His British colleague Anthony Giddens singled out the substitution of artificial environments for natural ones as a defining characteristic of modernity (Giddens 1991, p. 60), and Frederic Jameson saw the disappearance of nature as the hallmark of postmodernity: 'Postmodernism is what you have when the modernization process is complete and nature is gone for good' (Jameson 1991, p. ix).

That the humanities have so eagerly seized upon the Anthropocene concept has much to do with the fact that it resonates with these older debates. At the same time, however, the Anthropocene compels us to reassess them from our present vantage point. In the talk about the 'end of nature', several lines of argument converge which rest on very different premises. One important strand is the poststructuralist notion that the very idea of 'nature' is a paradox: a concept which denies its status as a concept, a linguistic sign purporting to denote that which exceeds the arbitrariness of language. Thus Roland Barthes remarked already in 1957 that 'nature' is always an 'imposture' (Barthes [1957] 1972, p. 101). For Barthes, the task of the humanities is to dissolve nature into the history of discourses. Many scholars in the humanities continue to see it as their most important task to show how things that used to be seen as 'natural' and taken for granted (e.g. sexuality, race, social hierarchy, aesthetic value, but also ecological limits) are in fact products of discourse and social power relations, or, more simply put: social constructions. This form of critique is primarily directed against the old idea that nature furnishes norms for human behavior, e.g. that gender roles are based on biological differences. In the West, this idea of nature as a norm can be traced back at least to classical Greece, but it has an equally long history in Asia (Daston and Vidal 2004, pp. 3–6). But the constructivist critique of nature also calls the authority of the natural sciences into question, insofar as they claim to represent the world as it is 'in and of itself', apart from human description and cultural differences.

Meanwhile, the project of protecting nature against the encroachments of society, which had fired up the environmentalist movement of the 1970s, turned out to be inadequate to the real complexity of the issues. As environmental protection policies were implemented, it became increasingly clear that they did not really protect nature *as nature*, but amounted to the management of processes in which the natural, the cultural, and the technical were hopelessly intertwined. In practice, environmental protection had little to do with pristine nature, and a whole lot to do with amphibian road tunnels, air quality standards, and certification guidelines for organic farming. What characterizes our era is thus not simply the disappearance of nature, but rather the proliferation of 'hybrids' which subvert the categorical distinction between nature and culture (Latour [1991] 1993, pp. 3–5). This is particularly obvious with regard to genetically modified organisms, farming, and medicine, but it also applies to areas where 'naturalness' might seem to be fairly uncontroversial. National parks, for example, are generally seen as places where nature can be encountered in a form untainted by human interference. In fact, these are zones which are heavily regulated and screened off from changes in their surroundings so as to maintain them in an idealized state. Here, nature is not that which spontaneously is what it is, but rather a kind of museum piece (Sieferle 2003, pp. 27–28, Cronon 1995).

However, such phenomena pose problems not only for a naïve conception of nature, but also for the constructivist critique of the latter: there are important differences between, say, a wild mouse and one that is genetically engineered for use in the laboratory—but these differences are not simply a matter of social construction (Haraway 1997). This problem led Donna Haraway and Bruno Latour, among others, to develop a new vocabulary for describing the *entanglement* of natural and social processes (see Ch. 7: Aesthetics). Rather than thinking of nature and culture as ontologically distinct, they argued, one needed to conceive of the world as a seamless fabric in which human and nonhuman actors are tightly interwoven (Latour [1991] 1993, p. 7). The world of things is not merely an inert object of or passive backdrop for human action. Society and its knowledge of the world constitute and reproduce themselves by enlisting nonhuman agents, shaping them and allowing themselves to be shaped by them.

With these efforts, Latour and Haraway were building on earlier work in the sociology of science and Science and Technology Studies (STS). Since the turn of the century, they in turn became the figureheads of a far-flung constellation of interdisciplinary approaches which fall under the larger conceptual umbrella of posthumanism. In the Western tradition, what distinguishes human beings from animals and machines is the fact that they have consciousness, which allows them to act purposefully—this is what lifts humans above nature. Posthumanists reject this belief: animals and other living beings have cognitive abilities that differ from ours only in degree, and our evolutionary success is not a single-handed accomplishment, but rather owing to the symbiotic relationships humans have entered into with a multiplicity of other species. This is the central premise of multi-species ethnography, which argues that any kind of society must be understood as a 'multi-species community' (Kirksey and Helmreich 2010, Tsing 2015). Other versions of posthumanism question the distinction between humans and machines: from a cybernetic perspective, 'mind' is present wherever information is processed. In all of its forms, posthumanism seeks to dissolve the boundary between humankind and nature, and to locate in the nonhuman world properties which used to be seen as uniquely human (Braidotti 2013, Wolfe 2010). The new materialists follow this line of argument to its most radical conclusions. They argue that all matter has 'agency'—and in their use of the term, the distinction between causal efficacy and intentional action is deliberately blurred so as to question not only the line that divides humans from other living creatures, but also living from inanimate matter (Alaimo 2010, Barad 2007, Bennett 2009, Coole and Frost 2010) (see Ch. 5: The *anthropos*).

For all of these approaches, nature is not simply a social construction. Nevertheless, they share the skepticism toward the concept of nature that also characterizes poststructuralist thought. Haraway and Latour, too, consider nature to be an 'imposture', because it obscures the ways in which the social and the natural order are entangled. The relationships between human beings, other living creatures and the material world are always political— but by drawing a categorical distinction between nature and culture, these relationships are placed beyond the pale of debate. In this manner, the concept of nature has always served to legitimize contingent social norms as 'natural'. Nature is therefore 'anti-politics' (Purdy 2015, p. 21). To invoke it is, in the words of Ulrich Beck, 'to answer the question *how do we want to live?* before it has even been posed' (1988, p. 93, trans. HB).

A concept of nature that would be adequate to the Anthropocene must build on these critiques. Nature can no longer be understood as the counter-pole of culture and turned into an object of nostalgic fantasy, nor can it be the exclusive province of scientific experts to whom society owes unquestioning allegiance. Rather, we must learn to take responsibility for a hybrid world and develop forms of coexistence with nonhuman beings. Haraway calls this 'multispecies flourishing' (Haraway 2016, p. 3), Anna Tsing speaks of collective survival in the contaminated ruins left behind by the project of modernization (Tsing 2015, pp. 17–9), and Latour admonishes us to learn to 'love our monsters', i.e. accommodate ourselves to the natural-cultural composite beings which modern technology is proliferating in ever-increasing numbers (Latour 2011).

Environmental history, too, has increasingly dispensed with the ontological distinction between nature and culture. Its precursors during the 1950s and 1960s had focused on the history of ideas about nature (e.g. Hays 1959, Nash 1967). From the 1970s onwards, however, ecology begins to figure as a historical agent in its own right (Crosby 1972, Worster 1979, Cronon [1983] 2003). In his ground-breaking monograph *The Columbian Exchange*, Alfred Crosby showed that the European conquest of the New World was a process in which biological and cultural factors were closely intertwined. The success of the European settlers was owed not so much to their technological or military superiority, but above all to the multitude of microbes, plants, and animals which they carried with them across the Atlantic (see Ch. 2: Definitions). Long before the notion of 'multi-species communities' became popular, Crosby coined the term 'portmanteau biota' for this phenomenon (Crosby 1986, p. 270). The genocide of the native population and the thorough transformation of the Americas along European patterns was an ecological joint venture. Much like posthumanist theory, environmental history thus pivots on the discovery of nonhuman agency. At the outset, however, it shared the normatively charged conception of nature that underpinned contemporary environmentalism: native populations were assumed to have coexisted in a harmonious relationship with their natural environment, which was destroyed by the European arrivals. For a long time, writing environmental history meant writing the history of destruction and ecological decline.

In the early 1990s, this consensus began to fracture. Wilderness, William Cronon argued in his seminal essay 'The Trouble with Wilderness', is a social construction which harbors a host of culturally specific meanings. The landscapes which the European settlers encountered in the New World were not empty and untouched, but had in fact been shaped by centuries of

Native American inhabitation. By declaring them to be wilderness, this history was erased and native claims to the land were voided. Thus the world was divided into two distinctive zones: pristine nature, where humans can only ever be sojourners, is counter-posed to the places where people actually live and work—places which, because they are already 'fallen', are no longer seen as warranting care and protection (Cronon 1995). But this makes it very difficult to answer the question of what a responsible way of inhabiting the land might look like. If one takes the idea that humans are a part of nature seriously, it makes little sense to grade different ways of using nature as more or less natural. Every society intervenes in its ecological environment, so instead of excoriating the destruction of nature by society, the aim must be to describe the particular ways in which the two mutually transform each other, and to account for their social and ecological consequences. Thus environmental history becomes a history of hybrids, as in Cronon's depiction of Chicago as *Nature's Metropolis* (1991) or Richard White's programmatically titled study *The Organic Machine* (1996), which describes the transformations of the Columbia River since the eighteenth century as a succession of strategies for harnessing the river's energy flows. The theory of sociometabolic regimes, which studies the ways in which societies supply themselves with energy and the resulting changes of the ecological environment, follows a similar approach (Haberl *et al.* 2016) (see Ch. 9: Energy).

This paradigm shift in environmental history also drew on concurrent developments in ecology which had transformed the discipline's understanding of nature. Since classical antiquity, nature had served as a normative foil for society: feudal hierarchy was seen as a link in the 'Great Chain of Being' (Lovejoy 1936), competition in the capitalist market economy mirrored the Darwinian 'survival of the fittest' (Hofstadter 1944), and ecological self-regulation was seen as modeling the checks and balances of liberal democracy (Mitman 1992). Underlying all of these conceptions was the belief that nature was fundamentally unchangeable, a stable, self-regenerating order which stands in contrast to the inconstancy of human beings. Early systems ecology, as well as the environmental movement which drew on the latter, remained enthralled by this view: in the 1950s, older notions of the 'balance of nature' were translated into a new, cybernetic vocabulary. Ecological cycles were understood as homeostatic systems in which the various elements (e.g. predator and prey populations) regulate each other, thus balancing material and energy budgets. Eugene P. Odum's diagram of the nitrogen cycle from his influential textbook *Fundamentals of Ecology* illustrates this mode of thinking (Fig. 4.1).

In this view, ecosystems resemble the famous mobiles of Alexander Calder in which 'everything is connected to everything else', as Barry Commoner put it in his much-cited 'First Law of Ecology' (Commoner 1971, p. 16). To derange any of the components is to put the whole system into disarray. This also suggests that nature itself prefers ordered states which can best be observed where nature has not been disturbed by

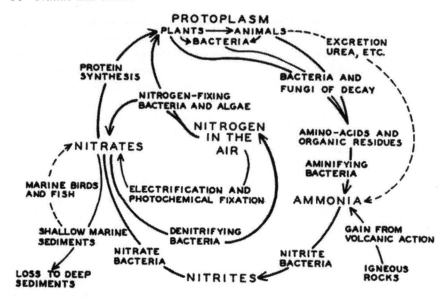

Figure 4.1 The nitrogen biogeochemical cycle, from Odum, E.P., 1953. *Fundamentals of Ecology.* Philadelphia: W. B. Saunders, 20.

human action—for example in the rainforests of the Amazon basin or the savannah of the Serengeti, which from the 1970s onwards became emblems of all things ecological.

This approach generally sidestepped the problem of how the stability of ecological systems was to be reconciled with evolutionary theory, which after all assumed that species are undergoing constant change (Kricher 2009, pp. 97–8). The more empirical data became available, the more clear it also became that not only individual species, but entire ecological processes are in a permanent state of flux (ibid., p. 16). Whether a natural system appears to be stable depends on the spatial and temporal scale at which it is observed. The incalculability of the weather is the stuff of proverbs, whereas climate is comparatively stable. However, if we examine how the climate changes over the course of millions of years, it turns out to be no less fickle than the weather. The same is true for ecosystems, in which stable phases alternate with periods of dramatic turbulence—even without human interference. The impression that nature is characterized by stable equilibria is thus an effect of the scale of observation (see Ch. 10: Scales I). For too long, scientists had taken their cue from snapshots of landscapes which, because they had been spared from modern forms of land use, were considered to be natural. The much-vaunted 'balance of nature' turned out to be a case of trompe l'oeil, visible only in the moment of its disappearance.

This idea of a nature that is restless and prone to sudden change also underpins the model of the planet and its spheres which Earth system science has developed over the past three decades or so (see Ch. 2: Definitions).

New techniques for collecting and computing data have enabled not only a fine-grained understanding of the Earth's deep past, but also of the complex interplay of the various components of the Earth system. We now understand that the Earth's crust (the lithosphere), atmosphere, and oceans (the hydrosphere) have undergone constant change since their formation about 4 billion years ago, that these changes were almost from the outset influenced by biochemical processes, and that they in turn heavily influenced the course of biological evolution. Earth system science builds on the cybernetic models of systems ecology, which conceive of ecological processes as self-regulating—but it scales them up to the level of the planet.

A decisive step in the direction of such a systems-theoretical perspective on the Earth was the Gaia hypothesis advanced by James Lovelock and Lynn Margulis (see Ch. 3: Genealogies). They started from the observation that the intensity of solar radiation had continuously increased over the more than 4 billion years of Earth's history, but that the planet's temperature had nevertheless remained within the narrow band suitable for organic life during this entire time. A planet's surface temperature depends fundamentally on the gases in its atmosphere. This suggests that the composition of the Earth's atmosphere must have changed in such a manner that it could effectively function as a planetary 'thermostat'. However, the high concentrations of nitrogen, oxygen, and carbon dioxide in the atmosphere constitute a geochemical anomaly that is itself only possible because of the presence of organic life. The situation thus entails a strangely circular logic: without atmosphere, there could be no organic life, but without organic life, the Earth's atmosphere could not exist. Lovelock and Margulis concluded that biosphere and atmosphere together constituted a homeostatic system which was able to compensate for fluctuations in its cosmic environment, thus actively producing and maintaining the boundary which separates the system from the lifeless reaches of interplanetary space (Lovelock and Margulis 1974). Within the ensemble of the spheres that form the Earth system—the atmosphere (the layer of gases enveloping the globe), the lithosphere (the rocks), the pedosphere (the layer of soil that enables plant growth), the hydrosphere (the oceans and fresh water deposits), the cryosphere (the ice), and the biosphere (the whole of living organisms)—the biosphere plays the role of the primary regulative force.

This conception of the Earth as a self-regulating system underpinned the 1986 US National Aeronautics and Space Administration (NASA) report *Earth System Science: Overview: A Program for Global Change*. The report instigated the formation of the International Geosphere-Biosphere Programme (IGBP) in the following year—the very institution whose annual conference would witness Paul Crutzen's outburst in 2000, catapulting the Anthropocene concept into the scientific debate. The 1986 report also contains the famous Bretherton diagram, which captures the idea of the Earth system in a single image (Fig. 4.2).

The Bretherton diagram depicts the Earth as a self-regulating system in which geophysical, geochemical, biological, *and* social processes interact with

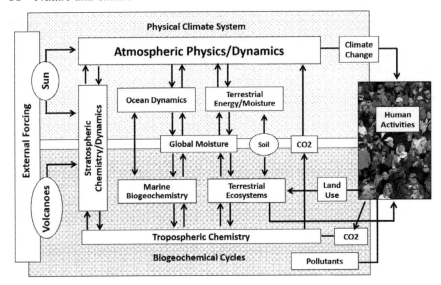

Figure 4.2 Redrawn by the authors from: National Aeronautics and Space Administration, 1986. *Earth System Science. Overview. A Program for Global Change.*
   Washington: NASA, 19.

each other. The latter point is of momentous import. This image of nature
departs from that of systems ecology not only with regard to the audacity of
its scope—the goal is to model the planet in its entirety!—but also in its
inclusion of the checkered little box at the right edge of the diagram:
'Human activities' are no longer viewed as extraneous, but understood as an
integral component of the Earth system. The blunt abstraction of the image
must not detract from the radicalism of the underlying idea: nature and
culture are no longer conceived as separate domains.

   The Bretherton diagram is not only the pictorial expression of a new
conception of the Earth, but also an organization chart for a mammoth scientific project: all components of the Earth system specified in the diagram
became subjects of international research programs—from the Global
Carbon Project (GCP) to Integrated Marine Biogeochemistry and Ecosystem
Research (IMBER) and Integrated History and Future of People on Earth
(IHOPE). In these efforts, the role of humans in the Earth system was not a
side issue, but the central point of interest. When IGBP scientists spoke of
'global change', they were referring to the large-scale transformation of the
Earth by human activities. In the words of the 'Amsterdam Declaration on
Earth Sciences', a quintessential statement of the conception of nature
advanced by Earth system science:

   Human activities are significantly influencing Earth's environment in
   many ways in addition to greenhouse gas emissions and climate change.
   Anthropogenic changes to Earth's land surface, oceans, coasts and

atmosphere and to biological diversity, the water cycle and biogeochemical cycles are clearly identifiable beyond natural variability. They are equal to some of the great forces of nature in their extent and impact. Many are accelerating. Global change is real and is happening *now*.

(Moore *et al.* 2001)

What Lovelock and Margulis had proposed as a hypothesis has since received ample confirmation from Earth system science. It also turned out that the coupling of biosphere and atmosphere is only one of many feedback loops which have kept the Earth system in a precarious balance over billions of years (Lenton 2016, p. 6). The weathering of rocks, the albedo of the polar ice caps, cloud formation, ocean currents and many other processes interact in a manner which has allowed the whole system to compensate for endogenous and exogenous disturbances (such as the development of oxygen-producing cyanobacteria, volcanism, meteorite impacts, and changes in the intensity of solar radiation), in such a manner that the conditions necessary for sustaining organic life remained in place. The feedback mechanisms which link biosphere, atmosphere, hydrosphere, and lithosphere have not only stabilized the surface temperature of the planet, but they have also ensured that materials which are vital to organic life, such as liquid water, carbon, phosphorus, oxygen, and nitrogen, remained in constant supply. Together, these processes constitute the 'metabolism' of the Earth system (ibid., p. 36). While the Earth system is not an organism in the ordinary sense of the term, its development is nevertheless inseparable from the development of life. Its capacity for self-regulation makes it different from any other known object in the cosmos. Hans-Joachim Schellnhuber has therefore described the discovery of the Earth system as a second Copernican revolution: whereas Copernicus demonstrated that the Earth is only one planet among many, Earth system science has shown that the Earth is unique among planets: 'It may well be nature's sole successful attempt at building a robust geosphere-biosphere complex (the ecosphere) in our Galaxy' (Schellnhuber 1999).

Earth system science forms the indispensable empirical foundation for an understanding of nature in the Anthropocene, yet its description of the Earth is in several ways 'unnatural'. First of all, it contradicts traditional conceptions of nature as passive, harmonious, or unchanging. The ability of the Earth system to maintain conditions conducive to organic life over billions of years is not based on its invariability, but precisely its capacity for constant transformation. In the history of the Earth, phases of stability are frequently interrupted by cataclysmic change, which are not only caused by external shocks, but also by life itself. A particularly dramatic instance of this is the Great Oxygenation Event, which propelled the Earth into a new geological era about 2.45 billion years ago (Holland 2006). Cyanobacteria developed the capacity for photosynthesis, using carbon dioxide as a new source of energy. The oxygen which this process released as a waste product

was lethal to most existing forms of life—but it also enabled the development of oxygen-breathing microbes which subsequently formed the evolutionary basis for all multicellular organisms (see Ch. 10: Scales I). And this
was probably not the only instance in which life skirted self-inflicted extinction. There are many indications that the Late Permian Extinction Event 250
million years ago, which eradicated about 90% of biological species, may
have been precipitated by methane-releasing microbes (Rothman *et al.* 2014).
The Earth system appears to be both incredibly robust *and* extremely sensitive to disturbance. From the perspective of geological history, the current
episode of global change which has accompanied the explosion in human
numbers is not unique—but that is not in the least reassuring. If we wish to
stick to the metaphor of 'Mother Earth', we need to understand that in the
Earth system we are dealing with an irritable, capricious mother that
demands unstinting attention and solicitude from her offspring (Stengers
2015, p. 45). Indeed, the murderous Medea might be a more apt mythologi-
cal model than the nurturing Earth goddess as which Gaia has often been
interpreted (Ward 2009).

The Earth described by Earth system science is also 'unnatural' in a
second sense: it has very little to do with the world of sensory experience.
The Earth system cannot be perceived with the senses of the natural body,
but is rendered perceptible and calculable only by way of elaborate technical
procedures. Without a global infrastructure of monitoring stations, satel-
lites, data processing and imaging systems (Edwards 2010, pp. 14–6), the
Earth system could be neither imagined nor represented. Our relationship to
this system thus cannot be conceived by way of analogy to the relationship
between human consciousness and particular natural objects (i.e., as a relationship between entities of a similar scale, see Ch. 10: Scales I). Its characteristic properties can only be comprehended with the help of
mathematical models, and they must be described at the level of probabilities and statistical correlations. This is the reason why climate scientists
keep insisting that no single weather event, however extreme, can ever *prove*
the reality of anthropogenic climate change. In order to understand this
process, we have to use computer simulations and compare current data
with counterfactual projections of how the system would have behaved
without human interference. Thus 'virtual realities' become the basis for
actual political decisions. That is an important reason why these decisions
are so controversial.

In the Anthropocene, the 'nature' of the Earth system is thus indeed a
social and epistemic construct. But the problem is no longer, as the post-
structuralists believed, that people mistake this construct for reality but, on
the contrary, the ease with which it can therefore be dismissed as a fraud, for
example by those who deny climate change. For Bruno Latour, this confu-
sion marks the fundamental break between modernity and the Anthropocene. Modernity was characterized by a sharp ontological divide between
nature and culture: the latter denoted the domain in which human subjects

act freely and articulate culturally specific perspectives on nature; the former stood for the realm of 'hard facts' which were beyond dispute (Latour [1991] 1993, pp. 27–32). The interminable debates over climate change show that this division of labor has broken down (Latour 2004). It is no longer possible to deny that scientific facts are the product of social processes—processes, however, which also involve nonhuman actors. According to Latour, Gaia theory and Earth system science are examples of a new form of scientific practice in which the production of knowledge is inseparable from political responsibility. The instruments with which scientists investigate the Earth also stake out the horizon of political action (this idea had already been developed by Michel Serres, see Ch. 6: Politics), and thus constitute them as a political force: 'earthbound scientists [...] belong to the territory outlined by their instruments. Their knowledge extends as far as their ability to finance, to control, to maintain the sensors that make the consequences of their actions visible. [...] They appear clearly as a new form of non-national power that is explicitly participating as such in geopolitical conflicts' (Latour 2017, pp. 252–3).

Latour and other posthumanist thinkers therefore believe that the Anthropocene is not only a moment of danger, but also an opportunity, because it forces us to finally let go of the ontological distinction between nature and culture—a distinction which, they argue, is at the root of modernity's ecological destructiveness. This critique of the nature/culture binary has become a mainstay of the environmental humanities. It is linked to the search for an alternative ontology 'beyond nature and culture', frequently modeled on indigenous cosmologies (Descola [2005] 2013). Such an ontology would not only put an end to the arrogance of modernity, but also to the 'arrogance of humanism' (Ehrenfeld 1978), while the notion that humans occupy an exceptional position within the natural world is denounced as a pathology of Western thought.

However, it is rather problematic to reduce the process of modernization to the imposition of a single categorical schema (Lindemann 2011)—a schema which, on closer inspection, turns out to be a bizarre misunderstanding and never coincided with actual practice, as Latour has always insisted (Latour [1991] 1993). To argue that modernity is an ontological aberration from which people are only now returning to the path of common sense (Latour also refers to this as the 'closing of the modern parenthesis', Latour 2013, p. 8) is to avoid the question of what is truly *novel* about the Anthropocene. Even more problematically, it suggests that ontologies are something that could be adopted or rejected at will.

Rather than drafting new ontologies or rehabilitating old ones, it may be more important to view them in close conjunction with the historical and ecological conditions of their emergence. The environmental historian Rolf-Peter Sieferle has proposed that the nature/culture binary should be seen neither as a distinctly modern, nor as a uniquely European phenomenon, but rather as a product of the experiential world of agricultural civilizations.

Agriculture entails the removal of vegetation from a bounded plot of land so as to produce conditions favorable to a privileged set of biological species. The growth of these species is fostered and their competitors are destroyed in order to monopolize the primary production of biomass. In its original Latin meaning, 'culture' referred precisely to this process of *cultivating the soil*—i.e., to the attempt to control ecological processes to the benefit of agrarian communities. A basic experience of such a form of life is that this work is never finished: as soon as one stops clearing, plowing and weeding the soil, nature quickly recoups what the farmer took from her 'in the sweat of his brow'. The distinction between nature and culture, Sieferle argues, reflects this fundamental reality of agrarian life: nature is that which is originally there and spontaneously regenerates itself. Culture, on the other hand, requires continuous exertion. Nature denotes a tendency that is inherent in things, and which culture must counteract (Sieferle 2003).

Both sides of this distinction allow for positive and negative valuations. Insofar as nature denotes the 'essence' of things as they are of their own accord, it can also be understood as a norm or as a measure of perfection. An example of this is Aristotle's teleological conception of nature, which informed much of European thought until the early modern period (Johnson 2005, pp. 15–29). Conversely, it can also represent that which threatens the basis of human life and must be subdued through cultivation, the shapeless chaos on which a rational order must be imposed. Culture offers protection from the vicissitudes of nature, but it also entails coercion and civilizational constraints. All the divergent interpretations of the nature/culture binary can be ranged along the spectrum marked by these semantic possibilities: 'There is the cruel barbarian versus the noble savage, the simple life of self-realisation versus privation and licentiousness, alienated artificial civilisation versus civilised urban life' (Sieferle 2003, p. 15).

With the shift to fossil fuels, the lifeworld which had supported these distinctions begins to fade. Farming withers into a marginal occupation and fundamentally changes its character: it no longer provides energy, but turns into just another branch of industrial production which depends, like all the others, on fossil fuels. The availability of cheap and plentiful energy and the concomitant mobilization of material resources (from base metals and cement to synthetic compounds and rare earths) leads to the loss of that fundamental experience which had made the distinction between nature and culture plausible in the first place: that nature resists the effort to bend it to human purposes. By contrast, a distinctive feature of contemporary society is the ease with which 'fantasies can be cast into a material form': 'The extremely low cost of material provision makes it possible to realize even the most simple ideas with an extravagant expenditure of raw materials. The symbolic world immediately coalesces into hard artifacts which are difficult to remove and clog landfills, urban landscapes, libraries, and museums' (Sieferle 2000, pp. 15–6; trans. HB).

The constructivist critique of nature as outlined above can thus also be viewed as reflecting this new relationship to the material world. Looked at in this way, however, the overcoming of the nature/culture binary is no longer an intellectual project, but an accomplished fact, and surely not one to be celebrated. The constructivist critique tends to look past the fact that with the disappearance of 'nature', its antonym also changes its meaning. In the agrarian world-view, the idea that nature needs to be protected from society would have been almost incomprehensible, because nature is defined by the fact that it is what it is, regardless of what humans do. Today, it seems, the situation is reversed. It is society which resists human efforts to shape and control it, which spontaneously regenerates itself and 'may be more recalcitrant to efforts at "rational" colonization than the old, vanquished nature' (Sieferle 2000, p. 16; trans. HB).

This is precisely what is meant when the Anthropocene is described as an age in which humanity encounters itself as a geological force. The processes which today inundate the Earth with an ever-increasing number of technically produced objects have gained a dynamics of their own whose consequences are comparable to those of the biosphere, atmosphere, or hydrosphere. This 'technosphere' can be viewed as a new, emerging sphere in the Earth system whose power is fully comparable to that which the agrarian world-view attributed to nature. And it is equally resistant to attempts at rational control (see Ch. 5: The *anthropos*). Its total mass—consisting of everything from buildings to roads, cables, transistors, ball-point pens, and rubber bands—is today estimated at 30 trillion metric tons, equivalent to about 50 kilograms per square meter of the Earth's land surface (Zalasiewicz *et al.* 2016) and more than five times the total terrestrial biomass (Bar-On *et al.* 2018). The Earth of the Anthropocene will be fundamentally different from that of the Holocene, which witnessed the birth of human civilization. But it may well be that it confronts humans with a very similar challenge: to defend islands of autonomous life against a pullulating force that is at once alien and deeply familiar.

HB

References

Alaimo, S., 2010. *Bodily Natures. Science, Environment, and the Material Self.* Bloomington: Indiana University Press.

Barad, K., 2007. *Meeting the Universe Halfway. Quantum Physics and the Entanglement of Matter and Meaning.* Durham: Duke University Press.

Bar-On, Y.M., et al., 2018. The Biomass Distribution on Earth. *Proceedings of the National Academy of Sciences of the United States of America*, 115(25), 6506–6511.

Barthes, R., [1957] 1972. *Mythologies.* Trans. A. Lavers. New York: Farrar, Straus & Giroux.

Beck, U., 1988. *Gegengifte. Die organisierte Unverantwortlichkeit.* Frankfurt am Main: Suhrkamp.

Bennett, J., 2009. *Vibrant Matter*. Durham: Duke University Press.

Braidotti, R., 2013. *The Posthuman*. London: Polity.

Commoner, B., 1971. *The Closing Circle. Nature, Man, and Technology*. New York: Alfred A. Knopf.

Coole, D., and Frost, S., ed., 2010. *New Materialisms. Ontology, Agency, and Politics*. Durham: Duke University Press.

Cronon, W., 1991. *Nature's Metropolis. Chicago and the Great West*. New York: W. W. Norton.

Cronon, W., 1995. The Trouble with Wilderness, or: Getting Back to the Wrong Nature. In: W. Cronon, ed. *Uncommon Ground. Rethinking the Human Place in Nature*. New York: W. W. Norton, 69–90.

Cronon, W., [1983] 2003. *Changes in the Land. Indians, Colonists, and the Ecology of New England*. New, revised ed. New York: Hill and Wang.

Crosby, A., 1972. *The Columbian Exchange. Biological and Cultural Consequences of 1492*. Westport: Greenwood Press.

Crosby, A., 1986. *Ecological Imperialism. The Biological Expansion of Europe, 900–1900*. New York: Cambridge University Press.

Daston, L., and Vidal, F., eds., 2004. *The Moral Authority of Nature*. Chicago: University of Chicago Press.

Descola, P., [2005] 2013. *Beyond Nature and Culture*. Trans. J. Lloyd. Chicago: University of Chicago Press.

Edwards, P.N., 2010. *A Vast Machine. Computer Models, Climate Data, and the Politics of Global Warming*. Cambridge: MIT Press.

Ehrenfeld, D., 1978. *The Arrogance of Humanism*. Oxford: Oxford University Press.

Giddens, A., 1991. *The Consequences of Modernity*. Cambridge: Polity.

Haberl, H., *et al.*, eds., 2016. *Social Ecology. Society-Nature Relations across Time and Space*. Berlin: Springer.

Haraway, D., 1997. *Modest_Witness@Second_Millennium.FemaleMan©_Meets_Onco-mouse*[TM]. London: Routledge.

Haraway, D., 2016. *Staying with the Trouble. Making Kin in the Chthulucene*. Durham: Duke University Press.

Hays, S.P., 1959. *Conservation and the Gospel of Efficiency. The Progressive Conservation Movement, 1890–1920*. Cambridge: Harvard University Press.

Hofstadter, R., 1944. *Social Darwinism in American Thought, 1860–1915*. Philadelphia: University of Pennsylvania Press.

Holland, H.D., 2006. The Oxygenation of the Atmosphere and Oceans. *Philosophical Transactions of the Royal Society B* [online], 361, 903–915. Available from: www.ncbi.nlm.nih.gov/pmc/articles/PMC1578726/pdf/rstb20061838.pdf [Accessed 14 February 2019].

Jameson, F., 1991. *Postmodernism, or the Cultural Logic of Late Capitalism*. London: Verso.

Johnson, M.R., 2005. *Aristotle on Teleology*. Oxford: Oxford University Press.

Kirksey, S.E., and Helmreich, S., 2010. The Emergence of Multispecies Ethnography. *Cultural Anthropology*, 25(4), 545–576.

Kricher, J., 2009. *The Balance of Nature. Ecology's Enduring Myth*. Princeton: Princeton University Press.

Latour, B., [1991] 1993. *We Have Never Been Modern*. Trans. C. Porter. Cambridge: Harvard University Press.

Latour, B., 2004. Why Has Critique Run out of Steam? From Matters of Fact to Matters of Concern. *Critical Inquiry*, 30(2), 225–248.

Latour, B., 2011. Love Your Monsters. Why We Must Care for Our Technologies as We Do for Our Children. *Breakthrough Journal*, 2, 21–28.

Latour, B., 2013. *An Inquiry into the Modes of Existence. An Anthropology of the Moderns.* Trans. C. Porter. Cambridge: Harvard University Press.

Latour, B., 2017. *Facing Gaia. Eight Lectures on the New Climate Regime.* Trans. C. Porter. London: Polity.

Lenton, T., 2016. *Earth Systems Science. A Very Short Introduction.* Oxford: Oxford University Press.

Lindemann, G., 2011. On Latour's Social Theory and Theory of Society, and his Contribution to Saving the World. *Human Studies*, 34(1), 93–110.

Lovejoy, A.O., 1936. *The Great Chain of Being: A Study of the History of an Idea.* Cambridge, MA: Harvard University Press.

Lovelock, J., and Margulis, L., 1974. Atmospheric Homeostasis by and for the Biosphere: The Gaia Hypothesis. *Tellus*, 26(1–2), 2–9.

McKibben, B., 1989. *The End of Nature.* New York: Random House.

Mitman, G., 1992. *The State of Nature. Ecology, Community, and American Social Thought, 1900–1950.* Chicago: University of Chicago Press.

Moore, B., *et al.*, 2001. *Amsterdam Declaration on Earth Systems Sciences 2001.* Global Change: International Geosphere-Biosphere Programme [online]. Available from: www.igbp.net/about/history/2001amsterdamdeclarationonearthsystemscience.4. 1b8ae20512db692f2a680001312.html [Accessed 13 February 2019].

Nash, R., 1967. *Wilderness and the American Mind.* New Haven: Yale University Press.

National Aeronautics and Space Administration, 1986. *Earth System Science. Overview. A Program for Global Change* [online]. Washington: NASA. Available from: www. nap.edu/catalog/19210/earth-system-science-overview-a-program-for-global-change [Accessed 14 February 2019].

Odum, E.P., 1953. *Fundamentals of Ecology.* Philadelphia: W. B. Saunders.

Purdy, J., 2015. *After Nature. A Politics for the Anthropocene.* Cambridge: Harvard University Press.

Rothman, D.H., *et al.*, 2014. Methanogenic Burst in the End-Permian Carbon Cycle. *Proceedings of the National Academy of Sciences of the United States of America* [online], 111(15), 5462–5467. Available from: www.pnas.org/content/pnas/111/15/ 5462.full.pdf [Accessed 14 February 2019].

Schellnhuber, H.J., 1999. 'Earth system' analysis and the second Copernican revolution. *Nature*, 402 [online]. Available from: www.nature.com/articles/35011515 [Accessed 15 June 2019].

Sieferle, R.-P., 2000. Im Einklang mit der Natur. In: B.-M. Baumunk, ed. *7 Hügel— Bilder und Zeichen des 21. Jahrhunderts. Dschungel.* Berlin: Henschel, 12–16.

Sieferle, R.-P., 2003. The Ends of Nature. In: E. Ehlers and C.F. Gethmann, eds. *Environment Across Cultures.* Berlin: Springer, 13–28.

Stengers, I., 2015. *In Catastrophic Times. Resisting the Coming Barbarism.* Trans. A. Goffey. Minneapolis: Open Humanities Press.

Tsing, A., 2015. *The Mushroom at the End of the World. On the Possibility of Life in the Capitalist Ruins.* Princeton: Princeton University Press.

Ward, P.D., 2009. *The Medea Hypothesis: Is Life on Earth Ultimately Self-Defeating?* Princeton: Princeton University Press.

White, R., 1996. *The Organic Machine. The Remaking of the Columbia River*. New York: Hill and Wang.

Wolfe, C., 2010. *What is Posthumanism?* Minneapolis: University of Minnesota Press.

Worster, D., 1979. *Dust Bowl. The Southern Plains in the 1930s*. Oxford: Oxford University Press.

Zalasiewicz, J., *et al.*, 2016. Scale and Diversity of the Physical Technosphere: A Geological Perspective. *The Anthropocene Review*, 4(1), 9–22.

5 The *anthropos*

Who is 'the human' from whom the Anthropocene takes its name? What capabilities or deficiencies, what historical developments have enabled human beings to change the Earth system so profoundly? Is it justifiable to name an entire epoch of the Earth's history after the species *homo sapiens*? And if so, on what basis? To interrogate the human as the 'onomatophore' (or 'name-bearer') of the Anthropocene (Szerszynski 2015) means to consider humans from the perspective of their power to transform their ecological environment. This implies seeing the human as a being that is at once natural *and* unnatural, both *a part of* nature and *apart from* nature. In this chapter, we therefore follow two lines of questioning that are connected but involve two entirely different ways of considering the human.

First, it is necessary to ask about the status of humankind as the cause and subject of the Anthropocene. In what way are humans the cause of the Anthropocene? How can their impact as a 'force in the Earth system' be adequately described (Moore 2000, p. 2)? This line of questioning must consider this specifically human capability, its historical development, its specific elements, institutions and driving forces—but also the context of the radically altered Earth system in which it unfolds. How does the paradoxical combination of immense power and lack of control, of goal-oriented action and unintended side-effects which characterizes human agency in the Anthropocene come about? And is it legitimate, in thinking about this agency, to attribute it to 'humanity', rather than asking about the specific economic systems, forms of consumption, lifestyles and technologies that have caused and continue to drive the ecological changes of the Anthropocene?

Secondly, one must think about the specificity of the species *homo sapiens*. What sets it apart from other, less invasive, species? On the one hand, humans are part of nature and establish themselves within structures composed of other life forms; but they have also developed the ability to create their own environments. This line of questioning approaches the question from an ecological and evolutionary perspective, considering the deep history of the human species, examining its peculiarities, as well as the decisive thresholds in the history of civilization which it crossed along the way to the

Anthropocene. This approach is 'anthropological', asking: *what is the human?* This question must be treated in the context of what we know today about the evolutionary and cultural development of humanity. What led it to become a dominant species that dramatically changes the living conditions of all other species?

These two approaches operate on different levels of abstraction and in different orders of magnitude (see Ch. 10: Scales I). While the first line of questioning focuses on small scales and examines the concrete ways in which people have changed their environments, the second asks about the specificity of the human relation to the world in contrast to that of other species. This latter question locates the problem at a much larger scale which encompasses ecology and the deep history of humanity, while the former is historical and political, referring to the history of human civilization and its technologies. If the point of departure of the second approach is what is common to all humans, the starting point of the first is, in contrast, the differentiated responsibility for this ecological transformation which is by no means shared by all of humanity. The core argument of this chapter is that these two perspectives on the human in the Anthropocene should be seen as addressing two complementary conceptions of the human: the first as a cultural and social being, the second as a biological species. In order to understand the role and the ambiguous structure of human agency in the Anthropocene as intentional power *and* unintentional force (Chakrabarty 2018), we believe, one needs to view these two conceptions as standing in an irresolvable but indispensable tension.

In the early days of the debate about the concept, these two lines of inquiry were presented as mutually exclusive alternatives. Either one asks about specific historical thresholds and agents responsible for ecological change, or one asks about the human species in general. A 'naturalistic' narrative addressing humanity as a species was thus juxtaposed with a 'historicizing' one devoted to political and economic differentiation. In fact, the first publications proposing the concept used a vocabulary that was bound to stick in the craw of humanities scholars. While the foundational articles by Crutzen and Stoermer speak generally and abstractly of 'mankind' as a force acting on the environment (Crutzen 2002, Crutzen and Stoermer 2000), two influential essays by Steffen *et al.* (2007, 2011) shift the perspective onto the human *species* and its deep history: 'The story begins a few million years ago with the genus *homo erectus*, which had mastered the art of making stone tools and rudimentary weapons' (Steffen *et al.* 2011, p. 846). In a problematic conflation of timescales, they posit a continuity from the production of tools and the control of fire to agriculture and eventually to globalization, industrialization, and fossil fuel use. Thus, the early definitions of the Anthropocene tended to draw a single arc joining evolutionary history to a Eurocentric history of culture and technology, as if the path leading into the Anthropocene had been a foregone conclusion, its trajectory inscribed in the essence of the species itself.

This sweeping account has come in for extensive criticism from the humanities. Holding humankind as a whole responsible for the Anthropocene has been criticized as a 'naturalizing' narrative. It not only obfuscates the contingent historical causes of the ecological crisis (such as colonialism and industrialization originating primarily in Europe), but also the vastly unequal contributions of different groups of humans to the crisis. 'The naturalising, species-centred [narrative]', writes the environmental historian Christophe Bonneuil, 'obscures the asymmetries among humans *about* nature—unequal access to environmental goods and exposure to environmental bads—and *through* nature—technical systems organise energy and material flows which co-produce a certain kind of "second", transformed, nature [...]' (Bonneuil 2015, p. 20). The kind of 'species-thinking' exhibited by natural scientists in the earliest publications on the Anthropocene creates the impression of an undifferentiated agency that blurs responsibility for the ecological crisis. Drawing a direct line from the control of fire to the use of fossil fuels, Andreas Malm and Alf Hornborg argue, confuses necessary and sufficient conditions: it is as if one tried, for example, to explain the success of Japanese fighter pilots in the Second World War with the evolution of stereoscopic vision and the opposable thumb (Gaddis 2002 cited Malm and Hornborg 2014, p. 64). This style of argumentation obscures the concrete social and economic arrangements that have destabilized the Earth system. The transition to fossil fuels, for example, initially took place in Europe and served to further European interests. And the driving factors for European industrialization—'a largely depopulated New World, Afro-American slavery, the exploitation of British labour in factories and mines, and the global demand for cotton fabric' (Malm and Hornborg 2014, p. 63)—can by no means be construed as essential attributes of the human species. The crisis of the Anthropocene, Malm and Hornborg argue, is therefore not caused by humankind, but by global capitalist society (see Ch. 2: Definitions). It is not anthropogenic, but *sociogenic*.

However, this polemic opposition between an undifferentiated 'species thinking' and a properly discriminating historical perspective has in fact confused rather than clarified the issue. Dipesh Chakrabarty—who has occasionally been consigned to the 'naturalist' camp (Bonneuil 2015, Sideris 2016)—has argued that the real challenge of thinking about the human in the Anthropocene consists precisely in the 'collision' of different conceptions of the human (Chakrabarty 2009, 2012, 2016). In the Anthropocene, the politically, culturally, and economically differentiated image of humanity which typically informs the social sciences and humanities is confronted with a scientific perspective that focuses on the cumulative impact of human action on the Earth system. According to Chakrabarty, this should not be interpreted as a new form of biologism sneaking into the discussion to make sweeping assertions about human nature. Rather, the focus on the ecological impact of humans exposes a blind spot of the humanities. In line with a tradition of thought going back to Giambattista Vico, they tend to conceive of humans exclusively in terms of what they themselves produce, that is, in social and cultural terms (Chakrabarty 2009, pp. 202ff). This 'homocentric' self-understanding of the human must now be supplemented by a 'zoe-centric' perspective on humans as one species living among others, as a life form embedded in the Earth system. Chakrabarty therefore proposes a terminological distinction between the human as '*homo*' and as '*anthropos*' (Chakrabarty 2015, p. 142). *Homo* designates the human of the humanities, differentiated by culture, gender, race, and economic situation, but also unified by the ability to think rationally and act morally, and by the possession of universal rights and freedoms. *Homo* is the human understood as the *other* of nature. *Anthropos*, on the other hand, refers to the human as a biological species, capable of modifying its environment but also subject to physical needs, exposed to natural forces and depending for its survival on coexistence with other species. The *anthropos* is a conception of the human as a natural being and force *within* nature.

This double conception of the human takes up a distinction in the concept of life already drawn by Aristotle and elaborated in recent years by Giorgio Agamben: *bíos* refers to 'life' as a form of social organization, to specifically human forms of life, whereas *zoé* denotes purely biological life of the sort that humans share with all other living beings (Chakrabarty 2015, p. 142f, Agamben 1998). In the modern age, as Agamben following Foucault argues, both aspects of life are subject to politicization (Foucault [1976] 1978). Understood as cultural and social life, *bíos* raises the problem of rights, of the freedoms and laws that organize human society. The politics of *bíos* is, in short, a question of culture. In contrast, *zoé*, physical life, is the object of biopolitical interventions and controls (see Ch. 8: Biopolitics). If *homo* corresponds to *bíos*, or socio-cultural life, then *anthropos* is equivalent to *zoé*, or biological life. This '*pragmatic* distinction', Chakrabarty argues, lies at the heart of debates about the human of the Anthropocene (Chakrabarty 2015, p. 156). Those who reject 'species-thinking' in favor of political, economic and cultural differentiation thus evade the real intellectual scandal of the Anthropocene: the unavoidable collision between these two conceptions of the human. The humanist *homo* needs the corrective of the ecological-biological *anthropos*. It is only through this tension that the ambivalent nature of the human assumes its distinctive contours. To be human is to be both detached from and attached to nature.

These two conflicting conceptions of the human also help to better understand two radically opposed ways of thinking about the role of humans in the Anthropocene: *ecomodernism* and *ecological posthumanism*. While the first position pushes the conception of the human as *homo* to an extreme, the latter radicalizes the conception of the *anthropos*.

(1) *Ecomodernism*. This position, advocated by the proponents of a 'Good Anthropocene', sees the role of humans in the Anthropocene as 'stewards' of the Earth system. It absolutizes the idea of the human as *homo*—a rational, self-determining being capable of making and carrying out ethical decisions. In this view, it is the task of humans to overcome the ecological crisis by

actively controlling both human action and maintaining or restoring the balance of the Earth system.

Precisely because of their power to transform the planet, it is argued, humans have a unique responsibility to control and regulate nature. As Stuart Brand puts it: 'We are as gods and have to get good at it' (Brand 2009, p. 1). The ecomodernist perspective on the human relies on two equally optimistic assumptions. On the one hand, it presumes that humans are sufficiently intelligent, prudent, and self-controlled to find and implement technical and social solutions which would allow them to reduce their environmental impact. On the other, it trusts in the resilience of the Earth system, which is taken to be capable of bouncing back from the destabilizing blows it has already sustained from human action. Ecomodernism calls for a new and different form of environmentalism which would no longer be based on the ideal of an 'untouched nature' (Nordhaus and Shellenberger 2005). It is not a matter of protecting nature from human intervention, but rather of managing it in a more sophisticated way by intensifying our use of 'green' technologies. This might include, for example, the replacement of fossil fuels with nuclear power, the extensive use of genetically manipulated organisms, and even active geo- and climate-engineering. It involves thinking of the planet as a vast ecological restoration project:

> The Anthropocene does not represent the failure of environmentalism. It is the stage on which a new, more positive and forward-looking environmentalism can be built. This is the Earth we have created, and we have a duty, as a species, to protect it and manage it with love and intelligence. It is not ruined. It is beautiful still, and can be even more beautiful, if we work together and care for it.
>
> (Marris *et al.* 2011)

The representatives of this position tend to express their views in grand programmatic statements such as the 'Ecomodernist Manifesto' (Asafu-Adjaye *et al.* 2015). Unlike traditional environmentalism, which they tend to dismiss, they eschew nostalgia and view the current situation in rigorously pragmatic terms: the comprehensive transformation of the planet is a situation from which there is no turning back, and we need to make the best of it. They believe that the ecological carrying capacity of the Earth leaves plenty of headroom for a growing human population and its ever-expanding needs—provided that the planet is properly managed (see Ch. 8: Biopolitics). The ecomodernists' optimism regarding technical solutions is often coupled with a conspicuous absence of social and cultural critique. They are neither interested in an analysis of industrial capitalism à la Jason Moore nor in programs of social and economic transformation towards de-growth. Mark Lynas, for example, writes: 'Global warming is not about overconsumption, morality, ideology or capitalism. It is largely the result of human beings generating energy by burning hydrocarbons and coal. It is, in other words, a technical problem, and is therefore amenable to a largely technical solution, albeit one driven by politics' (Lynas 2011, p. 66). Such a position presupposes that human beings are rational, responsible, far-sighted, and capable of taking the necessary steps to 'manage' the Anthropocene.

Clive Hamilton has criticized this position by noting that the human being of the ecomodernist imaginary is the anthropological counterpart to the benevolent, omniscient, and almighty God of classical theodicy (Hamilton 2015). Far from being non-ideological, their position is ultimately a metaphysical construction. Despite their supposed pragmatism, the ecomodernists tend to underestimate the irrationality, myopia, and haphazardness of human behavior. They also overestimate the resilience and plasticity of the Earth system. With a few well-placed interventions, they believe, the Earth could be steered back to the stable conditions which prevailed in the Holocene (Kareiva *et al.* 2011). This rosy view both of the Earth's resilience and of the rationality of human beings misconstrues, we argue, the specific structure of human agency in the Anthropocene, which consists in a paradoxical combination of enormous force and an equally profound loss of control. Understanding humans solely as *homo*, the ecomodernists tend to forget the non-rational, unintentional dimension of human behavior which is central to the conception of the *anthropos*.

(2) *Ecological posthumanism* presents the opposite extreme, albeit with a much higher degree of theoretical sophistication. Opposing the teleological and idealistic implications of classical humanism, ecological posthumanists propose to radically abandon any thought of human exceptionalism. They thus tend to consider the human exclusively as *anthropos*—as a life form among others, entangled in dependencies and symbioses which exhaustively define what it means to be human. As anthropologist Anna Tsing provocatively puts it: 'Human nature is an interspecies relationship' (Tsing 2012, p. 141). According to this position, humans have no essence that sets them apart from other biological species; rather they are defined by their position in a network of non-human life forms—from the bacteria and fungi colonizing their bodies to domesticated animals and plants. In contrast to the theory-averse ecomodernists, this conception relies on a theoretical framework that calls into question any sharp distinction between nature and culture. This 'zoecentric' perspective, as Chakrabarty calls it, wants to lead humans out of their anthropocentric arrogance into a world of mutual dependency and distributed agency. Humans are seen as one agent among many other, non-human, agencies—of other species, of inanimate forces such as climate or geology, and of 'matter' in the broadest sense. In short, the human is understood to be just one part in the assemblage of forces that is the Earth system.

Unlike the ecomodernists, the ecological posthumanist position takes both the power and the irritability of the Earth system seriously and accentuates the vulnerability of humans within that system. 'It is constitutive of our humanness', writes Nigel Clark, 'that we are inherently liable to be thrown off course by the eventualities of our planet' (Clark 2011, p. xiv). It is the very fragility of the Earth system, as well as of the humans in it, from which the sense of responsibility to other forms of life derives: 'But just as the Earth can perturb and excite us, so too are we receptive to the incitements of others who have been shaken up by the inconstancy of the ground they depend on. A volatile world can impinge upon ourselves directly, or it can present its demands and allures by way of others [...]' (ibid.). The ethical obligations of humans toward the non-human arise from their entanglement with other vulnerable species in the midst of an unstable nature.

However, this responsibility does not draw on the idea of a responsibility of the powerful for the powerless, or of consciousness for that which is without consciousness. Rather, both sides are seen as being on an equal footing, incurring obligations from their mutual dependence. For Donna Haraway, perhaps the most eloquent representative of this position, this means not only acknowledging the 'kinship' of humans with other forms of life but understanding other species as companions to which one has similar obligations as to one's own kind. Haraway writes: 'Kin-making is making persons, not necessarily as individuals or as humans. [...] Kin is an assembling sort of word. All critters share a common "flesh", laterally, semiotically, and genealogically' (Haraway 2016, pp. 103). Her biopolitical slogan—'Make kin, not babies!' (ibid.)—encapsulates this obligation to the non-human world. It lays the groundwork for a biopolitics not aiming to subdue and control life but striving for coexistence and multi-species flourishing (see Ch. 8: Biopolitics). It is this ethical and political attitude, rather than the much-discussed 'flat ontologies' (Bryant 2011), which may be the most promising and persuasive aspect of ecological posthumanism. Nonetheless, apart from the sometimes cozy, sometimes uncanny stories of symbioses with 'companion species' (Haraway 2003), it remains rather vague about what specific behaviors are to emerge from the acknowledgement of these interspecies relationships.

Pursuing Haraway's line of thinking, Anna Tsing has developed an alternative model of agency based on the mutual, symbiotic entanglement of species. She analyzes old and new human cultural practices—such as foraging, animal husbandry, agriculture, and the plantation system—as examples of the mutual interpenetration and transformation of species. Everything that we have mistakenly celebrated as achievements of unalloyed human ingenuity, Tsing argues, has arisen from such mutual transformations. Instead of explaining the beginning of agriculture with the cultivation of seed-bearing grasses at the hand of cunning humans, Tsing flips the script: 'Cereals domesticated humans' (Tsing 2012, p. 145). She shows how cereals brought about the shift from the varied diet of hunter-gatherer societies to a few staple foods, leading to a sedentary way of life, population growth, the development of cities and states—and thus to highly hierarchical social structures. In arranging for their own conquest of the Earth, cereals led humans down a path that was in no way good for us. Such a conception of agency may better be able to grasp the contingencies, as well as the dependencies, of human cultural development, than the established narratives of emancipation and progress. Tsing's account has the merit of an alternative narrative that corrects the anthropocentrism of classical cultural history. Nevertheless, her conception of an agency distributed among different biological species tends to underplay the extent to which their mutual transformations tend to be arranged for the benefit of humans rather than their domesticates. In denying the dominance of humans, it is ultimately unable to explain what this dominance consists in, how it came to threaten the existence of countless other species, and why it must be challenged.

If ecomodernism overestimates the human as *homo*, ecological posthumanism underestimates the human as mere *anthropos*. Both positions struggle to grasp the paradoxical structure of human agency in the Anthropocene. The world of *homo* is the world of purposeful human creation. Here, human agency is understood as rational action, as the intentional use of means to achieve specific ends, as well as the ability to assess the proportionality of means and ends. Seen as *homo*, humans are in control of their actions—and thus responsible for their consequences. This 'humanist' version of agency, however, does not give an adequate account of human agency in the Anthropocene. What is at stake in human agency as a planetary force is precisely *not* intentional (if perhaps reckless and misguided) actions, but rather their unintended, uncontrolled and unforeseeable consequences. The Anthropocene is about side-effects, unpredictable long-term impacts, or the upscaling of apparently innocuous individual activities into cumulative, collective and highly consequential behavior. Human agency betrays a fundamental ecological blindness that cannot simply be attributed to an ideologically blinkered modernity.

Rather than thinking of human agency in the Anthropocene in terms of *power*, it is better characterized as a *force* (Chakrabarty 2018). It has less to do with intentional, goal-oriented action than with what is called 'behavior' in biology. On a planetary level, the ecological consequences of human action are not planned but occur as unforeseen consequences or side-effects, obscured by periods of latency, invisibility and the considerable resilience of nature. This decoupling of intention and effect does not occur because people fail to properly reflect on what they are doing, but rather through the massive accumulation of individual actions. Only in their millionfold multiplication do isolated, everyday activities become ecologically relevant. Human agency as a geological force thus involves a scale effect, the translation from an individual to a global scale (see Ch. 10: Scales I). This is why it is so difficult to pin the responsibility for ecological impacts on individual actors. At the same time, the efficacy of human action can only be grasped at the level of the Earth system—a system we are only just beginning to understand, and which turns out to be far more complex and unpredictable than traditional conceptions of nature as regular and passive have led us to believe (see Ch. 4: Nature and culture). The massive effect of humanity therefore does not just depend on humans themselves but just as much on the irritability of the Earth system, on the capacity of its tangled feedback loops not only to dampen, but also to amplify the forces which impinge on it. In this regard, the new materialisms and ecological posthumanism, positions that strongly emphasize the agency of non-human actors, have a point: the planetary agency of human beings really can only be understood in their conjunction with the Earth system. As a 'geological force', humans appear to be just as 'blind' and aimless as other geological forces.

Human agency in the Anthropocene thus cannot be understood as a controlled, purposeful power, i.e. as a capacity that can be consciously used or withheld; it rather has the quality of a blind force. Politically and ethically, the challenge is to bring the ecological impact of *anthropos* under the rational, moral control of *homo*, or, in other words, to transform human force into human power. Criticizing 'species-thinking' in the Anthropocene is, we believe, an understandable but anthropologically naïve attempt to reinterpret the behavior of *anthropos* as the action of *homo*. Naming specific historical and economical culprits, such as European colonialism, industrialization, or capitalism tends to cast these as collective quasi-subjects acting with some level of purpose and intention. Thus understood, the ecological crisis of the Anthropocene is the knowingly and willingly incurred price of industrial progress (Bonneuil and Fressoz 2016, Moore 2016a). This perspective, however, confuses the two versions of the human—as if *homo* was indeed master in the house of the Earth system:

> The mode of being in which humans collectively may act as a geological force *is not* the mode of being in which humans—individually and collectively—can become conscious of being such a force. The talk of a 'conscious' or responsible 'force' collapses—ahead of any actual histories allowing for such a fusion—the two different modes of being human [...].
>
> (Chakrabarty 2018, p. 28)

Without the dual understanding of the human as *homo* and *anthropos*, as a being at once cultural and natural, the specific role of the human in the Anthropocene cannot be grasped. And this means—all the humanist polemics against 'human exemptionalism' notwithstanding (Bonneuil 2015)—that one must take the distinctiveness of the human species seriously.

It is in this context that a particular strand of anthropological thought acquires a new relevance: philosophical anthropology (see Ch. 3: Genealogies). This tradition of thought developed in Germany during the 1920s, inspired by the environmental theory of Jacob von Uexküll (1909) and by phenomenology. It sought to define the human on the basis of its ecological particularity (*Sonderstellung*). The most influential representatives of philosophical anthropology, Helmut Plessner and Arnold Gehlen, portray the human as a being that somehow managed to transform its physiological weakness into a source of strength. Their starting point is the fact that humans are not adapted to a specific environmental niche. According to Plessner, humans are characterized by their 'eccentric positionality', that is, by their ability to distance themselves from their existence and reflect on their own position in a given environment (Plessner [1928] 2019). Thus, the 'nature' of the human is their 'artificiality' (Plessner 1982, p. 15). The relation of humans to their environment is explained precisely by their 'nakedness', i.e. their lack of natural defenses and means of attack. Compared to other species, humans largely lack instincts to guide their behavior, and are thus burdened with the need to reflect on their actions (Plessner 1982, p. 25). Developing this line of thinking, Arnold Gehlen describes humans as 'deficient beings' (*Mängelwesen*), bare and unprotected but for that reason malleable and capable of learning. Their deficiencies compel them to develop cultural practices and social structures: language allowing for coordination and communication, social institutions to organize collective life, and finally technology as a compensation for physiological weakness (Gehlen [1940] 1988). Thus turning their weakness into strengths, humans became capable not only of creating specific environments (many species produce their own 'ecological niches'), but of constructing an entire world. To this end, they invent technology. But technology, according to Gehlen, has an ambivalent character. On the one hand, it supplements and protects humans, shielding them from the assaults of an overbearing nature. On the other hand, technology becomes a 'second nature' in which they eventually find themselves trapped and alienated (Gehlen [1957] 1980).

Yet from the viewpoint of traditional evolutionary theory, the idea that humans became a dominant species because of their lack of adaptation would appear very strange. The 'variability selection hypothesis' proposed by the American paleoanthropologist Rick Potts goes some way to providing a biological basis for the rather speculative claims of philosophical anthropology (Potts 1997). Potts notes that classical Darwinism conceived of evolution as a process of adaptation to relatively *stable* environmental conditions. Yet he points out that the development of *homo sapiens* did not take place in the stable environment of the Holocene but in the Pleistocene—an epoch that was characterized by enormous climatic and environmental fluctuations which often took place with breathtaking speed. Pollen deposits from France, Greece, and the Black Sea show that during the late Pleistocene, these areas were by turns covered with tundra and riparian forests, sometimes replacing each other over the course of a single decade (Potts 1997, p. 167). In order to survive this 'time of ecological trauma' (ibid., p. 216), it was advantageous not to fit too closely into a particular ecological niche, but to rather have the capacity to readily adapt to changing ones. Species survival was about being able to tap into resources in a quickly changing landscape, tolerating fluctuating environmental conditions, and differentiating into geographically distributed populations (ibid., p. 232). Symbioses with other species of the sort celebrated by Haraway and Tsing are, by contrast, rather risky in a volatile environment insofar as they require a high degree of specialization. An environment subject to abrupt change instead favors the evolution of ecological *variability*. Following Potts, this variability could be the key not only to the evolution of *homo sapiens*, but also of many other species to which humans have become closely bound, for example, rats, pigs, and, above all, cereals. All these species are able to quickly colonize disturbed ecosystems and tolerate a wide range of environmental conditions.

A closer look at the deep history of humanity may thus not only provide something of an ironic precedent for the Anthropocene—our species managed to eke out a living under turbulent climatic conditions before, only that this time they will be of our own making. But more importantly, it may hold the key to an evolutionary explanation of the 'natural un-naturalness' of humans. As Clive Hamilton has emphasized, such an understanding of human distinctiveness does not necessarily imply a *normative* claim to superiority or human exceptionalism (Hamilton 2017, pp. 53–4). In view of the altered constellation of humans and the Earth system in the Anthropocene—a more powerful human in the midst of a much more unstable, unpredictable nature—Hamilton advocates a 'moderate', non-teleological and non-normative 'new anthropocentrism':

> At the heart of the new anthropocentrism stands the 'embedded subject', a character who expresses the double truth of the human in the Anthropocene, that is, the possessor of autonomy but one always guided and constrained by its assimilation into the processes that govern the Earth system. It acknowledges that humans are agents more powerful than ever, yet confirms our ultimate inseparability from the forces of the natural world we inhabit.
>
> (Hamilton 2017, p. 52)

Hamilton's conception of human agency is thus based on the dual nature of the human we have argued for. Endowed with more power than other species, but also faced with a nature that is much more 'ticklish', at once more powerful and more prone to disturbance (Stengers 2015, p. 46), human beings bear a unique responsibility in the Anthropocene. Yet this responsibility may have less to do with implementing green technology than with adjusting to the new unpredictability of nature. The idea of a unified humanity in the Anthropocene, criticized as 'species-thinking' (see, for example, Malm and Hornborg 2014, Bonneuil and Fressoz 2016), can now be understood quite differently. Thinking about the human in the Anthropocene, it is not enough to identify specific culprits such as 'capitalism' or 'industrialized nations'. Beyond that, it is about negotiating a common future in the increasingly volatile and extreme natural conditions to which all human beings will be exposed (see Ch. 6: Politics).

Hamilton is rightfully skeptical about the ecomodernist belief that humanity will be able to stabilize the Earth system by implementing the proper kinds of technology. Yet, beyond ecomodernist techno-optimism and its critics, we believe that the role of technology for an anthropology of the Anthropocene has so far not been sufficiently analyzed. Philosophical anthropology, in particular Plessner and Gehlen, has long insisted that the compensation of physiological weakness by way of technology is an essential feature of our species—an aspect of human nature, as it were. In the modern age, this realm of technology has attained its own dynamic and mode of being, to the point of radically transcending, even marginalizing human intentions and needs. The question of the human as the 'onomatophore' of the Anthropocene thus cannot be answered without reference to technology, as the British sociologist of religion Bronislaw Szerszynski has pointed out in a brilliant piece of speculative fiction (Szerszynski 2015). Szerszynski's text describes an application by the human species to the interplanetary *Commission on Planetary Ages* (a whimsical riff on the international body that will have to decide on the formalization of the Anthropocene). *Anthropos'* request to name the present epoch after itself is examined with scholastic exactitude by the commission—and finally turned down. Instead, the commission resolves to define the emerging epoch as the *Phanerotechnic age*, in analogy to the *Phanerozoic age*, in which life appeared on Earth: 'Be it known that the Commission has decided: ... that the closing of the Phanerozoic aeon is also the opening of a new aeon in the Earth's immanent time, which ... shall be called the Phanerotechnic: the aeon of technological life, of organised inorganic matter ...' (Szerszynski 2015, p. 182). The emergence of technology, the commission argues, heralds an entirely new geological aeon—an age of machines which will emancipate themselves from their organic builders.

The power of this flight of fancy lies in the fact that it compels the reader to think of the Anthropocene on a truly planetary scale, i.e. in the context of the history of life on Earth. In so doing, it points to an 'agent' both omnipresent and curiously underappreciated in most reflections on humanity's role in the Anthropocene: technology. For the disruption of the Earth system by humans is only possible through technology, which arguably has come to constitute an entirely new realm: the 'technosphere'. Far from being celebratory, this perspective introduces a very different kind of 'posthumanism' into the debate, one that marginalizes not only the human but biological life more generally (Rosol *et al.* 2017, p. 3). According to geologist and environmental engineer Peter K. Haff, who introduced the term into the Anthropocene debate, the technosphere is an independent dimension of the Earth system, an autonomous sphere (see Ch. 4: Nature and culture), similar to the biosphere, atmosphere, hydrosphere and lithosphere (Haff 2013, 2017, p. 104). In some respects, the term resembles the 'noosphere' which Vernadsky and Teilhard de Chardin proposed as a dimension of the planet engendered by the human intellect (Vernadsky 1945, Teilhard de Chardin [1955] 1960) (see Ch. 3: Genealogies). Unlike the noosphere, however, the technosphere is not an immaterial dimension of human making, but a material system that physically interacts with the other spheres of the Earth system. Even more importantly, technology is no longer—as in philosophical anthropology—understood in instrumental terms, i.e. as a tool that serves humans to control and shield themselves from nature. Rather, the technosphere represents an emergent sphere of organized, inorganic matter whose dynamic is not determined by its human components. In the age of digital technology, technology is no longer simply an extension of the human. On the contrary, humans must now be understood as 'parts' of the technosphere (Haff 2013). Haff views the technosphere as an autonomous agent that encompasses all the material aspects of world society:

> The technosphere includes the world's large-scale energy and resource extraction systems, power generation and transmission systems, communication, transportation, financial and other networks, governments and bureaucracies, cities, factories, farms and myriad other 'built' systems, as well as all the parts of these systems, including computers, windows, tractors, office memos and humans. It also includes systems which traditionally we think of as social or human-dominated, such as religious institutions or NGOs [nongovernmental organizations].
>
> (Haff 2014, p. 127)

The technosphere might be created and maintained by humans, but the reverse of this statement is equally valid: humans are created and maintained by the technosphere. While humans service the system and ensure its energy supply, their own bodies run on technically produced calories, are kept warm, dry and healthy by machines. The dependency is mutual, and there is no reason to believe that the trajectory of the whole assemblage is determined by the actions of individual humans. Indeed, in this framework, humans are little more than 'minor components' of the technosphere (ibid.)., elements of a larger system to which, at the operative micro- and macro-levels, they ultimately have no cognitive access.

The ability of humans to interact with the technosphere is thus limited—and these limits are related to a scaling problem (see Ch. 10: Scales I). Haff argues that humans can only interact with things that are of the same order of magnitude as their own bodies, which he calls Stratum II. According to this schema, elements that are much smaller belong to Stratum I, elements that are much larger to Stratum III. Interactions with elements on Stratum I or III require complicated processes of translation (Haff 2014, p. 130). In a traffic system, for example, humans have access to the car they are driving and to its various interfaces (brakes, steering wheel, dashboard, etc.), all of which are of the same 'human' scale. But they do not have access to either the technical micro-level of Stratum I (the electronics, the physics and chemistry of the combustion process in the engine, etc.), or to the macro-level of Stratum III (the urban traffic system, the car market, or the carbon dioxide emissions of global traffic).

Humans in the Anthropocene thus can no longer be conceived of outside of the technosphere, even if they no longer really control the proliferation of technology or have access to the various scalar levels on which it operates and takes effect. The paradoxical form of human agency in the Anthropocene—the combination of immense force and loss of control—can now be seen in yet another light. Human force within the Earth system is exercised through and within the framework of the technosphere. The 'subject' of the Anthropocene is thus not the human being, nor certain societies or economic systems (capitalism), but rather a concrete 'assemblage' of people, infrastructures, forms of consumption, economies, and energy regimes within the technosphere (Woods 2014). Haff's concept of the technosphere also makes it possible to understand in more detail the problem of scale inherent in human agency in the Anthropocene. The technosphere—as the means of human intervention into nature—not only surrounds humans as an entire system of which they are a part, but also transcends human dimensions. If, to draw on Haff's terminology, the human being is located in Stratum II, the technosphere includes orders of magnitude that are both too small (Stratum I) and too large (Stratum III) to be directly accessible for humans. While they can act on the level of Stratum II—on their own scale—they lose control and oversight when it comes to the other strata: the carbon dioxide emissions of an individual combustion engine in Stratum I are as invisible to human beings as the accumulated consequences of these emissions for the global climate in Stratum III. Nonetheless, human involvement in the technosphere is constantly being translated between these different orders of magnitude. What humans do in the technosphere is scaled up to planetary dimensions. It is in this process of translation that the disjunction between individual actions and their unintentional, cumulative side-effects arises. Both the loss of control which characterizes human agency in the Anthropocene and the massive force of its impact are scaling effects of the technosphere (see Ch. 10: Scales I).

The notion of the technosphere, if taken seriously, displaces the human as the subject of the Anthropocene. And, as in Szerszynski's fiction, it also marginalizes the human historically. Maybe it is not humans who define the present epoch, but rather something that they have brought forth. The fictional *Commission on Planetary Ages* points towards a model of planetary history in which the spheres produce elements that, by destabilizing the Earth system, give rise to wholly new spheres. Thus the atmosphere emerged from the gases released by the lithosphere of the young Earth. The inorganic spheres—the lithosphere, the atmosphere and the hydrosphere—engendered the biosphere, the dimension of life on Earth. Human beings emerged as a late and initially unremarkable product of the biosphere (Szerszynski 2019). In the larger scheme of things, humans may be little more than catalysts for a new, autonomous sphere, the sphere of 'anorganic life', as it were. From this perspective, the transformation of the Earth system we are witnessing in the Anthropocene not only reflects the dual, contradictory nature of human beings, but also marks the emergence of the technosphere. It may well be that in the course of this transformation, the human being as the biotic midwife of the technosphere will eventually disappear—not so much like a 'face drawn in sand at the edge of the sea', as Foucault would have it (Foucault [1966] 1989, p. 387), but more in the manner of the trilobites, dinosaurs, and Tasmanian tigers.

EH

References

Agamben, G., 1998. *Homo sacer. Sovereign power and bare life.* Trans. D. Heller-Roazen. Stanford: Stanford University Press.

Asafu-Adjaye, J., *et al.*, 2015. *An Ecomodernist Manifesto* [online]. Available from: www.ecomodernism.org [Accessed 13 February 2019].

Bonneuil, C., 2015. The Geological Turn. Narratives of the Anthropocene. In: C. Hamilton, F. Gemenne and C. Bonneuil, eds. *The Anthropocene and the Global Environmental Crisis. Rethinking modernity in a new epoch.* New York and London: Routledge, 17–31.

Bonneuil, C., and Fressoz, J.-B., 2016. *The Shock of the Anthropocene. The Earth, History and Us.* London and New York: Verso.

Brand, S., 2009. *Whole Earth Discipline. An Ecopragmatist Manifesto.* London: Viking Penguin.

Bryant, L.R., 2011. *The Democracy of Objects.* Michigan: Open Humanities Press Imprint.

Chakrabarty, D., 2009. The Climate of History. Four Theses. *Critical Inquiry*, 35(2), 197–222.

Chakrabarty, D., 2012. Postcolonial Studies and the Challenge of Climate Change. *New Literary History*, 43(1), 1–18.

Chakrabarty, D., 18–19 February2015. *The Human Condition in the Anthropocene, The Tanner Lectures in Human Values* [online]. New Haven: Yale University. Available from: https://tannerlectures.utah.edu/Chakrabarty%20manuscript.pdf [Accessed 14 April 2019].

Chakrabarty, D., 2016. Humanities in the Anthropocene: The Crisis of an Enduring Kantian Fable. *New Literary History*, 47(2–3), 377–397.

Chakrabarty, D., 2018. Anthropocene Time. *History and Theory*, 57(1), 5–32.

Clark, N., 2011. *Inhuman Nature. Sociable Life on a Dynamic Planet.* London: Sage.

Crutzen, P.J., 2002. The Geology of Mankind. *Nature*, 415(6867), 23.

Crutzen, P.J., and Stoermer, E.F., 2000. The 'Anthropocene'. *Global Change Newsletter* [online], IGBP 41, May 2000, 17–18. Available from: www.igbp.net/publications/globalchangemagazine/globalchangemagazine/globalchangenewslettersno4159.5.5831d9ad13275d51c098000309.html [Accessed 14 April 2019].

Foucault, M., [1976] 1978. *The History of Sexuality.* Vol. 1. Trans. R. Hurley. New York: Pantheon.

Foucault, M., [1966] 1989. *The Order of Things. An Archeology of the Human Sciences.* Oxford and New York: Routledge.

Gaddis, J.L., 2002. *The landscape of history. How historians map the past.* Oxford and New York: Oxford University Press.

Gehlen, A., [1940] 1988. *Man. His Nature and Place in the World.* New York: Columbia University Press.

Gehlen, A., [1957] 1980. *Man in the Age of Technology*. New York: Columbia University Press.

Haff, P.K., 2013. Technology as a geological phenomenon: Implications for human well-being. *Geological Society: Special Publications*, 395(1), no pages.

Haff, P.K., 2014. Humans and technology in the Anthropocene: Six rules. *The Anthropocene Review*, 1(2), 126–136.

Haff, P.K., 2017. Being human in the Anthropocene. *The Anthropocene Review*, 4(2), 103–109.

Hamilton, C., 2015. The Theodicy of the 'Good Anthropocene'. *Environmental Humanities*, 7(1), 233–238.

Hamilton, C., 2017. *Defiant Earth. The Fate of Humans in the Anthropocene*. Cambridge: Polity Press.

Haraway, D., 2003. *The Companion Species Manifesto. Dogs, People, and significant otherness*. Chicago: Prickly Paradigm Press.

Haraway, D., 2016. *Staying with the Trouble. Making Kin in the Chthulucene*. Durham: Duke University Press.

Kareiva, P., *et al.*, 2011. Conservation in the Anthropocene. *Breakthrough Journal* [online], 2 (Fall), no pages. Available from: https://thebreakthrough.org/journal/issue-2/conservation-in-the-anthropocene [Accessed 14 April 2019].

Lynas, M., 2011. *The God Species. Saving the Planet in the Age of Humans*. London: National Geographic.

Malm, A., and Hornborg, A., 2014. The geology of mankind? A critique of the Anthropocene narrative. *The Anthropocene Review*, 1(1), 62–69.

Marris, E., *et al.*, 7 December2011. Hope in the Age of Man. *The New York Times* [online]. Available from: www.nytimes.com/2011/12/08/opinion/the-age-of-man-is-not-a-disaster.html [Accessed 14 April 2019].

Moore, B. III, 2000. Sustaining Earth's life support systems—the challenge for the next decade and beyond. *Global Change Newsletter* [online], IGBP 41, Mai 2000, 1–2. Available from: www.igbp.net/download/18.316f18321323470177580001401/1376383088452/NL41.pdf [Accessed 27 April 2019].

Moore, J.W., ed., 2016a. *Anthropocene or Capitalocene? Nature, History, and the Crisis of Capitalism*. Oakland: PM.

Nordhaus, T., and Shellenberger, M., [14 January2004] 2005. The Death of Environmentalism: Global Warming Politics in a Post-Environmental World. *Grist* [online]. Available from: https://grist.org/article/doe-reprint/ [Accessed 14 April 2019].

Plessner, H., [1928] 2019. *Levels of Organic Life and the Human. An introduction to philosophical anthropology*. Trans. M. Hyatt, introduction J. M. Bernstein. New York: Fordham Press.

Plessner, H., 1982. Der Mensch als Lebewesen. In: H. Plessner. *Mit anderen Augen. Aspekte einer philosophischen Anthropologie*. Stuttgart: Reclam, 9–62.

Potts, R., 1997. *Humanity's Descent. The Consequences of Ecological Instability*. London: Avon Books.

Rosol, C., *et al.*, 2017. In the machine room of the Anthropocene. *The Anthropocene Review*, 4(1), 2–8.

Sideris, L., 2016. Anthropocene Convergences: A Report from the Field. In: R. Emmett and T. Lekan, eds. *Whose Anthropocene? Revisiting Dipesh Chakrabarty's 'Four Theses'*. RCC Perspectives: Transformations in Environment and Society, 2,

89–96. Available from: www.environmentandsociety.org/sites/default/files/2016_2_
sideris.pdf [Accessed 13 February 2019].

Steffen, W., *et al.*, 2007. The Anthropocene: Are humans now overwhelming the great forces of nature? *Ambio*, 36(8), 614–621.

Steffen, W., *et al.*, 2011. The Anthropocene. Conceptual and historical perspectives. *Philosophical Transactions of the Royal Society A*, 369(1938), 842–867.

Stengers, I., 2015. *In catastrophic times. Resisting the coming Barbarism* [online]. Trans. A. Goffey. London: Open Humanities Press und Meson Press. Available from: https://meson.press/wp-content/uploads/2015/11/978-1-78542-010-8_In-Catastrop hic-Times_Stengers.pdf [Accessed 13 February 2019].

Szerszynski, B., 2015. Commission on Planetary Ages: Decision CC87966424/49: The onomatophore of the Anthropocene. In: C. Hamilton, F. Gemenne and C. Bonneuil, eds. *The Anthropocene and the Global Environmental Crisis. Rethinking modernity in a new epoch*. New York and London: Routledge, 177–183.

Szerszynski, B., 2019. Von den Werkzeugen zur Technosphäre. In: K. Klingan and C. Rosol, eds. *Technosphäre*. Berlin: Matthes & Seitz.

Teilhard de Chardin, P., [1955] 1960. *The Phenomenon of Man*. 4th ed. London: Collins.

Tsing, A.L., 2012. Unruly Edges: Mushrooms as Companion Species. *Environmental Humanities*, 1, 141–154.

Uexküll, J.v., 1909. *Umwelt und Innenwelt der Tiere*. Berlin: Julius Springer.

Vernadsky, V., 1945. The Biosphere and the Noosphere. *American Scientist*, 33, 1–12.

Woods, D., 2014. Scale Critique for the Anthropocene. *The Minnesota Review*, 83, 133–142.

6   Politics

The shape which the Anthropocene will assume depends on whether humanity manages to control its influence over the Earth system. This necessitates that different social actors—be they states, companies, munici-palities, or citizens' groups—bind themselves to rules and coordinate their interests. The Anthropocene is thus an eminently political question. How does the realization that humanity is an integral part of the Earth system change our conception of politics? What forms of social organization, what political structures will be necessary to *explicate* the relationship between society and the Earth system (see Ch. 7: Aesthetics) and to get a handle on the cumulative effects of human action? Or, put differently: is it possible to translate the geological *force* of the *anthropos* into a *power* that could be wiel-ded consciously and with restraint (see Ch. 5: The *anthropos*)?

Michel Serres's *The Natural Contract* opens with a powerful image for the way in which our new understanding of the Earth system has shifted the horizon of political action. Serres describes Francisco Goya's painting 'Duel with Cudgels' (Fig. 6): 'A pair of enemies brandishing sticks is fighting in the midst of a patch of quicksand' (Serres [1990] 1995, p. 1). While the observer is captivated by the struggle between the two men, the real drama takes place not *between*, but *underneath* them: 'With every move they make, a slimy hole swallows them up, so that they are gradually burying themselves together' (ibid.). In Serres's reading, the image is an allegory of political thought in the Anthropocene: it points to the limitations of traditional conceptions of pol-itics, which focus on the conflicts between people but sideline the very ground which makes these conflicts possible, in the first place—a shared ground which is not passive, but an active participant that now threatens to engulf the conflicting parties. The outcome of the struggle thus depends on a third party: the Earth system which is the basis of all life and whose dynamics affect the conflicts between humans. This requires a rethinking of the political. In modern thought, political order was conceived as resting on a social contract which regulates the relationships between people. This, Serres argues, is no longer sufficient: the social contract must be supple-mented by a *natural contract* which takes natural processes into account.

The Natural Contract was published in 1990, at the end of the Cold War. The struggle between the two duelists stands for social antagonisms in the most general sense, but it also refers to this geopolitical conflict in particular which had enthralled political thinking for almost half a century. For contemporaries of the Great Acceleration, which started at the end of the Second World War, the central motif of their era was not the transformation of the planet, but the struggle between communism and the 'free world'. All the processes which characterize the Great Acceleration—the nuclear tests, the massive proliferation of new consumer goods, the spread of artificial fertilizers and pesticides, the construction of highways and gigantic dams—were viewed as aspects of this contest over which political system would be better able to redeem the modern promises of progress and prosperity. Serres recognized that in the course of this struggle for geopolitical *power*, the combatants had turned themselves into a geological *force*.

Not only this 'global change' itself, but also the knowledge about it was a product of the Cold War. Already in the 1950s, there were inklings that the conflict between the superpowers was putting the ecological basis of all human life into question. This motivated early scientific cooperation across the Iron Curtain, most importantly the International Geophysical Year (1957–58) which prepared the way for the very first international treaty that explicitly aimed at the protection of the Earth (Edwards 2017, p. 36): the Nuclear Test Ban Treaty of 1963 put an end to the nuclear fallout which had, over the course of the preceding decade, covered the entire planet with a thin but stratigraphically significant layer of radioisotopes. Fear of the 'nuclear winter' which might follow a large-scale nuclear war drove research into the chemistry of the atmosphere (Hamblin 2013, pp. 237–41). This, in turn, helped to lay the groundwork for the Gaia hypothesis (Lovelock and Margulis 1974) and led to the discovery of the stratospheric ozone layer which protects the biosphere against ultraviolet (UV) radiation. In the 1980s,

Figure 6.1 Francisco Goya, 1820/23. *Duel with Cudgels*. Oil on canvas. © Museo del Prado.

POWER / FORCE

scientific experts warned that the chlorofluorocarbons used in refrigerators, air conditioners, etc. were destroying this protective layer. The international community reacted by passing the Montreal Protocol, which came into force in 1989 and outlawed the emission of ozone-depleting substances.

Against this historical backdrop, Serres's abstract notion of the natural contract takes on a very concrete meaning: the Nuclear Test Ban Treaty and the Montreal Protocol, but also the formation of the Intergovernmental Panel on Climate Change (IPCC) in 1988 are examples for the conjunction of 'Physics' and 'Law', of scientific and political institutions, that Serres has in mind (Serres [1990] 1995, p. 39). He thinks of the natural contract not as a legal document but, just like the social contract, an implicit agreement which makes actual contracts possible, in the first place. It is a collective acknowledgement of our dependency on a shared Earth which creates the conditions for binding rules. Serres assumed that such a natural contract was already in place and, indeed, the 1990s did turn out to be a 'golden age' for international environmental law (Pattberg and Zelli 2016, p. 6): the Montreal Protocol was followed by the United Nations Framework Convention on Climate Change (UNFCCC) in 1992, the Biodiversity Convention in 1993, the Kyoto Protocol for the reduction of carbon dioxide emissions in 1997, and a host of other multilateral and bilateral treaties, which gave environmental protection a broad foundation of international law.

The withdrawal of the US from the Kyoto Protocol in 2001 was only the most conspicuous signal that this phase was coming to an end. That the approach of addressing global environmental issues through international treaties reached its limits with the problem of climate change is not a coincidence. The use of fossil fuels is intimately linked with questions of political and economic power. Since the development of the steam engine in the eighteenth century, it had been a primary driver of modernization and a symbol of the geopolitical ascendancy of the West (see Ch. 9: Energy, Ch. 12: Conclusion). Even today, consumption of fossil fuels remains a reliable indicator for the level of affluence a society enjoys. Already in the early 1990s, critics had raised suspicions that international efforts to reduce carbon dioxide emissions amounted to a new form of 'environmental colonialism': they would slow the economic development of the newly industrializing nations and thus shore up the dominance of the established industrial powers (Agarwal and Narain 1991). A just climate policy, it was argued, must factor in the historical responsibility of the industrialized nations when calculating carbon budgets, and it must distribute the economic burdens of decarbonization accordingly. It cannot focus only on the cumulative emissions of entire nations, but must take into account the vast differences in individual emissions. Climate policy cannot be separated from questions of global distributive justice. The UNFCCC adopted this view: in the effort to protect the Earth's climate, signatories are said to bear 'common but differentiated responsibilities' (United Nations 1992). In practice, this meant that countries such as China and India would not be required to reduce their emissions—providing the US with a welcome pretext to withdraw from the Kyoto Protocol. Ultimately, the repeated failure of the UN climate conferences up until the Paris Agreement of 2015 reflects a refusal to subordinate national aspirations for political and economic power to the goal of protecting the Earth system.

The difficulties of coordinating the interests of the different parties with regard to climate policy are exemplary for the political challenges of the Anthropocene. In terms of their structure, they are an instance of what in the social sciences is known as 'collective action problems' (Olsen 1965, pp. 29–30), and in game theory as the 'prisoner's dilemma' (Axelrod 1984, pp. 7–9). Fundamentally, what is at issue is the possibility of reconciling individual and collective interests. Under what conditions will an actor forgo individual benefits in the interest of the group? How can cooperation be organized so as to be attractive to the individual? A formulation of this problem which became particularly influential in the debate over ecological issues was advanced by Garrett Hardin in his 1968 essay 'The Tragedy of the Commons'. Hardin uses the term 'commons' to refer to goods which are accessible to anyone, but for whose maintenance no one in particular is responsible. His example is an open pasture. For each herdsman, it makes sense to put as many heads of cattle on the pasture as possible, because the benefits of doing so will accrue only to him, whereas the damage to the pasture will be shared by all. Thus there is a permanent tendency to ruin the pasture through overgrazing (Hardin 1968, p. 1244). This behavior which, as it maximizes individual utility, may be described as rational, leads to detrimental (and thus irrational) outcomes for the group.

The Earth's atmosphere constitutes a 'commons' in precisely this sense. All people profit from it in one way or another (insofar as it serves as a sink for their greenhouse gas emissions while at the same time providing climatic stability), but there is no authority which would regulate access to it. The burning of fossil fuels is rational insofar as it has immediate benefits for the individual user. The damage which it causes, on the other hand, is distributed both spatially and temporally: the cycles through which carbon is exchanged between the atmosphere, biosphere, hydrosphere and lithosphere work at vastly different timescales such that the full consequences of anthropogenic climate change will become fully apparent only to subsequent generations. Indeed, all the components of the Earth system specified in Rockström's model of 'planetary boundaries' (see Ch. 2: Definitions)—including e.g. the phosphorus and nitrogen cycles, freshwater and biodiversity—can be conceptualized as 'common-pool resources'. In economics and the social sciences they are often summarily referred to as a 'global commons' (Brousseau et al. 2012).

When Hardin speaks of the destruction of the commons as a 'tragedy', his point is not that we should feel sad about it. Rather, he is referring to the logical structure of the tragic plot as defined by traditional theories of the genre: a tragedy is a fate which the actors accomplish unwittingly (Nixon

2012, p. 594). In Hardin's view, the only way to avoid this outcome is the conversion of the commons into private property and its legal protection through the power of the state. Hardin's argument remains a central reference point for all attempts to find 'market-based' solutions to environmental problems (Anderson and Leal 2015). Environmental organizations such as the Audubon Society or the Nature Conservancy have long pursued a policy of protecting species and landscapes considered particularly valuable by purchasing land and putting it under private management. Moreover, in economics and environmental law, it has become increasingly common to quantify the monetary value of the natural environment in terms of the 'ecosystem services' it provides to society (Costanza *et al.* 1997). Underlying all of these approaches is the assumption that what is for free has no value—and that if we wish to preserve nature, we must put a price tag on it.

One simple reason why such efforts are problematic is the fact that most natural things cannot be demarcated and counted in the same way as most commodities. From an ecological perspective, a tree, for example, is not only an individual organism, but also an element in the water and nutrient cycles of a larger ecosystem—an element which, viewed individually, happens to be almost irrelevant for the functioning of the whole. However, it is also a complex system in its own right, which is composed of further systems (e.g. the root system with its symbiotic fungi, or the foliage with its chloroplasts) and provides habitat for other species. Finally, it may also possess a symbolic meaning for the people in whose lifeworld it occurs. Because a tree can be viewed on many different levels which interact in complex ways, the tree's 'value' depends entirely on one's perspective. Because many of its functions are not substitutable, it makes no sense to determine their exchange value (Brennan 2006). Natural things thus have no natural price (Purdy 2015, p. 263). This is all the more true for the atmosphere and other components of the Earth system, which simply cannot be divided up and fenced off like a piece of pasture. A scheme such as emissions trading, which aims to create a market for atmospheric carbon dioxide and thus promote an economically efficient path to its reduction, can only succeed if all actors agree on a common pricing mechanism (Tirole 2017, pp. 213–6). But a central authority which would be able to implement such a mechanism on a global scale does not exist. This seems to lead to the conclusion that the Earth system will inevitably fall victim to the tragedy of the commons.

It was above all the work of economist Elinor Ostrom which demonstrated that Hardin's abstract model of the problem was at odds with empirical evidence. In her seminal book *Governing the Commons*, she discussed several examples of societies which had successfully managed 'common-pool resources' over many centuries without destroying them (Ostrom 1990). From these precedents, she distilled a list of eight design principles which made this possible. These included: (1) clearly defined group boundaries, i.e. access to the common-pool resource must be restricted to a particular community; (2) subsidiarity, i.e. those affected by the rules which govern the use of the resource need to have a say in drafting, modifying, and implementing them; (3) effective monitoring, i.e. all community members must be able to see that the other members cooperate; and (4) a system of 'graduated sanctions' for those who violate the rules. Ostrom further showed that the social structures which enabled the sustainable use of common-pool resources were often the result of spontaneous cooperation between the participants. They developed without the involvement of a central authority (Ostrom 1990, pp. 178–81). Indeed, it is often the intervention of state power and privatization which brings about the destruction of the commons.

One example for this process are the Maasai, a pastoral people in the dry savannah of the East African Rift Valley, who developed a system of collective land use which proved to be remarkably resilient even in the face of steep environmental challenges (Blewett 1995). This system, which also encompassed neighboring tribes, was based on an intricate web of mutual obligations, sustained by intermarriage and trade, and guarded by a strict code of honor. That some families owned a much greater number of cattle than others was an accepted feature of this system, because such large herds were able to ride out even long periods of drought and could subsequently be used to restock the herds of poorer tribesmen. Colonial administrators from Germany and Great Britain, which took political control of the Rift Valley in the 1890s, did not understand this system. They viewed the larger herds as the result of a self-destructive competition for social prestige, and the many unused tracts of land, which were essential to the ecological flexibility of a pastoral way of life, as a sign of inefficiency and waste. The most fertile pieces of land were distributed to white farmers. The network of social relationships which had tied the Maasai to their territory was ripped apart by the demarcation of administrative boundaries and the juridical production of fixed ethnic identities. The result was ecological degradation which, in accordance with Hardin's argument about the tragedy of the commons, was then used to justify further expropriations (Blewett 1995, pp. 486–8).

The point of this example is not to idealize exotic tribal societies. Similar cooperative arrangements can be found in traditional societies the world over, and indeed Ostrom draws her examples in *Governing the Commons* from Switzerland, Spain, and Japan. What the history of the Maasai illustrates especially well, however, is the destruction of such systems at the hands of state power and private economic interests, particularly in the context of colonialism. It therefore can serve as an example for a process that has played a key role in the genesis of the Anthropocene. Karl Marx had believed that the 'primary accumulation' of productive forces through the violent expropriation of land and labor power belonged to the pre-history of capitalism. Today, it is generally regarded as an intrinsic feature of the capitalist system which has continuously taken place throughout its history (Harvey 2003, Federici 2004). According to Simon Lewis and Mark Maslin, the conversion of the commons into private property, which begins in sixteenth-century England with the so-called 'enclosure movement', is one of the key drivers of the transformation of the Earth system (Lewis and Maslin 2018, pp. 173–5). The expropriation of common-pool resources produces a landless proletariat which migrates to the cities to sell its labor. At the same time, it prepares the ground for new forms of cultivation which are no longer geared towards social and ecological reproduction, but rather towards capital accumulation. Thus the logic of the commons is displaced by the logic of the plantation (Tsing 2015, p. 23). Traditional forms of land use such as the pastoralism of the Maasai (but also, say, of Swiss mountain farmers) are tuned to the ecological dynamics of the local environment. Their primary goal is not the maximization of yields, but long-term viability, and they must therefore be sensitive to the various rhythms of the natural systems on which they depend. Industrial agriculture, by contrast, must generate profits on a year-by-year basis. To that end, it must bank on the *scalability* of the processes of production, which requires that social and ecological relations be radically simplified (Tsing 2015, pp. 33–4, see Ch. 10: Scales I): the farmer becomes an entrepreneur or a wage laborer, the tree turns into so many board-feet of timber, and if oaks grow too slowly or erratically, they are replaced with quickly growing spruce. The ecological homogenization of the biosphere which sets in during the seventeenth century reflects this logic, leading Donna Haraway, Anna Tsing and others to refer to the new geological epoch as 'Plantationocene' (Bubandt *et al.* 2016).

But the example of the Maasai is not only of retrospective interest. Today, about 2 billion people, more than a quarter of the world's population, continue to make their living from traditional forms of fishing, pastoralism or farming. Such forms of subsistence generally depend on common-pool resources (Pearce 2012). In most cases, this means that the people engaging in them have no legal title to the land on which they depend, making them especially vulnerable to expropriation. Economic globalization has put their ways of life under increasing pressure. In Asia, South America, and Africa, governments are selling large tracts of land to international investors who produce palm oil, soybeans, sugarcane and other commodities for the world market (White *et al.* 2013). This rapidly destroys not only traditional societies, but also the ecosystems on which they depend—ecosystems which often are the last refuge for species that are displaced from the intensively managed monocultures of modern farms. These measures are often justified by pointing out the inefficiency of traditional forms of land use and the need for speedier economic development. Thus the very institutions which Hardin had expected to save the natural environment—private property and state power—are conspiring towards its destruction (Radkau 2008, p. 39).

Against this background, it also becomes clear why the traditional knowledge and historical experience of indigenous peoples assumes a new salience in the Anthropocene. Their social institutions and cosmologies reflect an intimate familiarity with local ecological conditions which foreign experts and aid workers often only come to recognize after the damage is already done (Lansing and de Vet 2012). Indigenous peoples thus play an indispensable role in the preservation of local ecosystems, and they provide important clues as to what kind of social structures might be able to prevent their destruction. In Serres's terms, they show what it might mean to base the social order on a natural contract. This is not only a matter of acknowledging the fragility of nature which was the primary concern of the environmental movement. It is just as much about recognizing the vulnerability of society to natural systems which it can influence but not control. Western modernity had conceived of the relationship between nature and society as a tug-of-war, in which an increase of society's power implied a weakening of nature and *vice versa*. The Anthropocene requires that we abandon this belief. That human action has now become coeval with 'the great forces of nature' (Steffen *et al.* 2007) does not entail that the older forces would simply abdicate. On the contrary, the more deeply humans intervene in the Earth system, the more they tangle with processes that are beyond their control. Humans have more power *and* nature has more power, as Clive Hamilton puts it (Hamilton 2017, p. 45). If it is true that humanity has become a geological actor, then so is the reverse conclusion: geology has become a political actor. At the heart of political thought in the Anthropocene stands the knowledge of a mutual dependency of natural and social processes, which implies that nonhuman actors have become involved in the political order. In this regard, the politics of the Anthropocene resembles indigenous cosmologies.

There is also another reason why the historical experience of indigenous peoples is of paradigmatic significance for the Anthropocene. Their conflicts with settler colonialism prefigure the situation in which their old opponents now find themselves. In the Anthropocene, the modernizing peoples, too, are confronted with a situation in which the ecological basis of their existence is rendered precarious (Latour 2018, pp. 7–8). The calamities to which the moderns still look forward in fearful expectation have long been a reality for indigenous peoples: 'the hardships many nonIndigenous people dread most of the climate crisis are ones that Indigenous peoples have endured already due to different forms of colonialism: ecosystem collapse, species loss, economic crash, drastic relocation, and cultural disintegration' (Whyte 2018, p. 226). If there is one thing to be learned from indigenous people today, it is not primarily a new humility before nature, but rather the search for social practices which allow a collective to bind itself to a particular territory even in the face of disaster.

All of this does not mean, however, that the lifeways of indigenous people provide a ready blueprint for the sustainable management of the global commons. To argue that they do would be to repeat one of the central fallacies of modernity: the belief that *one size fits all*. The arrangements which allowed indigenous peoples to avoid the tragedy of the commons are based on forms of social interaction which are only workable in relatively small groups and cannot easily be transferred to the level of world society. If a greedy Maasai refused to help his neighbors, his wives publicly humiliated him with mocking songs and gossip (because they would be among the first to suffer from his greed, Blewett 1995, p. 480). Due to the rise of social media, shame-based forms of social control are currently seeing a revival, but it seems unlikely that they could help countries to meet their national goals for reducing carbon dioxide emissions (however, if they were combined with other forms of monitoring consumer behavior, they might indeed be used to that end, see Ch. 12: Conclusion). There have been various attempts to translate indigenous cosmologies into the language of the modern legal system: Ecuador and Bolivia enshrined the rights of Mother Nature (in the form of the Inca-goddess Pachamama) in their constitutions, and more recently New Zealand's supreme court accorded the status of a legal person to the Whanganui River (Pecharroman 2017). These measures may very well lead to better environmental protection—but if they do, this will probably not be due to a genuine revitalization of indigenous cosmologies, but to the administrative effectiveness of the state. The fertility goddess which gave life to the inhabitants of the Andean highlands and the Pachamama of the Ecuadorian constitution have little more in common than the name.

The main question is whether and how the structures which allowed indigenous societies to protect local common-pool resources can be scaled up to the relationship between world society and the global commons. This is the problem to which Ostrom turned during the last decade of her life. Her solution was, in a single word: polycentrism (Ostrom 2014). Problems such as climate change are the cumulative result of countless actions on a whole range of different levels: individual consumer behavior plays a role, as do the decisions of municipal and national governments, of transnational corporations and international organizations. Each level features different incentive structures which an effective climate policy, for example, needs to take into account. In many cases, this will involve measures that do not take the protection of the climate as their primary goal, but rather seek to harness synergies and positive side-effects. If I ride my bike to work, I not only reduce my carbon dioxide emissions, but I also save money and improve my physical health. For a village in the African hinterland, solar panels make sense because the electricity they provide does not have to travel through long, easily disrupted power lines. Public transportation reduces air pollution and makes a city more livable, and city partnerships for climate protection (such as the UN-sponsored program *Cities for Climate Protection*) not only allow for the sharing of climate policy expertise, but also provide an opportunity for economic cooperation. In Ostrom's pithy summary: 'multiple benefits are created by diverse actions at multiple scales' (Ostrom 2014, p. 121). In order to be successful, climate policy must accept that local actors are best able to determine what works within the context that is immediately relevant to them. It must respect their autonomy and their superior knowledge of local conditions.

This emphasis on polycentric structures and 'multi-level governance' is also a characteristic of recent research on the subject of 'Earth System Governance' (Biermann *et al.* 2016). It is based on a fundamental insight of the theory of complex systems: the different levels of a hierarchy are linked, but at each level, different factors come into play (Berkes 2008, p. 2). Each level therefore requires different concepts and strategies. But this also means that cooperation between states will remain essential in the effort to protect the global commons. Only about a third of the reductions in carbon dioxide emissions which the IPCC considers necessary can be reached through measures which involve side benefits that make their voluntary adoption likely (Paavola 2012, p. 421). Many of the conditions which will be necessary in order to effectively govern the global commons can only be brought about through the action of the state: only the state is able to monitor emissions at a granular level, to put effective sanctions for rule violators into place, and to control the behavior of citizens in such a manner that it would be able to meet its international obligations. A treaty such as the Montreal Protocol, which prevented the destruction of the stratospheric ozone layer, would have been inconceivable without the administrative apparatus of the modern state. The state remains the most important institution that we have to regulate the behavior of large collectives and to protect such collectives against risks which would overtax the capacities of smaller political entities.

At the same time, the state remains our biggest problem. Its actions are frequently dictated by local egoisms and systemic imperatives, be it the desire for national greatness, the need of politicians to be re-elected, or the wishes of citizens for early retirement and cheap gasoline. The single most important challenge for the politics of the Anthropocene is to 'limit [...] the scope of human appetites' (Purdy 2015, p. 268). At some point, the world's economy will have to transition to a 'steady state', as Herman Daly argued already in 1973 (Daly 1993) (see Ch. 9: Energy). However, liberal democracies seem to be almost constitutionally unable to make decisions which would curtail the freedoms and the material prosperity their citizens have become accustomed to (Purdy 2015, p. 256). There are good reasons to doubt whether they can steer society towards ecological sustainability (Blühdorn 2013). And especially if one considers the development of international politics since the turn of the millennium, the valorization of local, regional, and non-state actors in the discourse of 'Earth System Governance' is poor consolation indeed. The period during which the Anthropocene turned from a technical term in Earth system science into a key concept of social critique was also a period that saw the proliferation of ethnic and religious conflicts and the emergence of new geopolitical fault lines. Whereas the collaboration between 'Law' and 'Physics' (Serres [1990] 1995, pp. 80–1) has advanced only haltingly, the military has eagerly embraced the prognostic power of Earth system science: while the diplomats continue to haggle over binding goals for the reduction of carbon dioxide emissions, military planners are already developing scenarios for the new conflicts that global warming is likely to bring (United States Department of Defense 2014, p. 8). To conclude, Serres's hope that the knowledge of Earth's vulnerability would restrain geopolitical rivalry was not fulfilled. But the poignancy of his allegorical formula for this situation has only grown: the duelists must lay down their cudgels if they don't wish to be swallowed by the quicksand. The question is whether they will realize this before it is too late.

HB

References

Agarwal, A., and Narain, S. 1991. *Global Warming in an Unequal World. A Case of Environmental Colonialism*. New Delhi: Center for Science and Environment.

Anderson, T., and Leal, D.R., eds., 2015. *Free Market Environmentalism for the Next Generation*. Basingstoke: Palgrave Macmillan.

Axelrod, R., 1984. *The Evolution of Cooperation*. New York: Basic Books.

Berkes, F., 2008. Commons in a Multi-Level World. *International Journal of the Commons*, 2(1), 1–6.

Biermann, F., *et al.*, 2016. Down Earth: Contextualizing the Anthropocene. *Global Environmental Change*, 39, 341–350.

Blewett, R.A., 1995. Property Rights as a Cause of the Tragedy of the Commons: Institutional Change and the Pastoral Maasai of Kenya. *Eastern Economic Journal*, 21(4), 477–490.

Blühdorn, I., 2013. The Governance of Unsustainability: Ecology and Democracy after the Post-Democratic Turn. *Environmental Politics*, 22(1), 16–36.

Brennan, A., 2006. Book Review: Bruno Latour 'Politics of Nature'. *Environmental Ethics*, 28(2), 221–223.

Brousseau, E., *et al.*, 2012. *Global Environmental Commons. Analytical and Political Challenges in Building Governance Mechanisms*. Oxford: Oxford University Press.

Bubandt, N., *et al.*, 2016. Anthropologists Are Talking—About the Anthropocene. *Ethnos*, 81(3), 535–564.

Costanza, R., *et al.*, 1997. The value of the world's ecosystem services and natural capital. *Nature*, 387(6630), 253–260.

Daly, H.E., [1973] 1993. The Steady-State Economy: Toward a Political Economy of Biophysical Equilibrium and Moral Growth. In: H.E. Daly and K.E. Boulding, eds. *Valuing the Earth: Economics, Ecology, Ethics*. Cambridge: MIT Press, 325–366.

Edwards, P.N., 2017. Knowledge Infrastructures for the Anthropocene. *The Anthropocene Review*, 4(1), 34–43.

Federici, S., 2004. *Caliban and the Witch*. Brooklyn: Autonomedia.

Hamblin, J.D., 2013. *Arming Mother Nature. The Birth of Catastrophic Environmentalism*. Oxford: Oxford University Press.

Hamilton, C., 2017. *Defiant Earth. The Fate of Humans in the Anthropocene*. London: Polity Press.

Hardin, G., 1968. The Tragedy of the Commons. *Science*, 162(3859), 1243–1248.

Harvey, D., 2003. *The New Imperialism*. Oxford: Oxford University Press.

Lansing, J.S., and de Vet, T.A., 2012. The Functional Role of Balinese Water Temples: A Response to Critics. *Human Ecology*, 40(3), 453–467.

Latour, B., 2018. *Down Earth: Politics in the New Climate Regime*. Trans. C. Porter. London: Polity.

Lewis, S.L., and Maslin, M.A., 2018. *The Human Planet: How We Created the Anthropocene*. London: Pelican.

Lovelock, J., and Margulis, L., 1974. Atmospheric Homeostasis by and for the Biosphere: The Gaia Hypothesis. *Tellus*, 26(1–2), 2–9.

Nixon, R., 2012. Neoliberalism, Genre, and 'the Tragedy of the Commons'. *PMLA*, 127(3), 593–599.

Olsen, M., 1965. *The Logic of Collective Action. Public Goods and the Theory of Groups*. Cambridge: Harvard University Press.

Ostrom, E., 1990. *Governing the Commons: The Evolution of Institutions for Collective Action*. Cambridge: Cambridge University Press.

Ostrom, E., 2014. A Polycentric Approach for Coping with Climate Change. *Annals of Economics and Finance*, 15(1), 97–134.

Paavola, J., 2012. Climate Change: The Ultimate Tragedy of the Commons? In: D.H. Cole and E. Ostrom, eds. *Property in Land and Other Resources*. Cambridge: Lincoln Institute of Land Policy, 417–433.

Pattberg, P., and Zelli, F., 2016. Global Environmental Governance in the Anthropocene: An introduction. In: P. Pattberg and F. Zelli, eds. *Environmental Politics and Governance in the Anthropocene. Institutions and Legitimacy in a Complex World*. London: Routledge, 1–12.

Pearce, F., 2012. *The Land Grabbers. The New Fight Over Who Owns the Earth*. Boston: Beacon Press.

Pecharroman, L.C., 2017. Rights of Nature: Rivers That Can Stand in Court. *Resources* [online], 7(1), no pages. Available from: https://dx.doi.org/10.3390/resources7010013 [Accessed 26 February 2019].

Purdy, J., 2015. *After Nature. A Politics for the Anthropocene*. Cambridge: Harvard University Press.

Radkau, J., 2008. *Nature and Power: A Global History of the Environment*. Trans. T. Dunlap. Cambridge: Cambridge University Press.

Serres, M., [1990] 1995. *The Natural Contract*. Trans. E. MacArthur and W. Paulson. Ann Arbor, MI: University of Michigan Press.

Steffen, W., *et al.*, 2007. The Anthropocene: Are Humans Now Overcoming the Great Forces of Nature? *Ambio*, 36(8), 614–621.

Tirole, J., 2017. *Economics for the Common Good*. Trans. S. Rendall. Princeton: Princeton University Press.

Tsing, A., 2015. *The Mushroom at the End of the World. On the Possibility of Life in the Capitalist Ruins*. Princeton: Princeton University Press.

United Nations, 1992. *United Nations Framework Convention of Climate Change* [online]. Available from: https://unfccc.int/resource/docs/convkp/conveng.pdf [Accessed 14 March 2019].

United States Department of Defense, 2014. *Quadrennial Defense Review 2014* [online]. Available from: http://archive.defense.gov/pubs/2014_quadrennial_defense_review.pdf [Accessed 26 February 2019].

White, B., *et al.*, 2013. *The New Enclosures. Critical Perspectives on Corporate Land Deals*. London: Routledge.

Whyte, K.P., 2018. Indigenous Science (Fiction) for the Anthropocene: Ancestral Dystopias and Fantasies of Climate Change Crises. *Environment and Planning E: Nature and Space*, 1(1–2), 224–242.

7 Aesthetics

How to conceive of an aesthetics for the Anthropocene? In the art world, the Anthropocene has proven to be a particularly productive concept. Yet, it has also shown a tendency to devolve into a fashionable buzzword. When an 'aesthetics of the Anthropocene' is invoked at exhibitions, seminars, and public discussions, it generally refers, in a broad-brush fashion, to 'ecological crisis', 'global warming', 'the human footprint', or to more specific problems such as pollution, species extinction, or issues of coexistence with other species. Yet such references hardly add up to a coherent aesthetic program. Rather, they reflect certain prevalent assumptions about the purpose and relevance of art. In the first place, art is supposed to make the abstract concept 'Anthropocene' thinkable and perceptible: 'As the vehicle of aesthesis, [art] is central to *thinking with and feeling through* the Anthropocene' (Davis and Turpin 2015, p. 3). Secondly, art is thought to provide forms of expression that offer an alternative to the discourse of science and politics: 'Art provides [...] a non-moral form of address that offers a range of discursive, visual, and sensual strategies that are not confined by the regimes of scientific objectivity, political moralism, or psychological depression' (Davis and Turpin 2015, p. 4). In other words, art should mobilize and 'raise awareness', conveying a sense of urgency in the face of the ecological crisis. Thirdly, art is supposed to provide new conceptual tools for approaching the problem. As the Field Book that accompanied the exhibition *Reset Modernity*, curated by Bruno Latour, reads: 'Modernity was a way to differentiate past and future, north and south, progress and regress, radical and conservative. However, at a time of profound ecological mutation, such a compass is running in wild circles without offering much orientation anymore. This is why it is time for a reset' (Latour 2016, p. 2).

None of this, however, takes us very far towards an aesthetic theory for the Anthropocene. It simply reformulates some fairly conventional expectations of art and its capacity to make the world a better place. 'Anthropocene art' is for the most part understood to represent certain *themes* such as climate change, the destruction of ecosystems, melting icebergs, species loss, and, more recently, geological history and stratigraphy. Many of the novels, films, and artworks that deal with climate change (such as climate fiction or

certain forms of landscape photography) belong to this category. For example, a study on *climate fiction* carries the title *Anthropocene Fiction*—without
so much as addressing the specific role of climate change in the context of
the more comprehensive problem of the Anthropocene (Trexler 2015).

A genuine aesthetics for the Anthropocene, however, cannot be satisfied
with thematic references and the rhetoric of political mobilization. It must
ask what it means to confront a deeper understanding of the Anthropocene,
not in the content but in the *form* of aesthetic representation. Such a reflection on form is exemplified by Bruno Latour's reading of a painting by
Caspar David Friedrich, reproduced on the cover of his *Gaia Lectures*
(Latour 2017, p. 222; Fig. 7.1): *The Great Enclosure Near Dresden* (1832).

The painting shows the muddy floodplain of a river at dusk or dawn,
speckled with pools of water. But, as Latour observes, this landscape
appears oddly warped, as if one were seeing the curvature of the globe itself.
The sky is similarly arched, displaying a concave upward curve. Only the
horizon line in the middle distance is straight and separates the two distorted
spaces of earth and sky. Because of this distortion of pictorial space, the
observer's vantage point is difficult to make out. The observer seems neither
to stand on the level of the curved floodplain in the foreground, nor on any
determinable higher ground. It is this strange double curvature of space that
for Latour epitomizes the disturbance in the human relationship to the

Figure 7.1 Friedrich, Casper David., 1831/2. *The Great Enclosure near Dresden*. Oil on
Canvas. © Staatliche Kunstsammlungen Dresden. Photograph by Jürgen
Karpinski.

world brought about by the Anthropocene. If the Anthropocene heralds nothing less than a *new way of being-in-the-world*, it solicits questioning on two levels: first, there is the epistemological question as to the modes of access to, and forms of knowledge of, the non-human; second, there is the question as to how this new relationship between the human and the non-human might be aesthetically represented. For Latour, these two questions are closely connected.

In Friedrich's painting, the classic formal convention of European art history, according to which space is to be rendered from a fixed vantage point, is suspended or distorted. This convention, according to Latour, perfectly expressed the Western relationship to nature: nature is subordinated to an objectifying gaze, as if it had no purpose other than to be thus represented (Latour 2017, p. 17). According to this paradigm, it is—implausibly—as if the subject-viewer and the object-viewed exist only *for one another* (Daston and Galison [2007] 2010). Although Friedrich's painting cites these conventions—its pictorial space is oriented towards a vanishing point—this only highlights the extent to which it deviates from them. As Latour writes: 'This is not a landscape that someone might contemplate. It offers no possible stability [...]' (Latour 2017, p. 222). Latour sees the curved, non-Euclidean space of the picture, the free-floating gaze of the disoriented viewer, as an allegory of the human standpoint with regard to a nature in which it no longer has a secure place. In the Anthropocene, nature can no longer be represented as a simple given which the observer could grasp with a single gaze, but must be recognized as something that can be neither totalized nor objectified. Friedrich's painting traps the viewer in this space, in a wavering, uncertain observer position. In Latour's words:

> What is brilliant about this painting is the way it marks the instability of every point of view, whether it's a matter of seeing the world from above, from below, or from the middle. With the Great Enclosure, the great impossibility is not being imprisoned on Earth, it is believing that Earth can be grasped as a reasonable and coherent Whole, by piling up scales one on top of another, from the most local to the most global—and vice versa—or thinking that one could be content with one's own little plot in which to cultivate a garden.
>
> (ibid., p. 223)

Latour's reading of the painting is exemplary of what an 'aesthetics of the Anthropocene' might involve. At a first glance, Friedrich's painting appears to be a fairly straightforward representation of a landscape; in fact, however, it introduces a small twist in its *form* that makes all the difference. The painting abandons the presupposition of a transparent, readily intelligible structure of the world which the work of art simply reflects or re-enacts. It is replaced by a disorientation which is as subtle as it is profound, encompassing both the position of the viewer and the space of representation. In this way, the painting performs a veritable 'mutation of the relation to the world' (ibid., p. 7) as well as of the categories of subject and object, human and non-human, whole and part. The Anthropocene fundamentally unsettles the dualisms that have long shaped not only our theoretical and practical access to the world, but also the conventions of aesthetics—even though aesthetics was often presented as a categorical alternative to the scientific relation to the world (Böhme 2002, p. 435). It is no accident that this unsettling effect is not an achievement of *what* the picture depicts, but rather of *how* it brings the world into a specific form and thus into a specific relation with the observer.

The modern construction of nature, which Latour sees unsettled in Friedrich's painting, was based on a fundamental dualism between subject and object. While the subject was traditionally understood to be a cognitive, reflective, and affective being, nature—as it was regarded by a subject—was conceived as lacking all of these qualities. Devoid of intention, perception, and consciousness, it was taken to consist of stable, inert matter which obeyed a fixed set of rules called the 'laws of nature'—laws which were furthermore believed to be fundamentally intelligible to the human subject. Leibniz famously summed up this belief in the maxim *natura non facit saltus*—nature does not make jumps. Because it was understood to be essentially immutable, continuous in space and time, and always acting in accordance with laws which can be expressed in mathematical form, nature could be systematically observed, broken down into its constituent parts, subjected to experiments and technologically manipulated. With the demise of this modern understanding of nature, a different nature emerges which not only is characterized by manifold, complex interdependencies, but also by discontinuities and surprises. Nature, we have come to understand, does indeed 'make jumps'. This nature cannot be objectified, i.e. epistemologically held at a distance, nor can it be divided up into parts without losing sight of the essential interconnectedness of its many active elements. Ecology played an important role in bringing into focus this interconnectedness, as well as the profound entanglement of human beings in the larger fabric of life. Cycles, interdependencies, feedback loops, and tipping points are the characteristic features of a new paradigm of nature (see Ch. 4: Nature and culture).

The modern dualism between this idea of an 'objectifiable' nature and a human observer, between object and subject, formed the basis of the modern aesthetics of nature (Böhme 2002). In his *Critique of the Power of Judgment* (1790), one of the most powerful and influential expressions of such an aesthetics, Immanuel Kant argued that aesthetic experience complements the scientific and technical approach to nature. Aesthetics mediates between the theoretical-scientific approach to the world as it is laid down in his *Critique of Pure Reason* (1781/87) and the sphere of free will which he had discussed in the *Critique of Practical Reason* (1788). According to Kant, the aesthetic experience of nature does not originate in the object itself but rather in the attitude of the subject when it experiences an object either as 'beautiful' or as 'sublime'. Whereas 'the beauty of nature' Kant writes, 'reveals to us a technique of nature', thus making known its inner purposiveness and coherence (Kant 2000, p. 129), the sublime is an experience of being overwhelmed by the object of contemplation. The 'mathematical sublime' overwhelms on account of being 'absolutely great' (ibid., p. 131), while the 'dynamic sublime' infuses the viewer with awe by the power or violence expressed. That which arouses in us a feeling of the sublime appears 'in its form to be contrapurposive for our power of judgment, unsuitable for our faculty of presentation, and as it were doing violence to our imagination' (ibid., p. 129). In the sublime, the human capacity for perception, imagination and judgment is pushed to its limits. The objects which occasion this experience of the sublime are above all natural phenomena such as mountains, glaciers, icebergs, thunderstorms, towering rocks, raging streams or desolate wastelands. Essential to such an experience, however, is the reflexive distancing performed by the viewer. The sense of the sublime attests both to the experience of being overwhelmed by the object and, at the same time, to the capacity of reflecting on that experience. For example, the vastness of a mountain range can, upon reflection, impart a sense of the infinity of the universe, thus impressing on us the 'superiority of the rational vocation of our cognitive faculty over the greatest faculty of sensibility' (ibid., p. 141). The sublime overpowers the senses, but it is mastered and contained by reason. Kant thus construes the negative experience of horror before the magnitude or violent force of an object as an occasion for the self-assertion of the subject's cognitive faculty.

Nature, however, need not only be regarded as beautiful or sublime; in modern aesthetics, it has often been seen as something which occasions a sense of loss or alienation. Aesthetic representation would then be concerned with the attempt to repair this loss—in the form of nature writing, for example, or in modern landscape painting and photography. Such a *negative aesthetics* insists on the non-representability of alienated nature. In modern aesthetics, Kant's claim regarding the subject's ability to distance itself from the experience of the sublime is thrown into question. Theodor W. Adorno, for example, understands the sublime less as an indication of *superiority over* nature than of *dependency on* nature: 'Rather than that, as Kant thought, spirit in the face of nature becomes aware of its own superiority, it becomes aware of its own natural essence. This is the moment when the subject, vis-a-vis the sublime, is moved to tears. Recollection of nature breaks the arrogance of his self-positing' (Adorno 1997, p. 276). Following in the footsteps of Adorno's reinterpretation of the sublime against Kant, Jean-François Lyotard sees in it the signature of a postmodern aesthetic that 'denies itself the solace of good forms, the consensus of a taste which would make it possible to share the nostalgia for the unattainable'. Instead, the postmodern sublime 'searches for new presentations, not in order to enjoy them, but in order to impart *a stronger sense of the unpresentable*' (Lyotard 1984, p. 81, emphasis added).

An aesthetic theory of the Anthropocene might well take up Lyotard's diagnosis of the sublime object's resistance to representation. It cannot, however, retreat to a Kantian aesthetics of nature, nor to figures of alienation or a 'nostalgia for the unattainable', e.g. by celebrating and mourning the loss of untouched nature. Instead, it must question the notion of nature as the other and opposite of the human. Timothy Morton has proposed that an aesthetic program adequate to the ecological crisis must do away altogether with any emphatic conception of 'nature'. To overcome the false sense of immediacy that is attached to the term, he advocates using the term 'ecology', to suggest a condition of radical mediation: 'Ecology without Nature' is the programmatic title of his book on the paradoxes of nature writing (Morton 2007).

Rather than discarding 'nature', however, it may prove more fruitful to proceed from the assumption that both the concepts of 'nature' and of the 'human' are fundamentally transformed. An aesthetics of the Anthropocene, we believe, needs to deal not so much with the alienation of humans from nature but with a more thoroughgoing alienation—the *becoming uncanny* of the life-world. The journalist Thomas Friedman, playing on the term 'global warming', has suggested the term 'global weirding' (Friedman 2010). As we have seen, in the Anthropocene nature can no longer be understood as a collection of inert objects, as a world of passive matter which is perceived and acted upon by an observing (human) subject but itself incapable of perceiving and acting, a world that occasions reflection but lacks reflexivity. On the contrary, as Amitav Ghosh has argued, nature now returns the gaze—it appears alive, threatening, unpredictable, sentient, and temperamental. As Ghosh writes, this is 'one of the uncanniest effects of the Anthropocene, this renewed awareness of the elements of agency and consciousness that humans share with many other beings, and even perhaps with the planet itself' (Ghosh 2016, p. 63). Nature demands 'recognition'—both in the sense of recovering a knowledge that has been repressed and in the sense of a renewed respect for the non-human as an idiosyncratic, heteroclite, unpredictable and potentially dangerous force. Once the emphatic concept of nature as the *other of culture* is abandoned, the sense of separation between the human and the natural disappears, disclosing the indissoluble interconnectedness of humans with and in the world—an existence 'within the thick of the world, life in a vortex of shared precariousness and unchosen proximities' (Cohen 2015, p. 107).

Humans thus no longer find themselves standing over and above a world of objects but rather caught *in the midst of things*—in the midst of climate change, of coexisting forms of life, of technologies and technological consequences—and, at the same time, dependent on capital flows and the circulation of material resources which ceaselessly and uncontrollably transform the economic and ecological conditions of human existence. The world *involves* and *affects* humans in all kinds of ways, imposing responsibilities and material risks on them, and continually overtaxing their capacity to perceive and understand. In the 'thick of the world' (Cohen 2015, p. 107), what is most important may well be that which remains *imperceptible*. Art in the Anthropocene, if it is to be more than a thematic comment on this or that aspect of our present condition, must address these cognitive and ethical difficulties as a question of *form*, in an effort to render visually, sensually, affectively, or conceptually phenomena which otherwise elude experience, not because of their distance from the observer but because of their proximity. Unlike in the aesthetics of classical modernity, unrepresentability, then, has nothing to do with a withdrawal into 'aesthetic distance'. On the contrary, it involves an uncanny—uncontrollable, unmanageable—intimacy with things, in the midst of a world that is hypercomplex and multidimensional. The 'things' of the Anthropocene are too close to be objectified, too big to be pictured, too complex to be fully accounted for.

On this basis, we can distinguish three fundamental difficulties which an aesthetics of the Anthropocene must tackle: (1) *latency*, the withdrawal from perceptibility and representability; (2) *entanglement*, a new awareness of coexistence and immanence; and (3) *scale*, the clash of incompatible orders of magnitude (Clark 2015). This last issue, the clash of scales, in turn presents itself on different levels: temporally (the short frame of human time vs. the 'deep time' of Earth history but also the deep future); spatially (local life forms vs. planetary changes of the life system); and in terms of agency ('harmless' individual actions vs. the cumulative effects of their billion-fold multiplication) (see Ch. 10: Scales I: The planetary and Ch. 11: Scales II: Deep time). For artistic representation, what latency, entanglement, and scale have in common is that they cannot be addressed simply as topics or themes but only as *problems of form*.

It is remarkable how many of the efforts to formulate an aesthetic theory and an artistic practice for the Anthropocene revert to the concept of the sublime (Guénin 2016, Kainulainen 2013, Williston 2016). As we have seen, Kant's concept of the 'mathematical sublime' had already explicitly addressed the problem of incommensurable scales: the sublime is that which is not great relative to something else, not 'greater than' but 'absolutely great' (Kant 2000, 131). One could argue that the tendency in aesthetic approaches to the Anthropocene to retread this familiar conceptual ground betrays a failure of the theoretical imagination. However, the reference to the sublime serves as a starting point for a set of strikingly divergent arguments.

Jean-Baptiste Fressoz, for example, has criticized the affinity between the Anthropocene and the sublime as the aesthetic signature of a relationship to the world that is characterized by a desire for demiurgic control and epistemic distance. The feeling of guilty pleasure, the penchant for violence (in the iconography of the catastrophic) and for displays of technological domination (in the modern phenomenon of the 'technological sublime'), which nowadays mark the experience of the sublime point to the apolitical, technocratic ideology which, Fressoz argues, lies at the core of the concept of the Anthropocene: 'It seems more exciting to wonder at the dynamism of a humanity that has become a telluric force than to think about the regression of an economic system' (Fressoz 2016, p. 49, trans. EH). Fressoz sees evidence for this view in the tendency of many contemporary works of art, especially in photography, to depict their objects from a great distance.

Yet it is by no means clear that the view from a distance, from 'above' or 'outside', necessarily feeds into a technocratic ideology of the sort Fressoz excoriates. In some artworks, often explicitly devoted to the Anthropocene (consider e.g. David Meisel, Edward Burtynsky or Andreas Gursky), it is precisely the view from above or from a distance that makes tangible the magnitude of ecological destruction, the massive transformation of the landscape, or the excesses of human consumption. Such works appear less to present a stance of demiurgic dominance than an attempt to visually capture the almost incomprehensibly vast—in Kant's terms: 'absolutely great'—scope of anthropogenic impact. The distant, devastated, yet devilishly beautiful landscapes shown in these photographs are thus lifted out of the latency of marginality and oblivion. The view from above, which can only be achieved through elaborate technical means, is the condition for their becoming manifest.

Other theorists of the aesthetics of the Anthropocene understand the sublime not as a hallmark of the superiority of the observer but rather of their inescapable *entanglement* in the world. The overwhelming, affective terror of the sublime stages a blurring of the boundaries between subject and object, self and other, the necessary and the contingent, foreground and background. According to this view, the sublime of the Anthropocene dramatizes the involvement with a *non-natural nature* in which humans are profoundly implicated without, however, being able to gain an overall 'objective' perspective. The sublime thus discloses a condition of responsibility without mastery. Maggie Kainulainen writes: 'A sublime encounter with climate change is marked by uncanny and unwanted potency, as one finds oneself implicated in the complex web of interactions that will produce some level of global catastrophe' (2013, p. 113). The ecological significance of the sublime in the Anthropocene lies in the experience of these unpredictable processes of implication and interaction. Here, no aesthetic or epistemic distance of the sort occasioned by the Kantian sublime is possible. Rather, the aesthetic experience is one of radical immanence. The reflexive freedom once associated with sublime experience gives way to a disturbing intimacy with a world that can no longer be taken for granted.

Timothy Morton, probably the most flamboyant theoretician of the Anthropocene, has turned this conception of an aesthetic experience which overwhelms and destabilizes the subject into an ontological category (Morton 2013). His amalgamation of object-oriented ontology and ecocriticism, philosophy and pop culture, presented in a playfully hyperbolic style, has made him one of the most popular authors on the topic (Blasdel 2017).

His most successful coinage, the 'hyperobject', takes up Kant's figure of the sublime, but turns it on its head. What for Kant had been an *experience of the subject* becomes, in Morton's account, the ontological *quality of an object*, albeit one that radically resists 'objectivity'. Hyperobjects, Morton writes, 'are things that are massively distributed in time and space relative to humans' (2013, p. 1). For Morton, anything that exceeds human sensory experience can be described as a hyperobject—a black hole, climate change, the Florida Everglades, or even the sum total of all the styrofoam in the world. Morton thus elaborates the experience of immanence disclosed by the sublime in the Anthropocene into an *ontology* of uncanny, 'dark' coexistence. The hyperobject shatters the categories of perception which define human access to the world—and thus the dimensions of the 'lifeworld' as such: 'The vastness of the object's scale makes smaller beings—people, countries, even continents—seem like an illusion, or a small colored patch on a large dark surface. How can we know it is real? What does real mean? The threat of global warming is not only political, but also ontological' (ibid., p. 32). Thus the *epistemological problem* posed by the clash of scales in the Anthropocene—the challenge of mapping human and non-human scales onto one another—is turned into an *ontological problem*. This ontologization of the sublime replaces questions of epistemology and aesthetic representation with a fundamental 'darkness' and 'withdrawal' of the *things themselves* (Morton 2016). From this perspective, the challenges of an Anthropocene aesthetics no longer emerge from epistemic or aesthetic forms but from the very existence of things. Questions of *form* become questions of *being*.

Let us illustrate this with an example. The American artist Tara Donovan uses industrial materials and everyday objects (plastic cups, industrial tubing, paper or foil) to construct large installations (Fig. 7.2 and Fig. 7.3). Plastic cups, stuck together by the thousands, are shaped into fractal objects that look like a frozen wave, a gigantic pile of foam, or cumulus clouds. On account of their massive accumulation, the translucent material of the cups becomes opaque and their conical shape is subsumed into the rounded surfaces. The resulting objects have the appearance of monstrously enlarged organic structures or natural forms.

Using some of the emblematic materials of the Anthropocene (plastic, polystyrene, cardboard, etc.) and the disposable articles produced from them, Donovan creates a new, entirely *post-natural nature*: forms that look like moss or mildew, vegetal growths, stones or clouds. Here is how Morton describes them: 'In massive piles, the cups reveal *properties hidden from the view* of a person who uses a single cup at a time, a viscous (in my terms) malleability' (Morton 2013, p. 114, emphasis added). Morton sees in Donovan's installations the revelation of a hidden property of the object itself. However, if we consider it in *aesthetic* rather than *ontological* terms, Donovan's operation can be understood primarily as a game of scales which reflects the cumulative scale effects of the Anthropocene: one plastic cup is just a flimsy shred of polystyrene, billions of them are an ecological disaster.

Figure 7.2 Donovan, T., 2006. *Untitled (Plastic Cups)*. Installation (plastic cups). At: New York: Pace Gallery. © Tara Donovan, courtesy Pace Gallery. Photo Kerry Ryan McFate, courtesy Pace Gallery.

In their thousand-fold multiplication, the transition from the small to the enormous, and in their arrangement into structures that cite organic forms, a new object emerges which solicits an entirely different experience of the everyday object, even as it inflates microscopic organic structures to unfamiliar magnitudes. Morton emphasizes the plasticity or 'malleability' of Donovan's works, but he overlooks the *form of the installation*—a form that twists the toxic plastic cup into the figure of a fascinating, shimmering natural object. Donovan's work thus both *amplifies* and *erases* the material properties of the object: out of industrially produced, mass-consumed waste, she conjures an illusion of organic growth and spontaneous emergence. The structures of her installations mimic those generated by natural processes of self-organization. Deliberately and with great precision, Donovan plays with the *form-giving processes of nature*, pulling them out of latency through a translation in scale. She does nothing other than what nature itself does, e.g. when grains of sand pile up into a dune, molecules arrange themselves into crystals, or birds into an undulating flock.

In contrast to Morton, who believes that an aesthetics for the Anthropocene must start with an inquiry into *modes of being*, we therefore argue that it must above all concern itself with questions of *form*. The visual arts have developed a panoply of different strategies for translating the transformative

Figure 7.3 Donovan, T., 2003/08. *Untitled (Styrofoam Cups)*. Installation (styrofoam cups and glue). *At:* Boston: Institute of Contemporary Art, 2008–2009. © Tara Donovan, courtesy Pace Gallery. © Photo charles mayer photography.

processes of the Anthropocene, such as climate change, from their latency into something tangible and manifest. This is the case in the massive scales employed by contemporary photography; in the post-natural installations of a Tara Donovan or of the British artist duo Ackroyd & Harvey; in the artificially constructed atmospheres of Philippe Rahm or Olafur Eliasson; or in such experimental installations and experiments as Thomas Saraceno's *Aerocene* project. Works in other media, sound installations for example, seek to make the inaudible audible, the non-perceptible perceptible. Felix Hess's infrasound installations make it possible to *hear* fluctuations of atmospheric pressure across the Atlantic (Hess 2001), while John Luther Adams's light-sound installation *The Place Where You Go to Listen* translates seismological, geomagnetic, and meteorological data from Alaska into electronic sound (Adams and Ross 2009).

Peter Sloterdijk uses the term 'explication' to refer to such strategies of making manifest that which is latent, of making explicit that which is implicit, of bringing to the fore a background which otherwise goes unnoticed. Historically, such explications were made possible by the disruption or destruction of tacit background conditions, such as breathable air, drinkable water, or the regenerative force of nature:

The background only breaks its silence when foreground processes exceed its burdening capacity. How many real ecological and military disasters were needed before it could be said with juristic, physical and atmotechnic precision how one can set up humanely breathable air environments?

(Sloterdijk 2016, p. 63)

As it grapples with problems of latency, entanglement, and the clash of scales, an aesthetics for the Anthropocene ultimately is not concerned with a world of objects that altogether resist representation, but rather with 'explication' in precisely this sense. It involves an analytical, often experimental and highly knowledge-based *making-explicit* of processes, objects and practices which are murky not for *ontological*, but rather for *epistemological* reasons. It addresses our inability to get these obscure zones of latency into proper focus, and the difficulty of casting them into a *form* which would allow us to deal with them—aesthetically, epistemologically, and also politically.

In the narrative arts—literature and film—the same problem arises, albeit in a medium which is always already culturally coded. Because it involves patterns of coded signs and cultural conventions, literature does not easily lend itself to ontological approaches such as Morton's, nor to the new materialisms advocated, for example, by Iovino and Oppermann, who attribute 'narrative agency' to matter itself (2012). As in the other arts, the task of a 'literature for the Anthropocene' is not so much a question of addressing particular themes (e.g. climate change, ecological disasters, species loss, etc.), as many critics have argued (Trexler 2015, Goodbody 2013, Kaplan 2016, Houser 2014), nor is it about producing certain affects in the audience, as Claire Colebrook suggests when she writes that 'climate change should [...] awaken us from our all-too-human narrative slumbers' (2013, p. 60). Rather, the challenge for literature lies first of all in the development of poetic and narrative forms which are adequate to the problems of latency, entanglement, and scale that the Anthropocene confronts us with.

In narrative, however, the formal problem of the 'explication' of the latent presents itself in a very different way. Narratives are always highly coded cultural projections which not only represent, but organize reality. They give structure to temporal sequences and causal relationships, distinguish between active protagonists and passive backgrounds, and they cannot but employ established symbolic systems; they establish a spatial order and boundaries that define the narrated world through which the characters move; and they determine the perspective from which phenomena can be observed and events narrated. The ways in which narratives structure their world reflect the aesthetic and social values of the societies in which they arise and circulate. Narratives are thus defined by laws of genre which prescribe what material is to be in- or excluded, which settings, characters and action can be described, and in what literary form. Literary texts which seek to narrate climate change are now frequently relegated to a distinctive genre: 'cli-fi', short for climate change fiction (Goodbody and Johns-Putra 2018). However, the vast majority of these texts would otherwise be categorized as science thrillers, science fiction, or dystopian fiction. For Amitav Ghosh, the fact that a subject as momentous as climate change is mostly confined to genres which many critics still consider 'sub-literary' points to a deeper problem with our conception of what constitutes 'serious' fiction.

According to Ghosh, the modern novel treated nature mostly as an aspect of 'setting'—a part of the background against which the narrative unfolds—rather than as an actor in its own right. Furthermore, the genre conventions of the novel require that the narrative be situated in a recognizable time and place and cover a time span no longer than the lives of a limited cast of characters. The focus lies on the psychological development of these characters, who exemplify a particular social milieu, and the plot must be plausible, i.e. reflect common assumptions about the world. As Ghosh writes:

> In novels discontinuities of space are accompanied also by discontinuities of time: a setting usually requires a 'period'; it is actualized within a certain time horizon. Unlike epics, which often range over eons and epochs, novels rarely extend beyond a few generations. The *longue durée* is not the territory of the novel. Novels […] conjure up worlds that become real precisely because of their finitude and distinctiveness. Within the mansion of serious fiction, no one will speak of how the continents were created; nor will they refer to the passage of thousands of years: connections and events on this scale appear not just unlikely but also absurd within the delimited horizon of a novel. […] But the earth of the Anthropocene is precisely a world of insistent, inescapable continuities, animated by forces that are nothing if not inconceivably vast.
>
> (Ghosh 2016, pp. 59–62)

In this passage, Ghosh addresses the problem of a narrative aesthetics of the Anthropocene: the difficulty of casting the *longue durée* of geological time, imperceptible transformations and catastrophic breaks, hyper-complex entanglements, and non-human forms of agency into narrative form. As an alternative to the strict limitations imposed by the modern novel, Ghosh proposes a return to older and non-European genres—especially the epic.

However, we believe that this argument both underplays the flexibility and capaciousness of the modern novel and puts too much stock in the contemporary relevance of the epic. Indeed, novelists have always experimented with the conventions of their genre, for example by unsettling narrative perspectives and introducing unreliable narrators, playing with narrative chronology, and introducing non-human actors. On the other hand, it is questionable whether a literary form that was as tightly embedded in traditional forms of life as the epic can actually be updated for a literary aesthetic of the Anthropocene (Bergthaller 2018). Is not the epic ultimately a genre that is profoundly bound up with the living conditions and value systems of the Holocene? To narrate 'global weirding' can only mean developing narrative forms that take up and continue the formal experiments which shaped the modern novel—but to do so in a way that responds to the specific challenges presented by the Anthropocene.

Such a poetics can pursue many different strategies. The hyper-complexity of the ecological relationships in which humans are implicated can be translated narratively into a de-centered, multi-layered web of narrative. This is the case, for example, in David Mitchell's novel *Cloud Atlas* (2004), whose interwoven plotlines unfold over centuries into a distant future, while the text incorporates a wide variety of literary genres, from diaries and letters to thrillers and science fiction (Baucom 2015). It can also take the shape of a narrative excavation, digging into the layers of deep time sedimented in a particular landscape, as in Don DeLillo's *Point Omega* (2010) or William Least Heat Moon's *PrairyErth* (1991). An Anthropocene poetics can furthermore attempt to locate the human being in the deep time of geological history, as in Max Frisch's *Man in the Holocene* ([1979] 1980). Employing the technique of literary collage, Frisch's short novel combines the reflections of an unreliable narrator with encyclopedia entries about paleoanthropology and geological history in order to reflect on humankind's precarious position as an observer of nature (Malkmus 2017). Alternatively, such an experimental poetics might indeed explore what an 'epic' might be in the Anthropocene—for example in David Brin's science fiction novel *Earth* (1990; Heise 2018) or in Allison Cobb's book-length poem *Green-Wood* ([2010] 2018), which turns a fabled cemetery in Brooklyn into a cosmological metaphor for the modern conquest of nature and its ruinous consequences.

In all of these literary experiments, the protagonists and their inner worlds, and the narrator as observer and organizer of events, lose their central significance in the text. The traditional placeholders for the 'human' in the text, the 'anthropomorphisms' of narrative, take a back seat. The background or 'setting' becomes the actual protagonist of the narrative, while the human actors function merely as nodes in the entanglements and transformations of a world that extends far beyond them. Anthropocene narratives will, we believe, continue to interrogate such anthropomorphisms and perhaps leave them behind as they expand the space of possibility for storytelling. The formal inventiveness of modern and postmodern literature—the many self-imposed interdictions, the experiments with focalization and narrative time, the intertextual and metafictional games, and the programmatic distrust of narrative—testifies to a desire for forms of representation that can stand up to the complexity of the world we find ourselves in. Whatever else they may be about, such texts also speak to the importance of not allowing ourselves to be taken in by our desire for a good yarn.

EH

References

Adams, J.L., and Ross, A., 2009. *The Place Where You Go to Listen*. Middletown, CT: Wesleyan University Press.

Adorno, T.W., 1997. *Aesthetic Theory*. Trans. R. Hullot-Kentor. New York and London: Continuum.

Baucom, I., 2015. 'Moving Centers': Climate Change, Critical Method, and the Historical Novel. *Modern Language Quarterly*, 76(2), 137–157.

Bergthaller, H., 2018. Climate Change and Un-Narratability. *Metaphora* [online], 2. Available from: metaphora.univie.ac.at/3-Edited_Volumes/23-Volume_2/29-climate_change_and_un-narratability [Accessed 14 April 2019].

Blasdel, A., 2017. 'A reckoning for our species': The philosopher prophet of the Anthropocene. *The Guardian* [online], 15 June. Available from: www.theguardian.com/world/2017/jun/15/timothy-morton-anthropocene-philosopher [Accessed 14 April 2019].

Böhme, H., 2002. Natürlich/Natur. In: K. Barck, *et al.*, eds. *Ästhetische Grundbegriffe*, Vol. 4. Stuttgart and Weimar: Metzler, 432–498.

Brin, D., 1990. *Earth*. New York: Bantam Books.

Clark, T., 2015. *Ecocriticism on the Edge. The Anthropocene as a Threshold Concept*. London and New York: Bloomsbury.

Cobb, A., [2010] 2018. *Green-Wood*. New York: Nightboat Books.

Cohen, J.J., 2015. The Sea Above. In: J.J. Cohen and L. Duckert, eds. *Elemental Ecocriticism, Thinking with Earth, Air, Water, and Fire*. Minneapolis: University of Minnesota Press, 105–133.

Colebrook, C., 2013. Framing the End of the Species: Images without Bodies. *Symploke*, 21(1), 51–63.

Daston, L., and Galison, P., [2007] 2010. *Objectivity*. New York: Zone Books.

Davis, H., and Turpin, E., 2015. *Art in the Anthropocene, Encounters Among Aesthetics, Politics, Environments and Epistemologies*. London: Open Humanities Press.

DeLillo, D., 2010. *Point Omega*. New York: Scribner.

Fressoz, J.-B., 2016. L'anthropocène et l'esthétique du sublime. In: H. Guénin, ed. *Sublime. Les tremblements du monde*. Exhibition catalogue. Metz: Centre Pompidou-Metz, 44–49.

Friedman, T., 2010. Global Weirding is Here. *The New York Times*, 17 February.

Frisch, M., [1979] 1980. *Man in the Holocene*. Trans. G. Skelton. New York: Harcourt Brace Jovanovich.

Ghosh, A., 2016. *The Great Derangement. Climate Change and the Unthinkable*. Chicago and London: The University of Chicago Press.

Goodbody, A., 2013. Melting Ice and the Paradoxes of Zeno: Didactic Impulses and Aesthetic Distanciation in German Climate Change Fiction. *Ecozon@*, 4(2), 92–102.

Goodbody, A., and Johns-Putra, A., 2018. *Cli-Fi: A Companion*. London: Peter Lang.

Guénin, H., ed., 2016. *Sublime. Le tremblement du monde*. Exhibition catalogue. Metz: Centre Pompidou-Metz Editions.

Heise, Ursula, 2018. David Brin's *Earth*. In: Axel Goodbody and Adeline Johns-Putra, eds. *Cli-Fi: A Companion*. London: Peter Lang, 195–201.

Hess, F., 2001. *Air Pressure Fluctuations* [CD]. Editions RZ and Kehrer Verlag.

Houser, H., 2014. *Ecosickness in Contemporary U.S. Fiction, Environment and Affect*. New York: Columbia University Press.

Iovino, S., and Oppermann, S., 2012. Material Ecocriticism: Materiality, Agency and Models of Narrativity. *Ecozon@*, 3(1), 75–91.

Kainulainen, M., 2013. Saying Climate Change: Ethics of the Sublime and the Problem of Representation. *symploke*, 21(1–2), 109–123.

Kant, I., [1787] 1998. *Critique of Pure Reason*. Trans. P. Guyer and A.W. Wood. Cambridge: Cambridge University Press.

Kant, I., [1788] 1997. *Critique of Practical Reason*. Trans. M.J. Gregor. Cambridge and New York: Cambridge University Press.

Kant, I. [1790] 2000. *Critique of the Power of Judgment*. Trans. E. Matthews. Cambridge: Cambridge University Press

Kaplan, E.A., 2016. *Climate Trauma, Foreseeing the Future in Dystopian Film and Fiction*. New Brunswick, NJ, and London: Rutgers University Press.

Latour, B., 2016. *Reset Modernity! Field Book* [online]. Available from: www.bruno-latour.fr/sites/default/files/downloads/RESET-MODERNITY-GB.pdf [Accessed 14 April 2019].

Latour, B., 2017. *Facing Gaia. Eight Lectures on the New Climate Regime*. Trans. C. Porter. London: Polity.

Least Heat Moon, W., 1991. *PrairyErth: A Deep Map*. Boston: Houghton Mifflin.

Lyotard, J.-F., 1984. *The Postmodern Condition. A Report on Knowledge*. Trans. G. Bennington and B. Massumi. Minneapolis: University of Minnesota Press.

Malkmus, B., 2017. 'Man in the Anthropocene'. Max Frisch's Environmental History. *PMLA*, 132(1), 71–85.

Mitchell, D., 2004. *Cloud Atlas*. London: Sceptre.

Morton, T., 2007. *Ecology Without Nature, Rethinking Environmental Aesthetics*. Cambridge: Harvard University Press.

Morton, T., 2013. *Hyperobjects, Philosophy and Ecology after the End of the World*. Minneapolis: University of Minnesota Press.

Morton, T., 2016. *Dark Ecology, For a Logic of Future Coexistence*. New York: Columbia University Press.

Sloterdijk, P., 2016. *Spheres Volume III: Plural Spherology*. Trans. W. Hoban. South Pasadena: Semiotext(e).

Trexler, A., 2015. *Anthropocene Fictions, The Novel in a Time of Climate Change*. Charlottesville: University of Virginia Press.

Williston, B., 2016. The Sublime Anthropocene . *Environmental Philosophy*, 13(2), 155–174.

Part III
Fault lines

8   Biopolitics

'For millennia, man remained what he was for Aristotle: a living animal with the additional capacity for a political existence; modern man is an animal whose politics places his existence as a living being in question' (Foucault [1976] 1978, p. 143). Half a century after their original publication, these famous sentences from Michel Foucault's *History of Sexuality* read like a lucid anticipation of the political challenges of the Anthropocene. It is the forms of our collective life, our political and economic order, which have turned the human species from an animal among animals into a geological actor, and which now endanger the ecological basis of its existence. The Anthropocene entails a transformation of the political which affects not only the domain of collective decisions (see Ch. 6: Politics) but also areas which we are accustomed to think of as the private sphere: private property, consumption, reproductive freedom and freedom of movement are not merely a matter between the citizens and the state, but must also be viewed with respect to their cumulative effect on the Earth system. How many children we have, what we eat, how we get to work or heat our homes—all of these are private decisions. Scaled up to the entire population, however, they potentially endanger the ecological foundations of society (in this case, too, we are thus dealing with a problem of scale, see Ch. 10: Scales I). In the Anthropocene, how people define their needs and how they go about satisfying them becomes a political issue. But it is no longer just the life of human beings that is thus placed in question, but that of countless other species, as well.

Foucault coined the term 'biopolitics' for such a politics that addresses the human being as a living creature, and he conceived of it as a specifically modern phenomenon which is linked to a fundamental change in the conditions of life:

> [The] pressure exerted by the biological on the historical had remained very strong for thousands of years; epidemics and famine were the two great dramatic forms of this relationship that was always dominated by the menace of death. [The] economic [...] development of the eighteenth century, and an increase in productivity and resources even more rapid

than the demographic growth it encouraged, allowed a measure of relief from these profound threats [...]. [The] development of the different fields of knowledge concerned with life in general, the improvement of agricultural techniques, and the observations and measures relative to man's life and survival contributed to this relaxation [...]. Western man was gradually learning what it meant to be a living species in a living world, to have a body, conditions of existence, probabilities of life, an individual and collective welfare, forces that could be modified, and a space in which they could be distributed in an optimal manner.

(Foucault [1976] 1978, pp. 142–3)

Thus the emergence of biopolitics is closely tied to a development which the historian Emmanuel Le Roy Ladurie had described, a few years earlier, as the overcoming of the 'Malthusian curse' (Le Roy Ladurie [1966] 1976, p. 311). Ladurie was referring to the cyclical pattern which the economist and Anglican cleric Thomas R. Malthus had outlined in his infamous *Essay on the Principle of Population* (1798): because the human population increases exponentially, it always outpaces the production of food. Demographic growth therefore invariably leads to misery, famine, and disease—and thus to a decrease in the population. According to Ladurie, the demographic development of France since the Middle Ages bore out this pattern: already at the beginning of the fourteenth century, the country's population had reached 20 million, the upper limit of what could be supported with traditional forms of agriculture. As a consequence of the Black Death, the population crashed to about 10 million. By the middle of the sixteenth century, it had recovered, and during the following two centuries it hovered between 18 and 20 million. Only after 1720—the year of the last large outbreak of the plague—did the country enter a sustained phase of demographic growth. Around 1800, the population had already increased to 30 million (Le Roy Ladurie [1973] 1977, pp. 123–4). It was precisely this 'demographic explosion' (Foucault [1975–1976] 2003, p. 249) which, in Foucault's account, instigated the development of new forms of power and was in turn fostered by them. In contrast to the sovereign power of the old monarchical state, this 'biopower' no longer addresses itself to a *people* constituted of legally defined subjects, but rather to a *population* of living beings whom it seeks to control through new statistical and administrative procedures. Its goal is to regulate the general conditions of life, the various factors affecting natality, morbidity, and mortality. Whereas sovereign power was first of all a 'subtraction mechanism' based on the right to seize 'services, labour, and blood' from the people, biopolitics seeks to 'incite, reinforce, control, monitor, optimize, and organize' life (Foucault [1976] 1978, p. 136). Foucault sums up the contrast in a pithy formula: 'the ancient right to take life or let live was replaced by a power to foster life or disallow it to the point of death' (Foucault [1976] 1978, p. 138).

Foucault's interest lies in the question of how biopower engendered new forms of control over *human beings*, and this has also been the focus of most recent debates over biopolitics. In the context of the Anthropocene, how-ever, biopolitics appears under a somewhat different aspect: it must be con-sidered in terms of a much more encompassing control of *biological processes*. Insofar as it seeks to prevent famine and disease, its calculations cannot be restricted to the human population, but must take into account the popula-tions of all the other species on whom the well-being of human beings depends. Biopolitics is also concerned with managing cattle and corn, microbes and mosquitos. Ultimately, it is concerned with regulating the ecological conditions of human existence. From the outset, biopolitics is perforce also ecological politics (Medovoi 2010). Modern factory farming provides a paradigm for the ever more sophisticated fine-tuning of biological processes which characterizes the biopolitics of the Anthropocene: livestock are bred with the most advanced reproductive technologies, the growth of their bodies is managed through hormones and a precise control of their living conditions (Wolfe 2013, pp. 48–51). Such biopolitical strategies have come to pervade life at a planetary scale. Since the beginning of the Indus-trial Revolution, the total biomass of terrestrial vertebrates has seen a ten-fold increase (Barnosky 2008). Humans and their domesticates account for more than 95% of this total (Williams *et al.* 2016, p. 44). One stratigraphic marker of the Anthropocene will therefore be chicken bones: since the 1950s, the number of chickens slaughtered annually for human consumption has increased from about 580 million to 9 billion, roughly by a factor of 15 (Pew Environment Group 2011).

Biopolitics enacts a kind of double movement that runs parallel to the distinction between *homo* and *anthropos*, *bíos* and *zoé*, and which is of essen-tial importance for the Anthropocene (see Ch. 5: The *anthropos*). On the one hand, it *naturalizes* the human species (as *anthropos*), i.e. it involves the knowledge that *homo sapiens* is one kind of biological creature among others. The threats which biopolitics seeks to ward off arise at the level of biological existence: hunger and disease are dangers which all living organisms are exposed to. Biopolitical forms of governance develop along with the realiza-tion that they are not 'acts of God', but have natural causes and can be controlled by natural means. Their result, however, is a radical *denaturaliza-tion* of the human and its ecological environment: once the biological mechanisms which had controlled the population in the past are rendered inoperative, their function is consigned to society. At the same time that biopolitics thus closes the ontological gap between the human and other biological species, it opens up a new divide between those forms of life whose flourishing is promoted and those who must die for the benefit of the latter. This biopolitical dividing line is drawn by society itself and can therefore no longer be 'natural' in any conventional sense—even if the necessity of drawing it is conceived and justified in terms of its naturalness. This, Foucault argued, was precisely the function of modern concepts of race and of racial degeneracy: to 'create caesuras within the biological continuum addressed by biopower' so as allow for the distinction between what must live and what must die (Foucault [1975–1976] 2003, p. 255).

In this context, the ideas which Thomas Malthus had laid out in his *Essay on the Principle of Population* play a central role. It is therefore quite remarkable that Foucault devoted hardly any attention to them (Tellmann 2013, p. 136). Malthus's *Essay* was first of all a polemic rejoinder to the optimistic view, promulgated by contemporaries such as William Godwin and the Marquis de Condorcet, that poverty could be permanently eliminated through public welfare programs. Population growth, Malthus argued, could be stabilized only through 'preventative checks', i.e. a reduction of the birth rate, or through 'positive checks', i.e. an increase of mortality, for example through famine, disease, and war (Malthus [1798] 1998, p. 20). Because public welfare alleviates the pressure to apply preventative checks, it leads to an increase in the number of the poor, eventually engendering a situation in which positive checks kick in, and thus an increase of human misery. Malthus's conclusion was that the poor must be left to their own devices. Thus Malthus supplied a 'natural' principle that could justify the exclusion of marginalized groups from the biopolitical protections of the state—a principle that allowed, in Foucault's terms, for the placement of a biopolitical 'caesura'. After Darwin had singled out the 'law of population' as the central mechanism of natural selection (see Ch. 3: Genealogies), it could also be seen as mandating the extermination of 'degenerates' and 'inferior races' in the name of progress. It fell to the British scholar Francis Galton to draw this conclusion: because civilization reduces the selective pressures that are necessary to ensure the dominance of biologically superior types, it leads to a 'degradation' of the human race that can only be countered through deliberate efforts to improve the 'racial stock' by selective breeding (Galton 1865). Thus Malthus's 'law of population' issues in biological race theory, and the *laissez-faire* of classical liberalism in the *laissez mourir* of eugenics and social Darwinism.

Foucault's failure to address Malthus is even more remarkable if one considers that he proposed the concept of biopolitics at the very moment when population growth had moved into the center of public debate. Paul Ehrlich's 1968 *The Population Bomb* (co-written with his wife, Anne), which painted a lurid picture of the consequences of the 'population explosion', had been a bestseller across the Western world. In the discussions sur- rounding the first 'Earth Day' in 1970, it was assumed as a matter of course that controlling population growth was the master key for resolving the environmental crisis (Mayhew 2016, pp. 265–6). Neomalthusian thought found its most influential expression in *Limits to Growth*, the 1972 report of the Club of Rome which employed computer models to predict a global ecological collapse unless the exponential growth of the world's population was quickly curbed (Meadows *et al.* 1972, see Ch. 3: Genealogies). On this basis, popular films projected a dystopian future in which overpopulation leads to cannibalism (*Soylent Green*, 1973), or is used to justify murderous state policies (*Logan's Run*, 1976, cf. Horn [2014] 2018, pp. 89–133).

The origin of these debates can be traced back to two books, both published in 1948, which had declared population growth to be the central challenge for the future of humanity: Fairfield Osborn's *Our Plundered Planet* and William Vogt's *Road to Survival*. Osborn's phrasing of the problem already anticipates the thinking of the Anthropocene: humans, he wrote, are now 'for the first time a *large-scale geological force*' (Osborn 1948, p. 29, emphasis in original, cf. Steffen *et al.* 2011, p. 844). Both Osborn and Vogt were trained biologists, and their argument transposed the concept of 'carrying capacity' from animal ecology into the realm of politics. History was full of examples of societies which had destroyed themselves by overtaxing their natural environment (Vogt 1948, p. 40). However, the rapacity of modern industrial society was historically unparalleled, and the idea of exporting this economic system to the rest of the world was a recipe for civilizational suicide: 'Like Gadarene swine, we shall rush down a war-torn slope to a barbarian existence in the blackened rubble' (Vogt 1948, p. 288).

This quotation already indicates how the discourse of overpopulation blends ecological concerns with questions of national security. That family planning and birth control became a central pillar of Western development aid was largely a consequence of the Cold War: it was feared that the misery engendered by overpopulation would make Third World countries receptive to communism (Nally 2016, pp. 217–9). There are good reasons for the accusation that such programs were steeped in neocolonial arrogance (e.g. Connelly 2008). While the Neomalthusians carefully avoided the vocabulary of eugenics and biological race theory, their aim was indeed nothing other than the placement of a biopolitical caesura. The Ehrlichs anticipated the need for compulsory sterilization programs in 'underdeveloped' countries (Ehrlich 1968, p. 165) and suggested that international food aid programs adopt a triage system: assistance should only be provided to countries which had already begun to implement measures for population control. Countries which refused to do, and where catastrophic famines were already unavoidable (such as India), should be left to their own devices (ibid., pp. 159–60). Garrett Hardin's infamous essay *Life Boat Ethics*, tellingly subtitled 'The Case against Helping the Poor', put the case in even harsher terms: by shielding Third World nations from the consequences of their own bad policies, foreign aid merely perpetuated their misery. Allowing their population to migrate to wealthier countries would degrade the natural resources of the latter without improving conditions in the former. The only prudent policy was therefore to stop foreign aid and close the borders (Hardin 1974, n.p.; this essay was in many ways a sequel to Hardin's argument in 'The Tragedy of the Commons', see Ch. 6: Politics).

Such arguments show how the Malthusian 'biopolitics of scarcity' leads to a logic of exception which suspends ethical obligations (cf. Horn 2013, p. 1003, Horn [2014] 2018, pp. 89–133). The tendency of Neomalthusian thinking to rationalize inhumane policies explains why the term 'overpopulation' has become taboo (and a favorite *ideé fixe* among cinematic villains, e.g. in *Inferno*, 2016, and *Avengers: Infinity War*, 2018). But that is not the only reason why the topic has gradually faded from view since the late 1980s (Campbell 2012). Most importantly, the catastrophic predictions of the Neomalthusians were not borne out by the course of events. Beginning in the 1960s, the so-called 'Green Revolution' dramatically boosted agricultural yields through the introduction of new strains of cereals and increased use of pesticides and artificial fertilizers (which were based on fossil fuels; see Ch. 9: Energy). Meanwhile, resource shortages failed to materialize. In 1980, Paul Ehrlich wagered with the economist Julian Simon that the prices of copper, tin, and other metals would rise over the following decade. Ehrlich lost the bet (Sabin 2013, p. 181). These developments seemed to confirm the views of the 'cornucopians', i.e. those who, like Simon, assumed that technological progress would allow even an increasing world population to enjoy rising standards of living. At the same time, population began to stabilize in many countries, in accordance with the widely received model of demographic transition, which stipulated that rising affluence reduced mortality well before it led to sinking birth rates. It thus seemed reasonable to believe that the growth of the world's population would level off in the course of economic development. This optimistic assumption also underlies the 1987 report of the United Nations World Commission on Environment and Development, better known as the Brundtland report, which enshrined 'sustainable development' as the central goal of international development aid (World Commission on Environment and Development 1987).

However, the discussion about the Anthropocene has put the issue of population back on the agenda, although often only in a roundabout way. The challenges of the Anthropocene are the challenges of a world in which humanity must learn to accommodate itself to the limits of the Earth system. If Johan Rockström *et al.* speak of a 'safe operating space for humanity', they are echoing the *Limits to Growth*—even when they explicitly distance themselves from their Neomalthusian predecessors, e.g. by emphasizing that they are not concerned with absolute population numbers or resource scarcity, but rather with the description of the Earth as a dynamic system (see Ch. 2: Definitions). Instead of 'hard' limitations, we are now dealing with complex feedback loops between the various components of the Earth system and with 'tipping points' which cannot be anticipated through linear extrapolation from current trends. Passing these tipping points will have effects that only become manifest over longer periods of time (Cornell 2015). Climate change can illustrate these differences between the *Limits to Growth* and Rockström's 'Planetary Boundaries': whereas the Neomalthusians were primarily concerned that fossil fuels would run out, we now know that the relevant boundary lies in the finite capacity of the Earth's atmosphere to absorb the greenhouse gases which are produced by burning them. We also understand that the consequences of crossing this boundary will only become fully apparent decades or even centuries in the future. An important characteristic of planetary boundaries is their latency. This has led some commenters to argue that sustainability is no longer a viable political and economic goal, because it assumes that the Earth system could be maintained in a stable, stationary state over the long term. In the Anthropocene, we should instead strive to make social and natural systems more resilient, i. e. we should strengthen their ability to react flexibly to fluctuating environmental conditions (Benson and Craig 2017).

Ultimately, however, these are differences in rhetoric rather than substance. Resilience has long been understood as an important aspect of sustainability (Caradonna 2014, pp. 243–4), and the idea that an 'overshoot' of the Earth's ecological carrying capacity would not be immediately apparent is an old staple of Neomalthusian thinking (e.g. Catton 1980, pp. 36–47). The biophysical models of Rockström *et al.* (2009) may be much more sophisticated than the primitive computer simulations used by the Club of Rome, but they lead to similar conclusions. Their refusal to factor demographic and economic projections into their calculations only means that Earth system science cannot answer the question of how world society needs to change if it is to support the lives of more than 10 billion people. In the Anthropocene, the concerns which the Neomalthusians had highlighted have only become more urgent.

The continuity becomes immediately apparent if one takes a closer look at the so-called 'Kaya identity' which the Intergovernmental Panel on Climate Change (IPCC) uses to calculate the development of global carbon dioxide emissions. According to this formula, anthropogenic carbon emissions are the mathematical product of four factors: population, gross domestic product (GDP) per capita, energy efficiency, and carbon intensity (Knutti 2014). Simply put: the total output of carbon dioxide depends on the amount of fossil fuels which must be burned in order to produce the energy that is required to sustain a particular standard of life, as well as the total number of people enjoying this standard of life. Basically, this is a revised version of the famous $I=P*A*T$ formula Paul Ehrlich and John Holdren proposed in 1971: the ecological impact (I) of human action is the mathematical product of population (P), the level of affluence (A) and technology (T) (Ehrlich and Holdren 1971). If our aim is to reduce the ecological impact of world society to a level that can be sustained by the Earth system, *all three of these factors* must be taken into account.

The different versions of a biopolitics of the Anthropocene can be viewed as so many different approaches to solving this equation. Neomalthusianism is usually understood as putting all the emphasis on reducing population (P; of course, the mere fact that Ehrlich tried to encapsulate the problem in the $I=P*A*T$ formula indicates that this is a gross simplification). Ecomodernist hopes for a 'Good Anthropocene' (Dalby 2015, see Ch. 5: The *anthropos*) rest on the assumption that technological innovation (T) will make it possible to increase energy efficiency to such a degree that humanity's ecological impact (I) can be reduced even while population (P) and affluence (A) continue to increase—a process which is referred to as 'de-coupling', and which has also been adopted as an important goal by the United Nations Environment Programme (UNEP 2011). Renewable energy sources and increased energy efficiency in industrial production, agriculture and transport, it is argued, will suffice in order to provide rising standards of living for all people without endangering the ecological basis of society.

In Europe, this program entered the political mainstream as early as the 1980s, under the title of 'ecological modernization' (Hajer 1995). In the debate over the Anthropocene, its most outspoken proponents are a group of writers associated with the Californian Breakthrough Institute. The geographer Erle Ellis, for example, paints the optimistic picture of a future in which a growing and increasingly affluent world population clusters in energy-efficient cities, while rising agricultural yields make it possible to free up space for wild species. In Ellis's view, this is merely the logical continuation of a process by which humanity has, over the course of many millennia, steadily expanded the biophysical limits of the ecological environment and sloughed off outdated forms of life: 'As we did at the end of the Palaeolithic, most of humanity is defecting from the older ways, which will soon become hobbies for the elite and nostalgic memories for the rest of humanity. Just as wild forests, wild game, and soon, wild fish disappear, so do the human systems associated with them' (Ellis 2011, p. 44).

In contrast to the Malthusian biopolitics of scarcity, Ellis is sketching a *biopolitics of abundance* which is predicated on the assumption that ecological carrying capacity can always be increased through a more intensive management of biological and social processes. From such a viewpoint, the Anthropocene merely marks the historical moment when the human species recognizes itself for what it always was: an ecological engineer who creates its own world. The total subordination of the Earth system to human purposes is sometimes described with the metaphor of 'stewardship', suggesting a responsible management of planetary resources for the benefit of future generations. However, as we have already seen, the need to increase efficiency and productivity has been used in the past to justify the enclosure of the commons. More often than not, the consequences were social and ecological degradation (see Ch. 6: Politics). On closer inspection, what Ellis innocuously describes as the 'disappearance' of human systems turns out to be violent expropriation and genocide. The biopolitics of abundance, too, requires the placing of caesuras, and it is far from obvious why an ecological modernization should turn out to be less coercive than previous phases of modernization.

This would seem to justify the deep suspicion that many scholars have articulated with regard to the notion of 'stewardship'. Bonneuil and Fressoz view it as little more than a rhetorical cover for 'geopower'—a term which, with direct reference to Foucault's concept of 'biopower', designates not only the technical systems for monitoring and modeling the Earth system, but also the attendant discourses of sustainability and ethical consumption.

They form different aspects of a new, planet-wide formation of power-knowledge. Just as Foucault's concept of biopower was meant to enable a critique of the ways in which modern political power seizes upon biological life, the concept of geopower names and critiques the project of geo-engineering (understood as the technical control of the Earth system). If the aim of biopolitics was to mobilize productive forces in the context of the nation-state, Bonneuil and Fressoz argue, then geopower must be seen as the tool of a new global, technocratic elite (Bonneuil and Fressoz 2016, pp. 87–94, similarly Luke 1995).

Still, there are good reasons not to dismiss biopolitics outright. After all, the overcoming of the 'Malthusian curse' is not an ideological fiction, but the empirical precondition for the phase of hyperexponential population growth that started with the Industrial Revolution. When Foucault writes that biopolitics seeks to 'maintain, ensure, and develop' life (Foucault [1976] 1978, p. 136), he is referring to a process that brought an end to a world in which about half of all children died before reaching five years of age (Roser 2017), in which the majority of people were suffering from malnutrition, and the average body weight was only two-thirds of what we consider as normal today (Fogel 1994, p. 10). Biopolitics concerns not only the optimal utilization of human capital, but also the development of modern systems of health care and social security, environmental regulation and consumer protections—in short, the entire network of protective and coercive measures by the state which safeguard the citizenry of the world's wealthier nations from hunger and disease. The blessings of biopolitical modernity are not so easily separated from its blights.

World population growth has slowed significantly since the 1970s. But according to current prognoses, it will continue to rise over the next three decades, from now 7.7 billion to almost 10 billion people (United Nations Department of Economic and Social Affairs 2017)—more than three times the number which had filled Fairfield Osborn with deep alarm in 1948 (Osborn 1948, p. 40). Most population growth today takes place in Africa and the Middle East—regions which will be hit especially hard by climate change and where states are often too weak to provide effective protection to their citizens. At the same time, prosperity is rising more quickly than ever before: in 1985, 1 billion people enjoyed a standard of living that met the Organisation for Economic Co-operation and Development's (OECD) definition of 'middle class'. Today, this global middle class encompasses 3 billion people, and if current trends continue, their number will have grown to 5 billion a decade from now. For the first time in world history, less than half of the world's population would live in poverty. Most of this growth in prosperity is due to economic development in Asia and especially in China (Kharas 2017, p. 11), i.e. in places that have seen a precipitous decline of birth rates. These numbers make clear why the concept of 'overpopulation' can be quite misleading insofar as it focuses attention only on the factor of population growth. However, global problems such as climate change and ocean acidification are largely caused by countries whose birth rates are at or below the replacement rate, i.e. where the population is already in decline. Nevertheless, it is misguided to conceive of the problem exclusively in terms of distributional justice. The high birth rates in poor countries exacerbate local environmental problems such as deforestation, overfishing, and loss of biodiversity, and they also make it exceedingly difficult to build effective education or health care systems. Thus they not only undermine the ecological basis of subsistence at a local level, but also contribute to social and ecological destabilization globally.

Neither the biopolitics of scarcity nor the biopolitics of abundance seems to be able to point towards a livable future, then. Ultimately, this leads to the question of whether a fundamentally different form of biopolitics can be imagined—a biopolitics which would not oppress or control life but contribute to its genuine flourishing. The possibility of such an 'affirmative biopolitics' has preoccupied philosophers such as Michael Hardt, Antonio Negri and Roberto Esposito for some time (Tierney 2016). However, the most concrete steps into this direction have been undertaken by Donna Haraway, who is also among the small handful of scholars in the environmental humanities who have explicitly addressed the 'Great Acceleration of human numbers' as a problem (Haraway 2016, p. 6). In Haraway's telling, the destructive effects of biopolitical modernity are rooted in a false view of life. Evolutionary theory since Darwin, and especially after the modern synthesis from the middle of the twentieth century onwards, conceives of life in terms of discrete units: genes, cells, and populations are modeled as unitary actors engaged in a competition over resources. Evolution is conceived as a zero-sum game (Haraway 2016, p. 62). Haraway contrasts this with the theory of symbiogenesis which, largely through the work of Lynn Margulis, has revolutionized evolutionary biology since the 1990s. Margulis provided evidence that mitochondria, chloroplasts and other organelles had originally been autonomous organisms which were incorporated by prokaryotic microbes (i.e. unicellular organisms lacking a nucleus). From such endosymbioses (i.e. symbioses in which one partner inhabits the body of the other) emerged the eukaryotic cells of which all complex, multicellular organisms are composed.

It has become increasingly clear that endosymbiosis is not a strange exception, but rather widespread in the biological world. Termites evolved from cockroaches which entered into a symbiotic relationship with microbes that were able to digest cellulose (Margonelli 2018, pp. 6–8), and the Hawaiian bobtail squid owes its ability to glow in the dark to the bioluminescent bacteria which colonize its skin (Haraway 2016, p. 66). The human organism, too, is not a clearly delimited individual, but a 'holobiont': it constitutes a complete ecosystem hosting a multitude of other species (such as the bacteria and fungi which populate our intestines and mucous membranes) on which it depends for its survival. Seen from this perspective, our bodies resemble a coral reef, in which corals and algae live in symbiosis, or a lichen, which consists of algae and fungi. In the words of biologist Scott Gilbert, whom Haraway quotes on multiple occasions: 'We are all lichens' (cited Haraway 2016, p. 30, see also Gilbert *et al.* 2012, p. 336)—that is to say, composite beings. It is not a coincidence that Margulis also played a central role in the development of the Gaia theory (see Ch. 4: Nature and culture), which effectively transposes the logic of endosymbiosis to a planetary scale (Clarke 2017, pp. 203–4). A biopolitics fit for the Anthropocene can no longer focus on the reproductive success of individual biological species. It must transform the human being from a parasite into a symbiont of the Earth (Serres [1990] 1995, p. 34). It must be based on the recognition of relationships of kinship and interdependence that cut across species lines and aim at the survivability of entire symbiotic networks. Thus Haraway's slogan, which encapsulates the task of biopolitics in the Anthropocene: 'Make kin, not babies!' (Haraway 2016, p. 102).

HB

References

Barnosky, A.D., 2008. Megafauna Tradeoff as a Driver of Quaternary and Future Extinctions. *Proceedings of the National Academy of Sciences of the United States of America*, 105(1), 11543–11548.

Benson, M.H., and Craig, R.K., 2017. *The End of Sustainability. Resilience and the Future of Environmental Governance in the Anthropocene.* Lawrence: University of Kansas Press.

Bonneuil, C., and Fressoz, J.-B., 2016. *The Shock of the Anthropocene. The Earth, History and Us.* London and New York: Verso.

Campbell, M., 2012. Why the Silence on Population? In: P. Cafaro and E. Christ, eds. *Life of the Brink. Environmentalists Confront Overpopulation.* Athens: University of George Press, 41–55.

Caradonna, J., 2014. *Sustainability. A History.* Oxford: Oxford University Press.

Catton, W.R., 1980. *Overshoot. The Ecological Basis of Revolutionary Change.* Urbana: University of Illinois Press.

Clarke, B., 2017. Planetary Immunity: Biopolitics, Gaia Theory, the Holobiont, and the Systems Counterculture. In: E. Hörl and J.E. Burton, eds. *General Ecology. The New Ecological Paradigm.* London: Bloomsbury, 193–215.

Connelly, M., 2008. *Fatal Misconception. The Struggle to Control World Population.* Cambridge: Harvard University Press.

Cornell, S., 2015. *Planetary Boundaries. Some Questions and Answers* [online], Stockholm Resilience Center. Available from: www.stockholmresilience.org/download/ 18.3110ee8c1495db744326bf5/1459560166869/Planetary+Boundaries+Q+and+A +Ja [Accessed 14 February 2019].

Dalby, S., 2015. Framing the Anthropocene: The good, the bad and the ugly. *The Anthropocene Review*, 3(1), 33–51.

Ehrlich, P.R., 1968. *The Population Bomb.* New York: Ballantine.

Ehrlich, P.R., and Holdren, J.P., 1971. Impact of Population Growth. *Science*, 171(3977), 1212–1217.

Ellis, E., 2011. The Planet of No Return. Human Resilience on an Artificial Earth. *Breakthrough Journal*, 2, 39–44.

Fogel, R.W., 1994. The Relevance of Malthus for the Study of Mortality Toda. Long-Run Influences on Health, Mortality, Labor Force Participation, and Population Growth. National Bureau of Economic Research, *Historical Working Paper* [online], 54. Available from: www.nber.org/papers/h0054 [Accessed 14 February 2019].

Foucault, M., [1976] 1978. *The History of Sexuality*. Vol. 1. Trans. R. Hurley. New York: Pantheon.

Foucault, M., [1975–1976] 2003. *Society Must Be Defended: Lectures at the Collège de France, 1975–76*. Ed. M. Betani and A. Fontana. Trans. D. Macey. New York: Picador.

Galton, F., 1865. Hereditary Character and Talent. *MacMillan's Magazine* [online], 12, 318–327. Available from: http://galton.org/essays/1860-1869/galton-1865-hereditary-talent.pdf [Accessed 14 February 2019].

Gilbert, S.F., Sapp, J., and Tauber, A.I., 2012. A symbiotic view of life. We have never been individuals. *The Quarterly Review of Biology*, 87(4), 325–341.

Hajer, M.A., 1995. *The Politics of Environmental Discourse. Ecological Modernization and the Policy Process*. Oxford: Oxford University Press.

Haraway, D., 2016. *Staying with the Trouble. Making Kin in the Chthulucene*. Durham: Duke University Press.

Hardin, G., 1974. *Lifeboat Ethics. The Case Against Helping the Poor* [online]. Available from: www.garretthardinsociety.org/articles/art_lifeboat_ethics_case_against_helping_poor.html [Accessed 14 February 2019].

Horn, E., 2013. Überlebensgemeinschaften. Zur Biopolitik der Katastrophe. *Merkur*, 67(773), 992–1004.

Horn, E., [2014] 2018. The Future as catastrophe. Imagining disaster in the modern age. Trans. V. Pakis. New York: Columbia University Press.

Kharas, H., 2017. The Unprecedented Expansion of the Global Middle-Class. An Update. *Brookings Global Economy and Development Working Paper* [online], 100. Available from: www.brookings.edu/wp-content/uploads/2017/02/global_20170228_global-middle-class.pdf [Accessed 14 February 2019].

Knutti, R., 2014. Keine Trendwende beim CO2-Ausstoß. *ETH Zukunftsblog* [online]. Available from: www.ethz.ch/de/news-und-veranstaltungen/eth-news/news/2014/09/keine-trendwende-beim-co2-ausstoss.html [Accessed 1 March 2019].

Le Roy Ladurie, E., [1966] 1976. *The Peasants of Languedoc*. Trans. J. Day. Champaign, IL: University of Illinois Press.

Le Roy Ladurie, E., [1973] 1977. Motionless History. Trans. J. Day. *Social Science History*, 1(2), 115–136.

Luke, T.W., 1995. On Environmentality: Geo-Power and Eco-Knowledge in the Discourses of Contemporary Environmentalism. *Cultural Critique*, 31, 57–81.

Malthus, T., [1798] 1998. An Essay on the Principle of Population, as it Affects the Future Improvement of Society with Remarks on the Speculations of Mr. Godwin, M. Condorcet, and Other Writers. *Electronic Scholarly Publishing Project* [online]. Available from: www.esp.org/books/malthus/population/malthus.pdf [Accessed 14 February 2019].

Margonelli, L., 2018. *Underbug. An Obsessive Tale of Termites and Technology*. New York: Farrar, Straus and Giroux.

Mayhew, R.J., 2016. The Publication Bomb: The Birth of Modern Environmentalism and the Editing of Malthus's Essay. In: R.J. Mayhew, ed. *New Perspectives on Malthus*. Cambridge: Cambridge University Press, 240–266.

Meadows, D., *et al.*, 1972. *The Limits to Growth. A report for The Club of Rome's project on the predicament of mankind*. New York: New American Library.

Medovoi, L., 2010. The Biopolitical Unconscious: Toward an Eco-Marxist Literary Theory. *Mediations*, 24(2), 122–139.

Nally, D., 2016. Imagine All the People: Rockefeller Philanthropy, Malthusian Thinking and the 'Peasant Problem' in Asia. In: R.J. Mayhew, ed. *New Perspectives on Malthus*. Cambridge: Cambridge University Press, 208–239.

Osborn, F., 1948. *Our Plundered Planet*. Boston: Little, Brown and Co.

Pew Environment Group, 2011. *Big Chicken. Pollution and Industrial Poultry Production in America* [online]. Available from: www.pewtrusts.org/en/research-and-analysis/reports/2011/07/26/big-chicken-pollution-and-industrial-poultry-production-in-america [Accessed 14 February 2019].

Rockström, J., *et al.*, 2009. Planetary boundaries. Exploring the safe operating space for humanity. *Ecology and Society*, 14(2), 32.

Roser, M., 2017. Child Mortality, 2017. *Our World in Data* [online]. Available from: https://ourworldindata.org/child-mortality/ [Accessed 14 February 2019].

Sabin, P., 2013. *The Bet. Paul Ehrlich, Julian Simon, and Our Gamble over Earth's Future*. New Haven: Yale University Press.

Serres, M., [1990] 1995. *The Natural Contract*. Trans. E. MacArthur and W. Paulson. Ann Arbor, MI: University of Michigan Press.

Steffen, W., *et al.*, 2011. The Anthropocene: Conceptual and Historical Perspectives. *Philosophical Transactions of the Royal Society A*, 369(1938), 842–867.

Tellmann, U., 2013. Catastrophic Populations and the Fear of the Future: Malthus and the Genealogy of Liberal Economy. *Theory, Culture & Society*, 30(2), 135–155.

Tierney, T.F., 2016. Toward an Affirmative Biopolitics. *Sociological Theory*, 34(4), 358–381.

United Nations Department of Economic and Social Affairs, 2017. *World Population Prospects* [online]. Available from: https://esa.un.org/unpd/wpp/Publications/Files/WPP2017_KeyFindings.pdf [Accessed 14 February 2019].

United Nations Environment Programme (UNEP), 2011. *Decoupling Natural Resource Use and Environmental Impacts from Economic Growth: A Report of the Working Group on Decoupling to the International Resource Panel* [online]. Available from: www.ourenergypolicy.org/wp-content/uploads/2014/07/decoupling.pdf [Accessed 1 March 2019].

Vogt, W., 1948. *The Road to Survival*. New York: William Sloane.

Williams, M., *et al.*, 2016. The Anthropocene: A conspicuous stratigraphical signal of anthropogenic changes in production and consumption across the biosphere. *Earth's Future*, 4(3), 34–53.

Wolfe, C., 2013. *Before the Law. Humans and Other Animals in a Biopolitical Frame*. Chicago: University of Chicago Press.

World Commission on Environment and Development, 1987. *Our Common Future*. Oxford: Oxford University Press.

9   Energy

In the earliest discussions of the concept, the Anthropocene was assumed to start in the eighteenth century (Crutzen 2002, Crutzen and Stoermer 2000, pp. 17–8, Steffen *et al.* 2011). This proposal was based on the well-known linkage between the use of fossil fuels and global climate change, but it had the additional advantage of lining up with familiar categories of socio-historical periodization. The transition to coal as primary energy carrier would thus mark *both* the beginning of modern industrial society *and* a turning point in the Earth's history. Although the lack of a clear stratigraphic marker associated with this date ultimately led the Anthropocene Working Group to reject the proposal, it remains eminently plausible: after all, the geological agency of humankind is directly linked to its ability to mobilize energy. In the scientific understanding, 'energy' is nothing other than the ability to perform 'work', i.e. to change the physical state of a body, for example by heating or accelerating it. If the Anthropocene is the geological epoch in which human activities begin to transform the Earth system in its entirety, then this must be linked to an increase in society's use of energy. Indeed, all the various proposals for a starting date of the Anthropocene (see Ch. 2: Definitions) correlate with shifts in the energetic base of society. The Early Anthropocene hypothesis argues that the transition to agriculture led to an increase in carbon dioxide and methane in the atmosphere, and the Great Acceleration after the Second World War coincides with the spread of an infrastructure based on oil and electricity. Even the Columbian Exchange constitutes an important watershed in energy history, because the spread of new crops such as maize and potatoes made agricultural production in the Old World much more energy efficient. Slave labor and the import of food from the New World allowed the European colonial powers to free up local land and labor, creating the necessary conditions for the Industrial Revolution (Pomeranz 2000, p. 264).

Joining cultural and social history to the history of human energy use is thus one of the central tasks for the humanities in the Anthropocene. Any such attempt must start with the insight that the human body, like that of any other living organism, can be considered as an 'energy converter' (Cottrell [1955] 2009, p. 35). This is a basic premise of modern biology: all living organisms absorb energy from their environment in order to build up and maintain their own physiological structure, and they release this energy in the form of waste or excrement. This process is called metabolism, and the various strategies which biological species pursue in order to keep their metabolism going define their relative position in the cycles of matter and energy that constitute the biosphere: plants use energy from solar radiation in order to convert water and carbon dioxide into sugars and other chemical compounds; the biomass resulting from this process is consumed by herbivores, which convert it into animal tissue, heat, and mechanical energy; their tissue in turn serves as food for carnivores. Ecology assigns all species to a particular level in this 'trophic pyramid'. According to the second law of thermodynamics, usable energy is lost at every step away from the base of this pyramid: the chemical conversion of plant tissues into animal protein consumes energy, and carnivores require copious amounts of energy not only in order to hunt, but also in order to masticate and digest. In both instances, energy is dissipated into the ambient surroundings as heat. Entropy is thus the reason why the number of predators in an ecosystem is always comparatively small. Energetically speaking, their way of life is less efficient.

From this perspective, what distinguishes humans from other animals is above all their unusual degree of flexibility with regard to the strategies for drawing energy from their environment. As an omnivore, *homo sapiens* lacks a clearly defined position in the trophic pyramid, but is able to shift between ecological levels depending on the circumstances, i.e. he can rely more on a herbivorous or a carnivorous diet. For that reason alone, ecological carrying capacity cannot be a fixed quantity with regard to human beings (see Ch. 8: Biopolitics). Even more importantly, however, humans supplement the energetic needs of their organic body with external sources of energy other than food (Nicolai Georgescu-Roegen refers to these forms or energy as 'exosomatic', Georgescu-Roegen 1971, p. 308). An especially relevant example of this is cooking with fire: cooking makes food more easily digestible. This means that the individual organism must expend less energy in order to metabolize it—making more energy available for other purposes, such as the maintenance of an unusually large brain. This gain in efficiency provided an important evolutionary advantage to our ancestors and had far-reaching consequences for the development of human physiology (Wrangham 2009). Such exosomatic forms of energy must be organized collectively. Even the use of fire requires a considerable amount of social cooperation: food is no longer consumed where it is caught or gathered, but must be transported to a communally used fire pit, and it must be prepared and divided among the members of the group. Tools used for hunting and gathering or for cultivating the soil must be produced and repaired, the necessary knowledge passed on from one generation to the next. Different forms of exosomatic energy require different divisions of labor. In this manner, they directly influence social structure.

The idea that the development of energy sources could thus provide an ordering principle for a theory of human history is almost as old as the concept of energy itself. As a shared measure for such different phenomena as heat, light, nutritional value, and movement, the neologism 'energy' established itself only around the middle of the nineteenth century (Harman 1982, p. 58). It became possible to think of energy as a 'common currency' for all phenomena of the physical universe—which could therefore also serve as a conceptual bridge between social theory and the natural sciences (Smil 2017a, p. 1). In his programmatic treatise *First Principles* (1862), Herbert Spencer proposed the increase of available energy as a unifying principle of biological and social evolution. In nature, more available energy leads to the development of increasingly complex organisms. In society, it leads to the internal differentiation of the 'social organism': a surplus of energy unburdens certain groups of people from physical labor and allows for increasingly complex forms of social organization (Spencer 1862, pp. 159–62).

Spencer's ideas developed under the aegis of the Industrial Revolution and Great Britain's newly acquired geopolitical primacy. For him, cultural history was synonymous with the history of progress, and progress was another name for the ascendancy of the Western industrialized nations. Over the next 100 years, most of the attempts to base a theory of culture on the concept of energy were characterized by such a triumphalist tendency. The opening up of new sources of energy was understood as a testimony of human (and more particularly: European) ingenuity, and the increase in the use of energy as an unambiguous marker of civilizational progress. From today's perspective, it is remarkable that the transition to fossil energies was not recognized as a historical rupture. It was well understood that energy from coal and oil was central to the transformation of modern society, and it was equally well known that these resources were finite. But it was also assumed as a matter of course that the use of fossil fuels was no more than a transitional phase. Thus the German chemist and philosopher Wilhelm Ostwald believed that future societies would rely on a 'photoelectric apparatus' to cover their energy needs (Ostwald 1909, p. 96), and the American anthropologist Leslie White anticipated the development of 'sub-atomic energy' well before the dwindling of coal and oil reserves would lead to an energy crisis (White 1943, p. 351).

In the social sciences, the notion that cultural differences could be explained on biological grounds fell increasingly into disrepute after the Second World War. As a consequence, theories which used the concept of energy to explain social development were also marginalized—at the very same historical moment when the Great Acceleration was picking up steam and fossil energies were beginning to transform the Earth system on an unprecedented scale. It thus fell to ecologists and economists to point out that modern industrial society was heading into a *cul-de-sac*. In his paper 'The Economics of the Coming Spaceship Earth' (1966), the economist Kenneth E. Boulding explained that the Earth had to be conceived as a materially closed system. This insight required a radical break with age-old habits of thought: during its entire history, humanity had lived in a 'cowboy economy', in which the consequences of ecological profligacy could be avoided by relocating to new territories. In the dawning 'spaceman economy', this would no longer be possible. Like an astronaut, humanity must now learn to keep house with the finite stocks of 'spaceship Earth' and find a place for itself within closed ecological cycles that put an absolute limit on production and consumption (Boulding 1966).

Theorists from Herbert Spencer onwards had considered the increase in energy efficiency as a hallmark of cultural progress: 'culture evolves as the productivity of human labour increases' (White 1943, p. 346). The same amount of labor produces a larger amount of material goods, and this is how society prospers. Boulding and his colleagues demonstrated that this view tends to overlook that increases in productivity often result from an increased reliance on finite resources. An especially pertinent example is industrialized agriculture: since the 1930s, the yields of American corn farmers have increased eightfold (Nielsen 2017). To a considerable extent, this staggering growth in productivity is owed to the use of artificial nitrogen fertilizer which is manufactured from natural gas, using copious amounts of electricity. Howard P. Odum, one of the pioneers of systems ecology (see Ch. 4: Nature and culture), therefore called the notion that modern farming techniques had increased ecological carrying capacity a 'sad hoax': 'industrial man no longer eats potatoes made from solar energy; now he eats potatoes partly made from oil' (Odum 1971, p. 116). Similar arguments can be made for many forms of industrial production, whose higher levels of productivity are based on the use of fossil fuels. Over the long run, traditional forms of production may in many cases turn out to be more energy efficient. These arguments led Boulding, Odum, and other scholars in the field of ecological economics to a radical conclusion. Because the planet's budget of renewable sources of energy was limited, the transformation of society that had set in with the Industrial Revolution could not be perpetuated. It was made possible only by the use of fossil fuels which cannot easily be substituted by other sources of energy, and whose long-term consequences outweigh the short-term benefits. Economists must therefore let go of the idea of economic growth. The only way to avoid an economic and ecological collapse is a gradual reduction in economic output and ultimately the transition to a growthless 'steady-state economy' (Daly [1973] 1993).

At the core of such arguments was the message that the wealthy industrial nations would have to tighten their belts, and the messengers had very little patience with their contemporaries who refused to heed this call. In a 1973 essay on the concept of the steady-state economy, Herman Daly called for a new 'moral consensus' and asked: 'Where is this moral consensus to come from? Not from the spineless relativism or from the hallucinatory psychic epiphenomena that seem to haunt complex mechanisms'. Daly hoped to counter the frivolity of consumer capitalism with the inviolable law of entropy and a 'dogmatic belief' in the absolute value of nature (Daly [1973] 1993, p. 357). But it became clear rather quickly that the second law of thermodynamics does not win political debates. If one wishes to understand the forces that pull modern society ever farther away from a steady-state economy, one needs to take seriously those 'psychic epiphenomena' which Daly dismissed out of hand. To put it differently: one must understand how fossil fuels have profoundly and comprehensively shaped the culture of modernity. This means that one must understand how the fossil-energy phase of modernity differs from all previous historical epochs.

To begin with, this requires an account which explains the dynamics of social development with reference to their energetic base. In the humanities, it is commonly cultural differences that are emphasized. From this perspective, however, structural parallels between different cultures are of particular interest. For example, the ancient civilizations of the Near East, China, and Mesoamerica all developed sophisticated calendrical systems, systems of taxation, forms of monarchic rule and bound labor, as well as monumental architecture (Sieferle 2010, p. 9). These similarities cannot be explained by cultural contact, but indicate developmental trajectories that are intrinsic to a way of life based on agriculture. The sources of energy and the energy converters used by society influence settlement patterns and population dynamics, political organization, and the organization of knowledge (Krausmann et al. 2008, p. 639). Based on this premise, it is possible to distinguish three great phases of human history which, following the Vienna School of Social Ecology, can be referred to as *sociometabolic regimes*: (1) a hunter and gatherer regime which is based on the *passive* utilization of solar energy, (2) the agrarian regime which harnesses solar energy *actively*, and (3) the fossil energy regime.

Hunter-gatherers fulfill their energy needs by tapping into the biomass production of their environment, but they have few means of controlling energy flows and storing surpluses. The low energy density of the resources on which they rely (i.e. wild animals and natural vegetation) usually forces them to adopt a nomadic lifestyle. This places a limit on the size of social groups. Breast-feeding lowers the birth rate, which is preferable because infants must be carried. There is little room for technological innovation, because tools and storage media also need to be transported. No nomad would ever get the crazy idea of inscribing laws on bulky clay tablets. The primary energy converters used by hunter-gatherers are fire and the tools used for procuring and preparing food. The 'metabolic rate' (or 'domestic energy consumption', DEC, Fig. 9.1) of such nomadic groups is comparatively low: according to an estimate by Marina Fischer-Kowalski et al., the annual per capita use of energy in a typical hunter-gatherer society is 11 Gigajoules, of which 4 Gigajoules are food and 7 Gigajoules firewood (Fischer-Kowalski et al. 2014, p. 22).

This energy regime dominated the life of our species from its emergence in the Pleistocene into the early Holocene. The transition to the agrarian

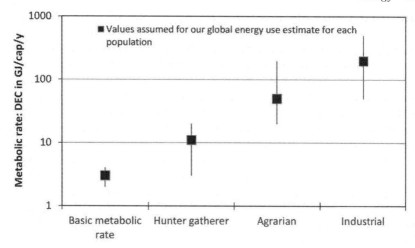

Figure 9.1 Metabolic rates of different energy regimes, from: Fischer-Kowalski, M., Krausmann, F., and Palua, I., 2014. A Sociometabolic Reading of the Anthropocene: Modes of Subsistence, Population Size and Human Impact on Earth. *The Anthropocene Review*, 1(1), 20.

regime occurred over a comparatively short period of a few thousand years. Because it took place more or less simultaneously in several, geographically distant regions, it is often interpreted as an adaptation to changing climatic conditions. Although this 'Neolithic Revolution' is still the subject of controversial debates, a common pattern can be discerned among the many different cultures which it brought forth: agrarian societies are based on the 'controlled use of solar energy flows [...], where people employ primarily biological converters (plants, animals) that are genetically modified for this purpose and whose habitats are actively transformed' (Sieferle 2010, p. 5, trans. HB). Compared to the hunter-gatherer regime, the agrarian regime fosters fast demographic growth and higher population densities. The shift to a more vegetarian diet implies that human beings also shift their trophic level, increasing the carrying capacity of their ecological environment. They become 'less wolflike, and more piglike' (Stiner and Feeley-Harnick 2011, p. 83). Fire continues to play a key role, but the development of ceramic vessels lends a new quality to it, because they allow not only for the storage of surplus food, but also the preparation of soups and mushes which can be fed to infants. They shorten the period of breast-feeding, allowing for a higher birth rate. This now becomes an advantage, because agriculture requires a much larger amount of physical human labor. For the same reason, many agrarian societies seek to control and maximize human reproduction, as can be seen in their predominantly pronatalist, patriarchal belief systems (Morris 2015, p. 85).

In accordance with the maxim of complexity theory that 'more is different' (see Ch. 10: Scales I), larger populations also brought a qualitative leap in social organization. The greater availability of human labor power made it possible to build up an infrastructure requiring ever larger amounts of material, such as roads, bridges, mines, irrigation systems, and fortifications. It also fostered the development of new mechanical energy converters, for example water- and windmills or sailing ships. Administering this infrastructure required expertise, leading to the formation of groups specialized in certain tasks (e.g. artisans, priests, judges, or soldiers). Combined with the fact that conflicts could no longer simply be resolved by walking away, this produced new forms of social inequality. Most agrarian civilizations developed political power centers which sustained themselves through the leveling of taxes. And this is not the only reason why, from the perspective of ordinary people, the transition to agriculture would have appeared to be a decidedly mixed blessing. There is plenty of archaeological evidence indicating that the inhabitants of early agrarian settlements worked harder, ate a less healthy diet, and suffered from a greater number of diseases than their hunter-gatherer brethren (Sieferle 1997, p. 73). James C. Scott suspects that during the initial phase of the agrarian regime, most of the people who took up farming had to be coerced into doing so, and that they therefore experienced the periodic collapse of the early states not as catastrophe, but as liberation (Scott 2017).

Agrarian energy systems vary considerably with regard to the extent to which they use animals as a source of labor and nutrition. The energy efficiency of crops and methods of cultivation is another factor differentiating such systems. Fischer-Kowalski *et al.* estimate that the annual per capita use of energy in agrarian societies lies between 20 and 80 Gigajoules (Fischer-Kowalski *et al.* 2014, p. 23). As much as they differ from one another, there is one thing they all have in common: they must operate within the narrow energetic constraints imposed by primary biomass production in the territory they inhabit. Economic growth is inseparable from growth in population and arable land, because most of the energy society uses comes from biomass, in the form of food and firewood. While over the course of millennia, technological innovation and intensification made it possible to produce more food per acre, in the end agriculture always remained bound by the law of diminishing returns: after a certain point, higher investments of labor no longer generate a commensurate increase in yields. The productivity of the land increases, but the productivity of human labor drops (Tainter 1988, pp. 91–8). Furthermore, increases of agricultural productivity tend to be offset by subsequent population growth, decreasing the amount of available energy per capita. Under such conditions, wealth accumulation is a zero-sum game in which the only way to increase one's own share is to subjugate and expropriate others. During the roughly ten millennia of the agrarian regime, living conditions for the vast majority of the people who were engaged in farming changed very little.

Only against this background can one get a sense just how profound a historical break was the transition to fossil fuels. Peter Sloterdijk has described the advent of fossil energy as a 'reprogramming of existential moods' based on an experience of 'de-scarcification' (Sloterdijk [2005] 2013, p. 227), essentially reiterating Emmanuel Le Roy Ladurie's point when the latter argued that Thomas Malthus formulated his 'principle of population' at the very moment when it had become obsolete (Le Roy Ladurie [1966] 1976, p. 311). With the use of coal, society escaped the limitations of the agrarian energy regime and broke the 'Malthusian curse' (see Ch. 8: Biopolitics). Already in the 1820s, energy from coal in Britain was equivalent to the biomass production of the entire island (Sieferle 2001, pp. 103–4). The steam engine was a new kind of energy converter which made it possible to transform thermal into mechanical energy (i.e. heat into motion). By revolutionizing industrial production and transport, such heat engines changed the way in which society could dispose of space and time. Cotton mills, for example, were no longer tied to water power and could be moved into the cities (Malm 2016); steamships and railways were able to deliver bulk goods on time even over great distances. Human labor was diverted from physical to mental activities, increasing the volume of communication. For more and more people, speaking, writing, reading, and calculating became a primary occupation (Weisz 2011, p. 332). All of this enabled radically new forms of social and spatial mobility. Much of what we mean when we describe modernity as a time of emancipation is a consequence of this transformation—in Dipesh Chakrabarty's pithy formula: 'The mansion of modern freedoms stands on an ever-expanding base of fossil-fuel use' (Chakrabarty 2009, p. 208).

In agrarian societies, landownership had been the most important basis of wealth and power. The fossil energy regime loosened the tie between land and political power, and it precipitated a phase of rapid urbanization which also led to the emergence of modern mass politics. While the new affluence was unevenly distributed, it nevertheless made plausible the idea of progress as a rising tide that would lift all boats. Economic growth came to be seen as a normal condition, and as remedy for every social ill. The geography of a coal-based infrastructure concentrated energy flows in a handful of strategic sites where large amounts of physical human labor were needed, such as coal mines, railroad stations and transshipment points. This allowed laborers to organize themselves and effectively enforce political demands (Mitchell 2011, pp. 26–7). A glance at Friedrich Engels's *The Condition of the Working Class in England* ([1845] 2005) suffices to see that the social and ecological consequences of this phase of industrialization were often devastating. However, they were also locally circumscribed and impossible to ignore, and therefore provoked reform movements which were able to substantially improve the lives of workers. The social safety net which most industrial nations put into place between the end of the nineteenth and the middle of the twentieth centuries are largely a product of this process.

Beginning in the early twentieth century, the fossil energy regime enters into a new phase whose most conspicuous feature is the ascendancy of oil. Stephanie LeMenager therefore refers to this configuration as 'petromodernity'

(LeMenager 2012, p. 60). Because oil has a higher energy density than coal and comes in liquid form, extraction and transport are much more energy efficient and require less human labor. Oil thus intensifies many of the effects that were already evident during the earlier phase of the fossil fuel regime. The combustion engine in particular allows for an unprecedented degree of individual mobility and engenders a new psychological habitus: 'We can no longer imagine a freedom that does not automatically include the freedom to risky accelerations, the freedom to move to the remotest of destinations, the freedom to exaggerate and to be extravagant, indeed the freedom to explode and self-destruct' (Sloterdijk 2010, n.p.). The feeling of individual empowerment that comes from driving a car is not just a figment of ideology: a simple step on the accelerator unleashes many times the kinetic energy available to a horseman, for example. The myth of freedom which surrounds the automobile in the twentieth century, culminating in the quintessentially American genre of the road movie, is inseparable from this fundamental somatic experience. The famous closing scene of Ridley Scott's *Thelma & Louise* (1991) powerfully illustrates the mythical image of the car as a machine for total emancipation from social constraints, even to the point of self-annihilation (Fig. 9.2).

Oil is not only a source of energy, however. It is also the raw material for a cornucopia of petrochemical products which shape the lifeworld of consumer capitalism in all of its dimensions, from nylon stockings to plastic packaging, chemical dyes, pharmaceuticals, lubricants, and cleaning agents. Only during this second phase did fossil energy also radically transform what remained of the preceding energy regime. Not only the Haber-Bosch process for fixing atmospheric nitrogen (patented in 1911), but also new pesticides and mechanization (e.g. through combines and tractors) enabled an increase in agricultural yields far beyond anything that was possible under the conditions of the agrarian regime. Thus coal and oil also precipitated the

Figure 9.2 Still from *Thelma & Louise*, 1991. Film. Directed by Ridley Scott. USA: Metro-Goldwyn-Mayer 1991, 129'. 1:43:35.

dramatic acceleration of population growth during the second half of the twentieth century.

But the second phase of the fossil energy regime is not only characterized by the increasing use of oil. It has just as much to do with a new energy converter: the dynamo made it possible to convert kinetic energy into electric current. Coal was not replaced as an energy source, but electrification increasingly *displaced* it from people's everyday lives. Economic historians view electricity and the combustion engine as the central drivers of a 'second industrial revolution' (Kander *et al.* 2013, p. 251). They allowed for the spatial disaggregation of residential and industrial areas. The smoke and soot which had polluted cities in the nineteenth century gradually disappeared. Electricity brought forth entirely new forms of entertainment, such as motion pictures and amusement parks, and transformed people's everyday lives (Nye 1990). During the first phase of the fossil energy regime, industrial production had been the primary source of pollution. Now, consumption catches up, even as the ecological costs of this development are geographically dispersed in such a way that they are easy to ignore, at least for the more affluent parts of the population—a process which Alf Hornborg describes as 'environmental load displacement' (Hornborg 2013, pp. 49–54).

Electricity and hydrocarbon energy bring forth an infrastructure that is tailored to smaller, more flexible social units, allowing for the privatization of public goods and inaugurating a new phase in the enclosure of the commons (see Ch. 6: Politics). Collectively used forms of transportation such as streetcars are replaced by the car, the city spills into the surrounding countryside. The dream of individual autonomy, nourished by the automobile, takes material shape in single-family homes which are equipped with electric machines (e.g. lawn mowers, washing machines, food processors, etc.) to the point where they resemble a factory floor. Matthew Huber has argued that the 'entrepreneurial subject' of neoliberalism is essentially a psycho-social reflex of this infrastructure (Huber 2013, p. 20). But the emphasis on individual autonomy which is such a characteristic feature of the fossil energy regime obscures the fact that these social changes also entail a process which Rolf-Peter Sieferle has described as 'de-autarkisation' (Sieferle 1997, p. 195). Under the auspices of fossil energy, individual households become more and more dependent on complex networks of distribution such as electric grids, petrol stations and supermarkets. Local means of subsistence (such as garden plots or wood stoves) are replaced by mobile, geographically dispersed flows of energy, material, and information. Most households nowadays own few tools which would be of use in the absence of electricity. It is therefore quite misleading to view the fossil energy regime primarily under the aspect of its emancipatory effects (as e.g. Ian Morris does, Morris 2015, pp. 162–3). The paradoxical combination of empowerment and impotence which characterizes the Anthropocene can be seen as reflecting a fundamental paradox of the fossil energy regime. On the one hand, modernity defines itself in terms of individual liberty and self-determination. On the other hand, it enmeshes people in an increasingly dense and inscrutable web of dependencies (Sieferle 1997, p. 201).

The proliferation of new technologies of energy conversion over the past 200 years makes it very difficult to determine the metabolic profile of society under the fossil energy regime. Fischer-Kowalski *et al.* have calculated that energy use in most industrialized countries today is roughly ten times higher than in agrarian societies (Fischer-Kowalski *et al.* 2014, p. 24). It is a socio-metabolic regime that cannot produce stable patterns—if only for the simple reason that its energetic base is finite. However, it has unleashed a dynamics which dissolves the social and ecological patterns of the Holocene at a furious pace. Today, we understand this process has catapulted us into the Anthropocene, yet an endpoint is not in sight. We can only speculate what Anthropocene society will look like. However, it is clear that it will have to rest on a different energetic base. Fossil fuels will be phased out. How long this will take is a different question. There are good reasons to believe that it will be a matter of several generations (Smil 2017b, pp. 176–7). World society has come to depend on fossil fuels in a way that makes them exceedingly difficult to replace, and the massive infrastructure that has been built up to produce and distribute fossil energy cannot easily be written off (Smil 2017b, pp. 199–203). Even more difficult to assess, but at least as important as the technical and economic impediments are those which are cultural and political. The conception of freedom that co-evolved with the fossil energy regime is today one of the greatest obstacles in overcoming it. If the task for engineers is to de-couple economic prosperity from fossil energy, humanities scholars face an analogous challenge: we need to decouple 'our notions of liberty from a life-style centred on the liberal dissipation of energy' (Bergthaller 2017, p. 430).

HB

References

Bergthaller, H., 2017. Fossil Freedoms: The Politics of Emancipation and the End of Oil. In: U.K. Heise, J. Christensen, and M. Niemann, eds. *The Routledge Companion to the Environmental Humanities*. London: Routledge, 408–416.

Boulding, K.E., 1966. The Economics of the Coming Spaceship Earth. In: K.E. Boulding and H. Jarrett, eds. *Environmental Quality in a Growing Economy*. Baltimore: Johns Hopkins University Press, 3–14.

Chakrabarty, D., 2009. The Climate of History: Four Theses. *Critical Inquiry*, 35(2), 197–222.

Cottrell, W.F., [1955] 2009. *Energy and Society*. Bloomington: AuthorHouse.

Crutzen, P.J., 2002. The Geology of Mankind. *Nature*, 415(6867), 23.

Crutzen, P.J., and Stoermer, E.F., 2000. The 'Anthropocene'. *Global Change Newsletter* [online], IGBP 41, May 2000, 17–18. Available from: www.igbp.net/publications/globalchangemagazine/globalchangemagazine/globalchangenewslettersno4159.5.5831d9ad13275d51c098000309.html [Accessed 14 February 2019].

Daly, H.E., [1973] 1993. The Steady-State Economy: Toward a Political Economy of Biophysical Equilibrium and Moral Growth. In: H.E. Daly and K.E. Boulding, eds. *Valuing the Earth: Economics, Ecology, Ethics.* Cambridge: MIT Press, 325–366.

Engels, F., [1845] 2005. *The Condition of the Working Class in England.* London: Penguin.

Fischer-Kowalski, M., *et al.*, 2014. A Sociometabolic Reading of the Anthropocene: Modes of Subsistence, Population Size and Human Impact on Earth. *The Anthropocene Review*, 1(1), 8–33.

Georgescu-Roegen, N., 1971. *The Entropy Law and the Economic Process.* Cambridge: Harvard University Press.

Haberl, H., *et al.*, eds., 2016. *Social Ecology: Society-Nature Relations across Time and Space.* Berlin: Springer.

Harman, P.M., 1982. *Energy, Force and Matter. The Conceptual Development of Nineteenth-Century Physics.* Cambridge: Cambridge University Press.

Hornborg, A., 2013. *Global Ecology and Unequal Exchange. Fetishism in a Zero-sum World.* London: Routledge.

Huber, M.T., 2013. *Lifeblood. Oil, Freedom, and the Forces of Capital.* Minneapolis: Minnesota University Press.

Kander, A., *et al.*, 2013. *Power to the People. Energy in Europe over the Last Five Centuries.* Princeton: Princeton University Press.

Krausmann, F., *et al.*, 2008. The Global Sociometabolic Transition: Past and Present Metabolic Profiles and Their Future Trajectories. *Journal of Industrial Ecology*, 12(5–6), 637–656.

LeMenager, S., 2012. The Aesthetics of Petroleum, after Oil! *American Literary History*, 24(1), 59–86.

Le Roy Ladurie, E., [1966] 1976. *The Peasants of Languedoc.* Trans. J. Day. Champaign, IL: University of Illinois Press.

Malm, A., 2016. *Fossil Capital: The Rise of Steam Power and the Roots of Global Warming.* London: Verso.

Mitchell, T., 2011. *Carbon Democracy.* London: Verso.

Morris, I., 2015. *Foragers, Farmers, and Fossil Fuels. How Human Values Evolve.* Princeton: Princeton University Press.

Nielsen, R.L., 2017. *Historical Corn Grain Yields for the US* [online]. Available from: www.agry.purdue.edu/ext/corn/news/timeless/yieldtrends.html [Accessed 14 February 2019].

Nye, D., 1990. *Electrifying America. Social Meanings of a New Technology.* Cambridge: MIT Press.

Odum, H.P., 1971. *Environment, Power, and Society.* New York: Wiley & Sons.

Ostwald, W., 1909. *Energetische Grundlagen der Kulturwissenschaft.* Leipzig: Werner Klinkhardt.

Pomeranz, K., 2000. *The Great Divergence. China, Europe, and the Making of the Modern World Economy.* Princeton: Princeton University Press.

Scott, J.C., 2017. *Against the Grain. A Deep History of the Earliest States.* New Haven: Yale University Press.

Sieferle, R.-P., [1982] 2001. *The Subterranean Forest.* Trans. Michael Osmann. Cambridge: White Horse Press.

Sieferle, R.-P., 1997. *Rückblick auf die Natur. Eine Geschichte des Menschen und seiner Umwelt.* München: Luchterhand.

Sieferle, R.-P., 2010. *Lehren aus der Vergangenheit* [online]. Berlin: Wissenschaftlicher Beirat der Bundesregierung 'Globale Umweltveränderungen'. Available from: www.wbgu.de/fileadmin/user_upload/wbgu.de/templates/dateien/veroeffentlichungen/hauptgutachten/jg2011/wbgu_jg2011_Expertise_Sieferle.pdf [Accessed 14 February 2019].

Sloterdijk, P., [2005] 2013. *In the World Interior of Capital: Towards a Philosophical Theory of Globalization.* London: Polity.

Sloterdijk, P., 2010. How Big is 'Big'? *Collegium International* [online], February 2010. Available from: www.collegium-international.org/index.php/en/contributions/127-how-big-is-big [Accessed 14 April 2019].

Smil, V., 2017a. *Energy and Civilization. A History.* Cambridge: MIT Press.

Smil, V., 2017b. *Energy Transitions. Global and National Perspectives.* 2nd ed. Santa Barbara: Praeger.

Spencer, H., 1862. *First Principles.* London: William and Norgate.

Steffen, W., *et al.*, 2011. The Anthropocene: Conceptual and Historical Perspectives. *Philosophical Transactions of the Royal Society A*, 369(1938), 842–867.

Stiner, M.C., and Feeley-Harnick, G., 2011. Energy and Ecosystems. In: A. Shyrock and D. Lord Smail, eds. *Deep History. The Architecture of Past and Present.* Berkeley: University of California Press, 78–102.

Tainter, J.A., 1988. *The Collapse of Complex Societies.* Cambridge: Cambridge University Press.

Weisz, H., 2011. The probability of the improbable: Society-nature coevolution. *Geografiska Annaler: Series B, Human Geography*, 93(4), 325–336.

White, L., 1943. Energy and the Evolution of Culture. *The American Anthropologist*, 45(3), 335–356.

Wrangham, R., 2009. *Catching Fire. How Cooking Made Us Human.* New York: Basic Books.

10 Scales I

The planetary

A problem we have encountered in all the preceding chapters is that of scale. Whether we are talking about conceptions of the human, of aesthetics, of politics or of energy regimes, a similar question arises: On what quantitative, spatial, and temporal scale should these issues be addressed? To speak of humans as a geophysical force implies a passage between incompatible scales—from individual actions to collective or cumulative behavior, and from collective behavior to a kind of agency that is effective on a global level. Such a transition is called a 'scale effect'. Timothy Clark has argued that such effects are constitutive of the Anthropocene:

> The Anthropocene is itself an emergent 'scale effect'. At a certain indeterminate threshold, numerous human actions, insignificant in themselves (heating a house, clearing trees, flying between the continents, forest management) come together to form a new, imponderable physical event, altering the basic ecological cycles of the planet.
>
> (2015, p. 75)

To understand the Anthropocene, we must understand how many of its most daunting challenges result from a clash of scales. These include the problem of the adequate representation of the Anthropocene (see Ch. 7: Aesthetics), of agency (see Ch. 5: The *anthropos*), and of responsibility (Ch. 6: Politics), or of assessing the risks and consequences of certain technologies. This clash of scales differentiates Anthropocene thought from the classical concept of sustainability, which mostly focused on local ecological problems within a very limited timeframe. Sustainability is about the protection of specific habitats or biomes for the benefit of coming generations (Horn 2017, Johns-Putra 2019). As Ursula Heise has pointed out, the ecological movement was mainly energized by a 'sense of place', which called for the preservation of particular locales, rather than by a 'sense of planet', involving a consciousness of ecological disruption on a planetary scale (Heise 2008, p. 21). Even in the oft-repeated ecological slogan 'think globally, act locally', the local turns out to be the place where the action is, whereas the global is shunted off to a purely theoretical level.

The global ecological diagnosis of the Anthropocene, however, requires that our perspective assume an entirely different scale: the planetary. It concerns not only particular ecosystems, but the entire Earth system (Hamilton 2015). It does not refer to human timescales of a few generations, but to geological scales of tens or hundreds of thousands of years. Lastly, it is not just about individuals and communities, but about a threat to all humans on the globe (see Ch. 1: Introduction). What is needed is thus a novel understanding of scale effects: 'Writing the causes of the Anthropocene means asking *how human agency stretches across the spatial and temporal scales of Earth*' (Woods 2014, p. 133l, emphasis EH). Indeed, a range of prominent thinkers have proposed that issues of *scale* and *scale variance* are of paramount importance in coming to terms with the Anthropocene (Heise 2008, Chakrabarty 2012, 2014, 2018, Woods 2014, Clark 2012, 2015, Clarke and Wittenberg 2017). This raises questions not only about the *quantitative* scales of human agency, but also about the *spatial* scales on which we must conceive the Anthropocene; the *temporal* scales on which to think about the epochal rupture between the Holocene and the Anthropocene, and about the 'deep time' of the Earth's geological past and future (see Ch. 11: Scales II). And these questions entail other questions concerning, for example, the epistemic and aesthetic modes in which we may think and represent these massive temporal and spatial scales (see Ch. 7: Aesthetics).

While the next chapter will be dedicated to the temporal scales of 'deep time', this chapter is focused on spatial and quantitative scales, and on the questions they raise. What are the distinctive spatial properties of the Anthropocene? What is the relation between the micro- and macro-scale, between the local, the regional, and the planetary? Where would the proper place of humans be located in this space? How can particular instances of culturally and economically differentiated human behavior, located in specific ecological contexts, be brought into conjunction with an undifferentiated, global 'humankind' which affects planetary ecological parameters? And what role does scale play in the effort to regulate this planetary agency, to negotiate some kind of settlement that could rein it in?

Let's start with two examples. The first one is the famous carbon footprint. It is used to put an ecological 'price tag' on specific practices (such as traveling by plane), consumer goods (such as cars or cell phones), lifestyles, or national economies (such as the carbon footprint of China or the UK). In order to arrive at such a price tag, a particular amount of carbon dioxide is set in relation to the total amount of carbon emissions worldwide, and an estimate of the total costs incurred as a consequence. By itself, the carbon footprint of a particular action is quite meaningless. Only when it is multiplied by many millions (e.g. as the American way of life, or the ecological footprint of a smartphone, etc.) does this number become relevant. And in order to evaluate it properly, it must also be compared with the ecological price tag of alternative products, lifestyles, and economies. The very notion of the carbon footprint thus implies working across different scales of magnitude, as Clark points out: 'The phrase "carbon footprint" becomes a very peculiar catachresis, collapsing huge and tiny scales upon each other' (2015, p. 72). The use of a small scale—i.e. the carbon footprint of an individual product or practice—serves to make a much larger scale—i.e. the planetary impact of certain goods, practices or technologies—amenable to political negotiation or exchange, as in the case of emissions trading. To decide at which scale a given fact is represented also means to decide whether, and how, it can be addressed politically.

Our second example comes from Timothy Morton:

> Every time I start my car or steam engine I don't *mean to* harm Earth, *let alone cause* the Sixth Mass Extinction Event in the four-and-a-half billion-year history of life on this planet. [...] Furthermore, I'm not harming Earth! My key turning is statistically meaningless. [...] But go up a level and something very strange happens. When I scale up these actions to include billions of key turnings, [...] harm to Earth is precisely what is happening. I am *responsible* as a member of this *species* for the Anthropocene.
>
> (2016, p. 8, emphasis EH)

With a good deal of rhetorical hyperbole, Morton evokes huge scales of various kinds: the 4.5 billion years of life on the planet, the sixth mass extinction, the human species. The point of this passage, however, is to draw a direct line from the micro-scale of individual practices to the macro-scale of geo-history: 'go up a level', as he writes. Without further ado, Morton asserts a direct causal connection between them, which of course is grossly misleading. His example, however, indirectly hints at a real problem: the problem of accumulation. It is in the mode of massive accumulation that individual actions add up to a planetary problem. Morton's formulations rather obscure the problem, i.e. the translation between small and large scales. Yet it is precisely this difficulty which turns the relation between agency and responsibility in the Anthropocene into such an intractable problem: there is no straightforward causal link between the individual act and the ecological crisis, between the actor's intentions and the effects of her behavior. The actors *exert* geological force—but they do not *exercise* it as a power (see Ch. 5: The *anthropos*). Their relation can only be established via *a transition between scales* (in this case, by aggregating individual actions into a widely shared lifestyle). Only when it is multiplied by billions can the act of switching on a car's ignition become a cause of climate change or biodiversity loss. But understanding this causal force also requires us to reconstruct the interconnections of such practices at the local and the global scale, such as the link between the combustion engine, carbon dioxide emissions, the structures of suburban life, and the greenhouse effect.

Such scale transitions can be found everywhere in Anthropocene thought. As in the case of the carbon footprint, they can be put to very different uses.

On the one hand, they can be justified by the need to downscale a highly complex problem to a level at which it becomes amenable to economic quantification and political negotiation. On the other hand, by upscaling a problem from the individual to the planetary level, they can also be used to generate a sense of extreme (albeit factitious) moral urgency, effectively short-circuiting the different scales. Whatever one may think of their rhetorical uses, it is important to recognize that scale transitions are indeed a central epistemological challenge of the Anthropocene and must be understood and analyzed as such.

What are scales? Scales are not a given measure (such as a measure of length) but exist only in relation to one another, as variation of orders of magnitude (such as between centimeters, meters, and kilometers). Scales make themselves felt only when we pass from one to another, at the point of transition—i.e., as *scale variation* in the process of *upscaling* or *downscaling*. In this regard, Peter Haff offers a helpful conceptual tool. He assigns entities at various levels of scale to distinct 'strata'. Stratum II refers to entities on the same level, that is, having a similar size to the reference entity S; Stratum I means that entities are on a much smaller scale unit; and Stratum III means that they are on a much larger scale (Haff 2014, p. 130). If S is a human being, other humans, as well as objects accessible to humans (cars, houses, certain animals, tools), are on Stratum II. Elements that are much smaller than humans (such as atoms, cells, nanoparticles) are on Stratum I. All components that are much larger (such as a city, traffic, a continent, the planet) occupy Stratum III. While items on Stratum II are readily accessible to humans (that is, perceived, used, interacted with, etc.), the elements of Strata I and III need complicated processes of translation to become accessible at all.

Epistemologically speaking, scale variation becomes interesting at the very moment when size begins to matter, that is, when the *quantitative* upscaling leads to entirely new and different *qualities* of the object. In the case, for example, of the translation of an architectural model of 1:100 to the real building, the building will not just be a hundred times bigger than the model but have entirely new structural qualities or problems. In some forms of representation, such as maps, the difference between a large and a small scale can seem unproblematic—they just serve different purposes. While a large measure allows for an overview of a larger region, a small measure will serve to designate local detail and facilitate orientation in the given area. Mapping scales only become a problem if the wrong scale is used for a specific problem at hand, such as finding a street address with a map of the entire country. Such an incongruence of scale and function is what defines a scale effect. The architectural model is a classic case of a scale effect, as small models of buildings or machines have entirely different structural qualities than the object in real size. Already Galileo Galilei had demonstrated that, if the surface dimensions of an object increase by a factor of two (x^2), the object's mass increases cubically (x^3) (West 2017, pp. 35–42). In other words,

by upscaling an object in size the mass of this object increases dis-
proportionately, thus entirely changing its static properties. There are countless examples of such scale effects, which frequently demonstrate the limits of
upscaling and downscaling. A body of the height of Godzilla (ca. 100 meters)
would collapse under its own weight; a mammal smaller than the shrew mouse
would perish from the viscosity of the blood in its miniscule veins. Results
from medical tests using model organisms such as mice often prove not to be
transferrable to human bodies because of their much larger mass.

Biological organisms thus often have an 'optimal size' and are not amenable
to arbitrary up- and downscaling (Haldane 1926, Bonner 2006). Only animals
which are very small and lightweight, such as insects, can climb walls, carry a
multiple of their own body weight or jump remarkable distances in relation to
their size. The laws of optimal size, however, are less clear when it comes to
technical objects and social structures. The world population has been
increasing massively for the past 50 years, apparently without exceeding the
Earth's carrying capacity; many cities have multiplied in size tenfold or more
within the past decades without logistically collapsing (although more than a
few appear to be on the verge of just such a collapse); multinational corporations seem to be growing without encountering any limits in efficiency of the
sort known to exist in biological processes. In many of these cases, upscaling
entails more energy efficiency and more complexity without necessarily
resulting in dysfunctionality (West 2017, pp. 269–334).

Scale effects mark the limits of a seamless scaling (i.e. an upscaling without
changes in the qualities of an object or organism). They appear when the
process of upscaling or downscaling beyond a given threshold brings about
problems in functionality, structure, resilience or even vitality. This change
of qualities, which cannot be explained by the linear growth in quantity, is
called 'emergence'. Its principle was captured succinctly by the mathematician Phil Anderson in the formula: 'more is different' (Anderson 1972). The
Anthropocene is precisely this effect of a 'more' giving rise to something
entirely 'different', leading from a growing array of local ecological damages
to a global change in the Earth system. This is a problem to which we will
return.

How has ecology addressed scale problems in the past? For a long time,
scale problems were generally seen as problems of space. What is the right
scale for the observation of a given biotope? How much detail is needed, and
where does a macro-scale—such as global climate change—enter the picture
(Jenerette and Wu 2000)? It is not by chance that the emerging discipline of
systems biology started out by describing clearly bounded biotopes such as
lakes and islands (Warren *et al.* 2015), which served as models for bigger and
less clearly delimited ecological entities. The scale problems in transitioning
from smaller models to bigger areas are addressed at the exact moment when
it becomes clear that the functioning of a specific ecosystem cannot be
understood without taking into account the global factors impacting it. In

turn, global ecological processes started to be investigated for their local origins and effects:

> Global and regional changes in biological diversity, in the distribution of greenhouse gases and pollutants, and in climate all have origins in and consequences for fine-scale phenomena. The general circulation models that provide the basis for climate prediction operate on spatial and temporal scales [...] many orders of magnitude greater than the scales at which most ecological studies are carried out.
>
> (Levin 1992, p. 1945)

Changing the scale of observation, however, not only changes the categories of description and observation for the scientists. Scale is a dimension intrinsic to the interactions between the organisms of a biotope. Organisms have to be understood as attuned to a certain scale of observation and activity. An ecological description of a particular area therefore needs to take into account the different scales of perception and activity of the many organisms that inhabit this space.

If humans themselves are understood as ecological agents, it becomes apparent that both their (self-)perception and their agency have to be considered across a range of different scales. The question of agency is inseparable from the conception of space, from the 'world' in which people situate themselves. Chakrabarty has articulated this issue as precisely a problem of scaling: 'The current conjuncture of *globalization* and *global* warming leaves us with the challenge of *having to think of human agency over multiple and incommensurable scales at once*' (2012, p. 2, emphasis EH). These divergent scales correspond to equally incommensurable conceptions of the human (see Ch. 5: The *anthropos*). On the one hand, there is the human as *homo*, as a cultural and social being, differentiated in terms of gender, culture, race, or economic circumstance. On the other hand, the human appears as *anthropos*, as a biological species among others, but also as an abstract geophysical force. The distinction between *homo* and *anthropos* is also a distinction between scales. The human considered as *homo* is situated in Stratum II—on the scale of their natural body and perception. As *anthropos*, as a biological and geophysical force, the human is viewed from the macro-perspective of Stratum III (or, possibly, the micro-perspective of Stratum I, as when Haraway and Tsing propose that we think of the human as a largely microbial multi-species assemblage).

What is at stake in the Anthropocene is above all the *global* agency of the human as *anthropos*. The space in which the human being is situated now is no longer that of a local environment, but that of the *world as a whole*. Since the Early Modern period, this relationship to the world found its most potent expression in the spatial model of the globe. The globe was both the instrument and an emblem of the European expansionary project insofar as it translated planetary space into a manageable scale, thus putting the Earth as a whole at the disposal of those who would master it: 'The affair between occidental reason and the world-whole unfolded and exhausted itself in the sign of the "globe". Globalization began as the geometrization of the immeasurable' (Sloterdijk [1999] 2014, p. 45). As a representation of the world as a whole, the globe not only became the practical and symbolic foundation of an imperial world order. It also drew on an unacknowledged theological inheritance, according to which particular regions or places were understood to be merely subordinate aspects of the whole. Initially, the epistemic counterpart of this 'whole world' is God. Beginning in the Early Modern period, this position is gradually usurped by 'Man'. Well before it became technically possible to look at the Earth from space, the fantasy of such a gaze served as the epistemic foundation of the geographic globe (Cosgrove 1994). Tim Ingold has described this world picture as one where the subject is positioned as an external observer, with the world as his object of contemplation: 'With the world imaged as a globe, far from coming into being in and through a life process, it figures as an entity that is, as it were, presented to or confronted by life. The global environment is not a lifeworld, it is a world apart from life' (2000, p. 210).

This external perspective on the planet, from a distance which had to be produced through ever more elaborate technologies, found its fullest and most eloquent expression in the photographs of Earth from space first made public in the late 1960s. This technological gaze on the globe is itself based on a massive scale effect: it enacts a magnitude of distance which formerly was only accessible by way of cartographic construction. Particularly the 'Blue Marble' photograph, shot by the Apollo 17 mission on 7 December 1972, created a sensation (Cosgrove 1994, p. 274) (Fig. 10.1). In the midst of the Cold War, this photograph quickly became the emblem of a new planetary consciousness: it was taken to symbolize a common humanity that transcended political or economic differences. More particularly, it became the emblem of a global ecological movement which proposed a shared human responsibility for the entire planet and eventually motivated slogans such as 'think globally—act locally'.

The image was widely read as visual shorthand for the singularity and finitude of the planet. It seemed to illustrate the metaphor of the 'spaceship Earth' which Kenneth E. Boulding and R. Buckminster Fuller had popularized in the 1960s (Boulding 1966, Buckminster Fuller 1968) (see Ch. 9: Energy). As early as 1966, Stewart Brand had pushed the National Aeronautics and Space Administration (NASA) to release photographs of the Earth from space by handing out buttons with the slogan 'Why Haven't We Seen a Photograph of the Whole Earth Yet?' In 1968, he began publishing the *Whole Earth Catalog*, an intriguing blend of counter-cultural digest and mail order catalog which bore the eponymous image on its cover. With its effort to promote an understanding of 'whole systems', it became an intellectual focal point of the early environmental movement (Clarke 2011). Significantly, the 'Blue Marble' has now also become an omnipresent emblem

Figure 10.1 Blue Marble. Image of the earth photographed from Apollo 17 (7 December 1972). Credit: Earth Science and Remote Sensing Unit, NASA Johnson Space Center, AS17-148-22727.

of the Anthropocene. In this context, however, it serves not only to convey the totalizing gaze for which the concept of the Anthropocene is so frequently criticized (see Bonneuil and Fressoz 2016), but also the vulnerability of a wounded, torched, or otherwise damaged planet (Schneider 2018) (Fig. 10.2).

If the globe embodies the idea of an all-encompassing, totalizing, and external gaze on the Earth, it also suggests that such totalization can be achieved only by maximizing the scale of representation, i.e. in the manner of a world map. What is lost in this spatial model are the details, the dimensions of the regional and the local. The macroscopic gaze thus calls for the microscopic gaze as its necessary complement. For that reason, the vision of the global has always been haunted by the dream of a medium of representation which would allow for a smooth transition between all scales, from a maximal scale with low resolution to a minimal scale that can picture even the smallest details. This is the dream of a medium that permits scale variation *without* scale effects.

In 1977, five years after the famous 'Blue Marble', the designer couple Charles and Ray Eames published an instructional film which gave a particularly powerful expression to this dream (Eames and Eames 1977). *Powers of Ten* opens with the image of a couple having a picnic on the shore of Lake Michigan. The camera then zooms outward, marking each time the distance

Figure 10.2 Burning Earth globe west hemisphere (elements furnished by NASA) (Shutterstock/Boris Ryaposov).

has increased by a factor of ten, from 10 meters, to 100 meters, to 1,000 meters, etc., until Chicago appears as a mere speck, the Earth as a blue orb, the solar system as a bright dot. After this trip into interstellar space, the camera reverses direction, zooming back and inwards into the subatomic realm, down to a scale of 10^{-16} meters, until the screen is filled with static. All of this is presented in a manner that simulates a continuous zoom shot, without a single cut—and, more importantly, without scale effects (Woods 2014, 2017). In 2001, after countless digital remakes of *Powers of Ten* (Woods 2017, p. 73), the dream of a universally accessible representation of the globe which would allow for a smooth transition between scales was finally realized by the software application Google Earth (Heise 2008, p. 21). As an age of digital cartography, the Anthropocene is also the age of the global zoom, where the largest and the smallest features of the Earth can be taken in at one fell swoop.

Arguably, however, such a totalizing gaze and the very idea of universal scalability remain instantiations of a fundamentally *modern* conception of space, rather than being something genuinely new. After all, scaling is not merely a strategy for *representing* the world, but rather a fundamental mode of *producing* it. As Anna Tsing has pointed out, scalability—the possibility of enlarging or reducing the size of something without changing its basic structure or having to reckon with qualitative differences—was a conceptual premise of European expansion and growth from the Early Modern period. According to Tsing, the colonial plantation system must be understood as a product of *upscaling*, as it transferred forms of cultivation that had long been practiced in the Old World and expanded them into gigantic cash crop monocultures in the New World. The plantation provided the blueprint for modern systems of production such as factories that were geared towards continuous growth and expansion (see Ch. 6: Politics). The basis of such systems is the use of standardized, maximally fungible units—not only raw materials and products, but especially laborers: 'workers become interchangeable and self-contained elements of the factory [...]. The scalability of labour thus lies at the foundation of capitalism' (Tsing 2012, p. 513). Importantly, certain commodities and practices are not amenable to upscaling, demanding a theory of what Tsing calls *nonscalability*. This property of nonscalability can serve as a rallying point for the forces that seek to thwart the imperatives of expansion and global homogenization, and for practices that preserve and reproduce local diversity. The decisive question is then how such spaces or worlds would have to be designed in order to be able to resist scalability.

This also indicates how the scales inherent in different conceptions of the world are linked to the issue of human agency—or, more exactly, to the different conceptions of the human which underpin our understanding of such agency. If, following Tsing, we assume that the modern project of scalability was directed at human beings—and not only as workers, but just as significantly as consumers of commodities, services, energy flows, etc.—then it becomes clear that the geological agency of the human has to do with the possibility of multiplying and upscaling economic, technical and social modules. However, this process of upscaling, which helped to usher in the Anthropocene, does not primarily target the human being as an individual or as an organism, but rather as a structural element of systems of production and consumption. It targets, one might say, the human being as an element of the technosphere (see Ch. 5: The *anthropos*). In this vein, Derek Woods has proposed that the subject of the Anthropocene is not *homo sapiens* as a dominant species, but rather an assemblage of humans, technologies and non-human actors—an assemblage whose most important characteristic is precisely (just as Tsing argues) the capacity for unlimited expansion:

> The subject of the Anthropocene is not an individual or species-based 'intelligence' that, without mutation, projects across scales to shape the matter of the Earth. [...] Scale critique shows that the subject of the Anthropocene is not the human species but *modern terraforming assemblages*. [...] What is necessary to accommodate scale variance is a horizontal, assemblage theory of the relations among humans, nonhuman

species, and technics rather than a vertical, phylogenetic account that traces all causal chains back to the embodied intelligence of *homo sapiens*.

(Woods 2014, p. 138)

The agency of such a subject would be a *distributed* agency—its crucial quality being the much discussed paradoxical combination of enormous potency and increasing loss of human control. This form of agency would not be a property of the human—least of all of the human as a *species*—but rather an effect of the interplay between technologies, geophysical forces, and biological organisms, both human and non-human.

Much of Bruno Latour's work over the past few decades has been devoted to elaborating just such a concept of distributed agency. The crux of his argument is that distributed agency is not smoothly scalable and that a theory of distributed agency (or actor networks) should therefore be skeptical towards gestures of globalization and homogenization, instead foregrounding singularity and diversity: 'Far from trying to "reconcile" or "combine" nature and society, the task, the crucial political task, is on the contrary *to distribute agency as far and in as differentiated a way as possible*—until, that is, we have thoroughly lost any relation between those two concepts of object and subject that are no longer of any interest any more except in a patrimonial sense' (Latour 2014, p. 15, emphasis EH). To describe distributed and differentiated agency is to describe the specific qualities of such assemblages and configurations. What this does not permit, however, is the drawing of a straight line (as suggested by Morton) connecting, in the name of moral responsibility, the individual use of a car with global climate change. Rather, we need to attend to the particular patterns that assemble flows of energy and matter, commodities and people across various dimensions, so as to affect the ecological environment in ways we are still only beginning to grasp. And, following Tsing, we need to identify and characterize those forces within these networks which facilitate or resist the massive upscaling of ecologically destructive practices (such as automobility).

To this end, an alternative concept of spatiality is needed—a concept that, in contrast to the modern model of the globe, we designate as *the planetary*. Although the adjective 'planetary' is often used synonymously with 'global', there are nevertheless fundamental conceptual differences between the two terms (Auer 2013). In contrast to the global, the planetary does not aim at a totalizing gaze, but instead focuses on networks of interdependency and the technologies which produce them, particularly technologies of communication (Bergermann 2012). The planetary also implies a *comprehensive* conception of the Earth but, as the etymology of the term suggests (the Greek word πλανήτης refers to 'that which strays or wanders'), this conception is informed by principles of exchange, of connection, interaction, and synergy.

The planetary *also encompasses the observer*, enveloping rather than externalizing her. In precisely this sense, Tim Ingold has opposed the spatial model of the 'sphere' to that of the 'globe':

> Unlike the solid globe, which can only be perceived as such from without, *spheres* [...] *were to be perceived from within*. The global view, we might say, is centripetal, the spherical view centrifugal. [...] *The lifeworld, imaged from an experiential centre, is spherical in form*, whereas a world divorced from life, that is yet complete in itself, is imaged in the form of a globe.
>
> (2000, pp. 210–11, emphasis EH)

A spherical cosmology suggests that we are not *on* but *in* the world. Spherical space curves back on itself, enveloping and enclosing the human, and bringing every place and every spatial scale into contact with other places and scales—without, however, assimilating them to a single homogenous and scalable space. Conceived in planetary terms, the Earth is not purely 'natural'. Rather, it assumes recognizable contours only as it is disclosed by logistic systems and media of communication (see Ch. 4: Nature and culture). Already in the early stages of the Great Acceleration, one can find the dawning recognition of such a planetary dimension which undercuts customary distinctions between the natural and the artificial (see, for example, Teilhard de Chardin [1959] 1964).

It is this planetary space that Bruno Latour opposes to the global (Latour 2014, 2017). In a pointed reading of Lovelock's Gaia theory, he sketches this space as a self-regulating, self-stabilizing system of dynamic interdependencies and processes of exchange which, however, is not governed by a unifying principle or a central, controlling agency. Latour rejects as misguided any attempt to understand Gaia in teleological terms—as, for example, a 'superorganism' or a guiding intelligence—interpretations which Lovelock had himself invited by adopting the name 'Gaia'. In the traditional understanding of evolutionary biology, it was assumed that organisms change their *internal* structure in order to adapt to an *external* environment. With Lovelock, Latour points out that many species also 'bend' their environment to their own ends, making it 'more favourable' to them (2017, p. 99). The human capacity to transform the world is thus definitely not a unique feature of our species—and as with all other species, it is complemented by a capacity to be affected and transformed by the world. This 'general property of living things' (ibid.) manifests itself not only at a micro- or meso-level (i.e., in the interactions of organisms and ecosystems), but most importantly at the planetary level, where it brings about the improbable phenomenon of a self-stabilizing Earth system. Lovelock makes this very clear:

The nearest I can reach is to say that Gaia is an evolving system, a system made up from all living things and their surface environment, the oceans, the atmosphere, and crustal rocks, the two parts tightly coupled and indivisible. It is an 'emergent domain'—a system that has emerged from the reciprocal evolution of organisms and their environment over the eons of life on Earth. In this system, the self-regulation of climate and chemical composition are entirely automatic. Self-regulation emerges as the system evolves. No foresight, planning or teleology [...] are involved.

(Lovelock 2000 cited Latour 2017, p. 133)

When Lovelock designates Gaia as an 'emergent domain', he is describing a scale effect. Emergence refers to the appearance of new properties in a system that cannot be derived from the properties of the constituent parts, but which only come into being after a certain critical mass or density of elements has been reached. From this perspective, life itself is a scale effect, a qualitative leap out of mere quantitative accumulation, validating Anderson's maxim that 'more is different' (1972). When certain chemical elements combined into the self-replicating molecules which eventually evolved into DNA, they acquired new properties that are irreducible to their components and cannot be understood on the basis of mere addition ('more is more'). The capacity for self-regulation, which defines life at all scales, from the cellular to the planetary, is an emergent phenomenon. Emergence always depends on thresholds or synergies, i.e. it occurs only once a certain number of elements is reached and particular environmental factors converge.

The fact that emergent phenomena are irreducible to their elements not only implies that they are unpredictable (Horn 2009). It means, first of all, that they are not 'caused' by any single agent but arise from the *interrelations between several agencies*. Secondly, one can anticipate (but not determine in advance!) tipping points where quantitative change (e.g. an increase of atmospheric oxygen) will jolt the system into a qualitatively different state. The Great Oxygenation Event 2.45 billion years ago is an example of this (see Ch. 4: Nature and culture): the newly evolved cyanobacteria pumped massive amounts of oxygen into the atmosphere, which not only destroyed much of the existing microbial fauna, but also reacted with iron molecules in the oceans and with methane in the atmosphere. This created most of the iron ore deposits in the Earth's crust, but it also led to the Huronian glaciation event that covered almost the entire planet with ice. It took many millions of years before oxygen levels stabilized at their current levels, allowing for the evolution of complex, multicellular forms of life as we know them today.

To describe the Anthropocene as a scale effect is to emphasize its emergent properties. It is characterized by qualities that cannot be understood as long as one focuses on individual actors, specific localities or particular technologies. A *single* steam engine, airplane, plastic cup or person changes nothing. It is only in their massive accumulation and planetary coupling that these agents acquire a force that must be analyzed and explained in its own terms. A concept of 'world' which can take the proper measure of the planetary emergency that is the Anthropocene must account for these entanglements, these cumulative and emergent effects. Such a perspective makes paradoxical demands: on the one hand, it requires that we pay particular attention to the local as a singular site of assemblage, a site where processes of upscaling and accumulation (of capital, of consumption and mobility) originate, but also as a locus of resistance to such processes (in the form of environmental movements, of experiments with new lifestyles, etc.). The local has the potential to be both a rallying point for resistance against the homogenizing drive of globalization *and* a site where this drive comes fully into force (as in the air-conditioned metropolises that have flourished since the Great Acceleration, or the burning rainforests of Kalimantan; see Ch. 12: Conclusion, and Horn 2016). Either way, the local always needs to be viewed in conjunction with the planetary, in light of the interdependencies between localities, actors, technologies, and ecological processes. Planetary thinking must comprehend the particularity of the local along with the Earth system as a whole—not in order to reduce the former to a subordinate part of the latter, but in order to understand the emergent effects, the escalations and causal cascades that bind them all together.

EH

References

Anderson, P.W., 1972. More is different: Broken symmetry and the nature of the hierarchical structure of science. *Science: New Series*, 177(4047), 393–396.

Auer, M., 2013. *Wege zu einer planetarischen Linientreue? Meridiane zwischen Jünger, Schmitt, Heidegger und Celan*. Paderborn: Wilhelm Fink.

Bergermann, U., 2012. Das Planetarische. In: C. Bartz, ed. *Handbuch Mediologie: Signaturen des Medialen*. München: Fink, 215–220.

Bonner, J.T., 2006. *Why Size Matters. From Bacteria to Blue Whales*. Princeton: Princeton University Press.

Bonneuil, C., and Fressoz, J.-B., 2016. *The Shock of the Anthropocene. The Earth, History and Us*. London and New York: Verso.

Boulding, K.E., 1966. The Economics of the Coming Spaceship Earth. In: K.E. Boulding and H. Jarrett, eds. *Environmental Quality in a Growing Economy*. Baltimore: Johns Hopkins University Press, 3–14.

Buckminster Fuller, R., 1968. *Operating Manual for Spaceship Earth*. Carbondale: Carbondale Southern Illinois University Press.

Chakrabarty, D., 2012. Postcolonial Studies and the Challenge of Climate Change. *New Literary History*, 43(1), 1–18.

Chakrabarty, D., 2014. Climate and Capital: On Conjoined Histories. *Critical Inquiry*, 41(1), 1–23.

Chakrabarty, D., 2018. Anthropocene Time. *History and Theory*, 57(1), 5–32.

Clark, T., 2012. Scale. In: T. Cohen, ed. *Telemorphosis: Theory in the Era of Climate Change 1* [online]. Available from: https://quod.lib.umich.edu/o/ohp/10539563.

0001.001/1:8/–telemorphosis-theory-in-the-era-of-climate-change-vol-1?rgn=div1; view=fulltext [Accessed 8 January 2019].

Clark, T., 2015. *Ecocriticism on the Edge. The Anthropocene as a Threshold Concept.* London: Bloomsbury.

Clarke, B., 2011. Steps to an Ecology of Whole Systems: Whole Earth and Systemic Holism. In: H. Bergthaller and C. Schinko, eds. *Addressing Modernity: Social Systems Theory and U.S. Cultures.* Amsterdam: Rodopi, 259–288.

Clarke, M.T., and Wittenberg, D., eds., 2017. *Scale in Literature and Culture.* London: Palgrave Macmillan.

Cosgrove, D., 1994. Contested Global Visions: One-World, Whole-Earth, and the Apollo Space Photographs. *Annals of the Association of American Geographers*, 84(2), 270–294.

Eames, C. and Eames, R., 1977. *Powers of Ten.* Film. Directed by Charles Eames and Ray Eames. USA, 9 minutes.

Haff, P.K., 2014. Humans and technology in the Anthropocene: Six rules. *The Anthropocene Review*, 1(2), 126–136.

Haldane, J.B.S., 1926. On Being the right size. *Harper's Magazine*, March.

Hamilton, C., 2015. Getting the Anthropocene so Wrong. *The Anthropocene Review*, 2(2), 102–107.

Heise, U., 2008. *Sense of Place and Sense of Planet. The Environmental Imagination of the Global.* Oxford: Oxford University Press.

Horn, E., 2009. Das Leben ein Schwarm. Emergenz und Evolution in moderner Science Fiction. In: E. Horn and L. Gisi, eds. *Schwärme—Kollektive ohne Zentrum: Eine Wissensgeschichte zwischen Leben und Information.* Bielefeld: Transcript, 101–124.

Horn, E., 2016. Air Conditioning. Taming the Climate as a Dream of Civilization. In: J. Graham, ed. *Climates: Architecture and the Planetary Imaginary.* Zürich and New York: Lars Müller Publishers, 233–243.

Horn, E., 2017. Jenseits der Kindeskinder: Nachhaltigkeit im Anthropozän. *Merkur* [online], 71(814), 5–17. Available from: www.merkur-zeitschrift.de/2017/02/23/jenseits-der-kindeskinder-nachhaltigkeit-im-anthropozaen/ [Accessed 8 January 2019].

Ingold, T., 2000. Globes and Spheres: The Topology of Environmentalism. In: T. Ingold. *The Perception of the Environment.* London and New York: Routledge, 209–218.

Jenerette, G.D., and Wu, J., 2000. On the Definition of Scale. *Bulletin of the Ecological Society of America*, 81(1), 104–105.

Johns-Putra, A., 2019. *Climate Change and the Contemporary Novel.* Cambridge: Cambridge University Press.

Latour, B., 2014. Agency in the Time of the Anthropocene. *New Literary History: A Journal of Theory and Interpretation*, 45(1), 1–18.

Latour, B., 2017. *Facing Gaia. Eight Lectures on the New Climate Regime.* Trans. C. Porter. London: Polity.

Levin, S.A., 1992. The Problem of Pattern and Scale. *Ecology*, 73(6), 1943–1967.

Lovelock, J.E., 2000. *Gaia: The Practical Science of Planetary Medicine.* Oxford: Oxford University Press.

Morton, T., 2016. *Dark Ecology. For a Logic of Future Coexistence.* New York: Columbia University Press.

Schneider, B., 2018. *Klimabilder. Eine Genealogie globaler Bildpolitiken von Klima und Klimawandel.* Berlin: Matthes & Seitz.

Sloterdijk, P., [1999] 2014. *Globes: Spheres II.* Trans. W. Hoban. London: Polity.

Teilhard de Chardin, P., [1959] 1964. *The Future of Man*. New York: Harper and Row.

Tsing, A.L., 2012. On Nonscalability: The Living World is Not Amenable to Precision-Nested Scales. *Common Knowledge*, 18(3), 505–524.

Warren, B., *et al.*, 2015. Islands as model systems in ecology and evolution: Prospects fifty years after MacArthur-Wilson. *Ecology Letters*, 18(2), 200–217.

West, G., 2017. *Scale. The Universal Laws of Life and Death in Organisms, Cities and Companies*. London: Weidenfeld & Nicholson.

Woods, D., 2014. Scale Critique for the Anthropocene. *The Minnesota Review*, 83(1), 133–142.

Woods, D., 2017. Epistemic Things in Charles and Ray Eames' Powers of Ten. In: M. T. Clarke and D. Wittenberg, eds. *Scale in Literature and Culture*. London: Palgrave Macmillan.

11 Scales II

Deep time

The problems of scale raised by the Anthropocene are by no means restricted to questions of magnitude and the spatial dimensions of human agency (see Ch. 10: Scales I). The term denotes a *geological* epoch, but to the extent that it has now become an important issue for the humanities, it must also be viewed as a *historical* one. Geology and historiography, however, operate on radically different temporal scales. The scale of geological time is extremely compressed, such that processes which unfold over hundreds, thousands or millions of years, such as glaciation or the evolution of *homo sapiens*, can be comprehended as a coherent sequence. A characteristic feature of geological time is its relative uneventfulness, if by events we mean fast, systemic changes. By contrast, the temporal scales employed in the humanities are usually calibrated to the historical pace of social structures, political conflicts, and cultural change. History primarily considers developments of the last 6,000 years, with a particular focus on the modern period, i.e. roughly the past 400 years. At a higher resolution, literary scholars or social historians may hone in on the time of individual human experience (with a timescale measured in generations of about 25 years) or the even shorter intervals of political cabinets and legislatures (which rarely exceed ten years).

But the problem of timescales has implications that go far beyond historiography. It is a properly 'metahistorical' problem. Timescales determine what can count as an event: are they long-term processes such as the 'Neolithic Revolution', that is, the slow transition to a sedentary way of life, or do we count only relatively brief incidents such as the French Revolution as events? And how do we define the sites in which they occur? Do we limit ourselves to specific localities, or do we train our gaze on entire geographical regions, or even on the planet as a whole? Finally, timescales also define what kinds of actors come into play: the human species, technologies, a social class or specific communities, or even particular individuals (as in the 'great men' school of historiography). These questions of scale are important for how we conceive of historical causality. Depending on the temporal perspective, we see or do not see a causal link between the genesis of states and the emergence of sedentariness, which happens over the course of several millennia, or we perceive or fail to perceive a link between the French Revolution and France's economic malaise in the decades prior to 1789. Timescales are not just a matter that concerns the past, they are equally important for our relationship to the future. How do the events that have shaped the lives of a particular generation—what Reinhard Koselleck calls the 'space of experience'—affect their hopes and desires for the future, their 'horizon of expectation' (Koselleck 2004, p. 255)? In modernity, both the space of experience and the horizon of expectations are geared towards progressive change and the management of an immediate future which can be planned and controlled (Assmann [2013] 2019, Horn [2014] 2018). Today, the 'horizon of expectation' implies timescales that are utterly incommensurable with those of our historical space of experience, which rarely encompasses more than two or three generations, and with the short-term horizons of political or individual decision-making.

In the Anthropocene, both the past and the future unfurl into a deep time which can no longer be comprehended in terms of individual or collective human experience. The effort to imagine this deep time cannot rely only on the kinds of historical documents and artifacts on which traditional approaches to historiography are based. In the Anthropocene, time is out of joint. Even the discussion over the start dates of the Anthropocene situates the origins of the present epoch in timescales that vary between mere decades (Great Acceleration) and many millennia (Early Anthropocene) (see Ch. 2: Definitions). The future, too, suddenly opens onto temporal vistas that stretch far beyond the lives of those 'grandchildren' who play such an important symbolic role in the discourse of sustainability (Horn 2017) and in the 'ethics of posterity' (Johns-Putra 2019). Considering the timeframes in which atmospheric carbon dioxide will cycle back into the geosphere, for example, we have to think in terms of tens of thousands of years (Archer 2009, Stager 2011)—a 'deep future' that vastly exceeds modern strategies for managing futurity. Deep time plays havoc with modernity's traditional ways of taming risk, from the monetization of damages through actuarial calculations, to prevention and the precautionary principle (Chakrabarty 2014, pp. 4–9). Political decisions today have to deal with a 'long-termism' that exceeds the timescales of traditional policies of sustainability or trans-generational justice (Nordblad 2017).

This tension between the short timescales of history and geological deep time has important implications for our understanding of the Anthropocene as an *epoch*. Stratigraphy defines a geological epoch as the interval between two distinct stratigraphic markers which define the lower boundary of a stratigraphic layer, the so-called 'golden spikes' (or, more formally, GSSP: Global Boundary Stratotype Section and Point). These boundaries point to characteristic environmental changes—the emergence or disappearance of certain biological species, for example—that have left a traceable layer of material around the globe. The geochronological system of periodization is strictly hierarchical, such that a sequence of ages (each corresponding to a stratigraphic 'stage') forms an epoch (corresponding to a series of stages), a sequence of epochs forms a period, etc. In stratigraphy, an epoch (or 'series', referring to strata of rock) usually encompasses millions of years, although the epochs of the current period, the Quaternary, are already much shorter than those of the preceding Neogene and Paleogene.

In the humanities, 'epoch' has a very different meaning, and our current understanding of the term is of rather recent vintage. In its original sense, 'epoch' referred to an *event* or a break (in Ancient Greek, ἐποχή means 'pause' or 'turning back'). Around the end of the eighteenth century, the meaning of the term changed: it was now used to denote the interval *between* events. Only then did it become a genuinely historiographical category. Epochs have a beginning and an end, and this enables historians to compare them with each other (Blumenberg [1966] 1983, pp. 457–82). However, these beginnings and ends can be much blurrier than the idea of a lower boundary in stratigraphy. Historical time can be marked by asynchronicities or temporally overlapping processes, depending on the type of history being examined (e.g. epochs in art, social, or intellectual history can differ from epochs in technological or political history). As the examples of the Renaissance or the Enlightenment show, certain periods display a heightened 'epochal consciousness' as times of transition. This also holds true for the Anthropocene (Chakrabarty 2015). For these reasons, the debate over the starting date of the Anthropocene (see Ch. 2: Definitions) is of essential importance, as it determines the historical break which would define the Anthropocene as a distinctive epoch. Unless we follow the proponents of an Early Anthropocene, who conflate the Anthropocene with the Holocene, we must fix criteria which distinguish the two epochs. However, this involves radically different kinds of historical change: on the one hand, there is the transition to the warm period of the Holocene which began about 11,700 years ago; on the other, there are social transformations such as the early phase of globalization in the seventeenth century (with the Columbian Exchange), nineteenth-century industrialization, or the global spread of consumer capitalism after the Second World War (the Great Acceleration), whose duration can be measured in decades. Long-term trends in environmental and climate history are thus linked with cultural and economic, scientific and technological developments—developments that are grasped by different narratives, with different settings and agents, and unfold at vastly different temporal scales. This collision of scales entails a radical heterogeneity in the forms of historical description: climate history rubs up against the history of cultural practices, economic history and the history of technology sit alongside geological history.

In conventional historiography, longer historical ages are usually represented as large 'containers' into which the shorter historical periods are fitted, just as in stratigraphy a sequence of series forms an epoch, and several epochs combine into a period. In such a chronology, Hellenism and the Roman Empire, for example, figure as constituent parts of Classical

Antiquity. With regard to the Anthropocene, however, this way of fitting smaller temporal units into larger ones—referring to industrialization as a segment of time *within* the Holocene, or to the Great Acceleration as a late phase *within* the process of industrialization—encounters certain problems. The sheer heterogeneity of the processes involved (cultural and social history, but also environmental, ecological and geological history) and of the timescales at which they unfold makes it very difficult to squeeze the (pre-) history of the Anthropocene into a coherent, uniform narrative. It makes more sense to cast Anthropocene history as a heterogeneous sequence of thresholds or 'leaps': the transition to sedentariness as a long, protracted process towards the transformation of landscapes, but also towards different forms of energy, economic and social regimes; the onset of industrialization as an asynchronous transition between an energy regime of cyclical energy sources (such as wind, water, and sun) towards fossil fuels, but also as an era of new forms of technology and social organization.

Looked at in this way, the Anthropocene appears as a series of tipping points rather than as an epoch among others: 'The idea of a tipping point introduces a perspective that the "past" that led up to the current crisis is only partially understood, and that the current transformation is a state of flux where we have departed from past conditions, but have not yet arrived at a "new normal"' (Veland and Lynch 2016, p. 4). From such a perspective, history can be described as a succession of tipping points, and the present as an open-ended process that is perpetually in transition, always 'on the threshold', as it were. But the notion of historical tipping points also requires a shift in scale—from long, slow and apparently gradual transitions of deep history to sudden, condensed and accelerated processes. Clearly, the Anthropocene involves such shifts between different timescales; the Great Acceleration, for example, demands an entirely different temporal representation than the slow, protracted and dispersed transformations of the Holocene.

Given the heterogeneity of the narratives and timescales which characterize the Anthropocene, it makes sense to describe it as an 'epoch' in the older sense of that word, i.e. it is not a discrete *segment* of time so much as an *event* (cf. Clark 2015, Bonneuil and Fressoz 2016). This suggests that it would be preferable not to settle on a single starting date, and perhaps that the Anthropocene ought not to be officially adopted into geological nomenclature: 'the Anthropocene, so long as it is seen as a measure of humans' impact on the planet, can have only plural beginnings *and must remain an informal rather than a formal category of geology*, capable of *bearing multiple stories* about human institutions and morality' (Chakrabarty 2018, p. 20, emphasis EH). If the Anthropocene is conceived as an event, it is a process that takes place across a range of spatial and temporal dimensions, and at different rates. As Rob Nixon has argued, the temporality of the Great Acceleration is both accompanied by and stands in contrast to a 'slow violence' which inconspicuously corrodes ecological environments and the traditional ways of life that depend on them (Nixon 2011). This form of destruction proceeds in small increments, and its full consequences only become apparent over the long term. For that reason, it resists representation in the popular media—not only because public attention cycles are driven by abrupt, spectacular events, but also because many of the relevant phenomena (for example, increased rates of cancer due to environmental pollution or disruptions of the water cycle) can only be grasped statistically and involve periods of latency which make it difficult to establish a clear connection between causes and their visible or measurable effects (Horn [2014] 2018, pp. 163–73). The Anthropocene encompasses divergent, often incommensurable temporalities: on the one hand, the frenetic increase of consumption, technological innovation, mobility and communication; on the other, comparatively slow-paced ecological and social changes which are difficult to represent, and which therefore tend to remain below the radar of public and political discourse.

To think of the Anthropocene as an event also indicates that it is not a temporary crisis after which things will go back to normal, but rather an irreversible break. This is most obvious with regard to climate history: the Anthropocene disrupts the Holocene period of relative climatic stability. Yet framed as the end of the Holocene, the Anthropocene points us towards the even larger timescales of the Quaternary period, and more specifically of the Middle Pleistocene (between 781,000 and 126,000 years ago), during which *homo sapiens* emerged. Whereas average temperatures during the early history of our species ranged between 8°C below and 2°C above those of today, they varied by no more than 1.5°C in the Holocene, during which time most of what we recognize as human history and civilization took shape. In the larger scheme of climate history, this relatively warm and stable period constitutes an anomaly. Only now that the potential end of this phase is in sight, can we recognize a stable, temperate climate as the well-tempered cradle of civilization. To leave the Holocene is to break with the conditions that gave birth to the process of which we ourselves are the product.

The Anthropocene thus not only changes our view of the present, but also casts the deep past in a new light. The Holocene no longer appears as the historical stage on which 'man makes himself', to quote Vere Gordon Childe's titular summary of the 'Neolithic Revolution'—referring to the combination of agriculture, animal husbandry, and urbanism that gradually began to emerge about 12,000 years ago (Childe 1941). With hindsight, the Middle Holocene appears as a phase when important ecological thresholds were beginning to be crossed (Smith 1995): once a sedentary, agricultural lifestyle is adopted, once cities and states have been formed, there is no path that would lead back to a hunter-gatherer society, other than catastrophic collapse. James C. Scott has shown that far from being a triumph of human self-fashioning, this transition was more like a fall from grace: in contrast to hunter-gatherer groups, life in the new agrarian societies was steeply hierarchical, disease-ridden, and prone to malnutrition and famine (Scott 2017).

Our own present, understood as the onset of the Anthropocene, can be similarly conceived: it is not so much a crisis as the barely noticeable, but fundamentally irreversible, crossing of a threshold.

This heterogeneity of timescales and temporalities calls for completely new forms of historiography. As Dipesh Chakrabarty has pointed out, climate change challenges traditional categories of historical thinking: 'Anthropogenic explanations of climate change spell the collapse of the age-old humanist distinction between natural history and human history' (2009, p. 201). Yet this distinction is, in fact, not so very old. It dates back only to the early nineteenth century, to the historical moment when the natural sciences and the humanities parted ways and a sharp division was made between the timescales of human history and those of natural history. Until then, biblical chronology had furnished a shared temporal framework which linked human history to the history of the world. Only with the modern discovery of geological time, which was measured in millions of years and in which the appearance of the human species seems like an afterthought, did the Earth's history become a 'plot without man' (Beer 2000, p. 17). Thus nature turned into the mute and immobile background for the agitations of human history. Charles Lyell's *Principles of Geology* ([1830–1833] 1997), a founding text of the discipline, articulated a set of basic assumptions which have shaped geological science up to the present. His theory of geological change excluded both abrupt alterations and causal forces that cannot be observed in the present. The first of these principles is usually referred to as 'gradualism'. It proposes that changes in nature occur slowly and continuously, not in sudden leaps. The second principle of 'uniformitarianism' states that the processes which shaped the Earth in the past must also be at work today. It basically excludes the emergence of entirely new forces and influences. Because geology changes at a vastly slower pace than human society, Lyell rejected the idea that human action could bring about a lasting transformation of landscapes and climates (Lyell [1830–1833] 1997, p. 102).

The split between natural and human time was also amplified by parallel developments in the humanities. With the advent of historicism in the early nineteenth century, the study of human culture is decisively uncoupled from nature, which is seen as relatively static and passive, as either a material resource or an obstacle to human endeavor. Human history was henceforth defined as unfolding within an ever-expanding domain of self-determination, progressing towards an emancipation from, and ultimately a 'victory' over, the forces of nature. The historian Jules Michelet expressed this mindset with drastic metaphors:

> With the world, a war began that will end with the world, and not before: the war of man against nature, of spirit against matter, of liberty against fatality. History is nothing but the story of this endless struggle. [...] And it will go on, without any doubt, for as long as human will braces itself against the influence of race and climate [...]. Of the two adversaries, one

never changes, the other changes and becomes stronger. Nature remains the same, while man daily gains some advantage over her.

(Michelet 2013, p. 24)

Man changes, nature remains the same—at least on the timescales that matter for human beings.

This sharp distinction between nature and culture, between natural and human history, between the slow pace of geological change and the quick pulse of human action, lies at the origin of the humanities as they have been practiced since the nineteenth century. If the Anthropocene requires us to overcome this split, such an effort can build on several historiographic approaches that have developed over recent decades. Among them are environmental history, which enquires into the relationship between societies and their ecological environments (see Ch. 4: Nature and culture), and the closely related fields of energy history and social ecology, which examine the social and ecological consequences of changing energy regimes (see Ch. 9: Energy). These approaches contribute directly to a history of the Anthropocene. However, they generally remain within familiar historical timeframes and chronologies.

A more radical departure from traditional historiography is proposed by the advocates of Deep History. They focus not only on the history of the human species, but especially on the earliest cultural practices (e.g. tool use, hunting, fire), and their transformative effects on the physiology, environments and social structures of *homo sapiens* and their immediate ancestors (for a popular account of Deep History, see Harari [2011] 2014; for an indepth discussion of its methodological implications, see Shryock and Smail 2011, pp. 16–49). Deep History draws attention to the long process by which *anatomically* modern humans gradually eclipsed other hominids and developed into *behaviorally* modern humans (see Ch. 5: The *anthropos*). It operates within a temporal horizon of roughly 2.5 million years. The decisive question is how such a history can be narrated and integrated into an account of the transformative processes that constitute modern history.

One point of convergence is the emphasis on thresholds and qualitative leaps in the historical process: Deep History, too, is 'punctuated by momentous leaps in population, energy flow, efficiency, levels of political organization and degrees of connectivity' (Shryock and Smail 2011, p. 247). Deep History neither believes that 'man made himself' (Childe 1941), nor does it try simply to 'naturalize' the human species. Instead of familiar historiographic tropes such as 'genesis' or 'revolution', Shryock and Smail propose the model of a *coevolutionary spiral*, so as better to describe the dynamic processes of mutual transformation that bind humans to other biological species and to their physical environments (2011, p. 19).

Perhaps the most ambitious form of historiography that seeks to integrate the various timescales not only into a single narrative but even into a unitary model of historical development is Big History (Christian [2004] 2011, Spier

1998). David Christian, a leading advocate of this approach, describes Big History as

> the attempt to understand the past *at all possible scales*, up to those of cosmology, and to do so in ways that do justice both to the contingency and specificity of the past [...]. [Big History] will treat human history as one member of a large family of historical disciplines that includes biology, the Earth sciences, astronomy and cosmology. By doing so, it will blur the borderline between history and the natural sciences [...] as history rediscovers an interest *in deep, even law-like patterns of change.*
>
> (Christian 2010, p. 7, emphasis EH)

Christian proposes, rather immodestly, that Big History can play the role of a 'modern creation myth' (Christian [2004] 2011, p. 1). What is in fact at stake in this approach, however, is not the mythical quality of its narratives but rather the question of whether all the divergent, seemingly disparate, forms of knowledge in modern society can be combined into a meaningful whole: 'Beneath the awesome diversity and complexity of modern knowledge, there is an underlying unity and coherence, ensuring that different timescales really do have something to say to each other' (Christian [2004] 2011, p. 3). In stark contrast to traditional historiography, which focuses mainly on the roughly 5,500 years of documented history, Christian suggests that the history of humankind must be narrated within the larger history of life, which in turn is nested in the history of the solar system, and then in the history of the universe. In his bestselling *Maps of Time* (2004), Christian foregrounds cosmological and geological timescales, thus pointedly de-emphasizing human history.

The coherence of this macroscopic perspective is underwritten by the recurrence of similar patterns of change as ever higher states of complexity emerge from a shapeless background. Thus, Christian compares the development of early human settlements with the process of star formation:

> In the early universe, gravity took hold of clouds of atoms, and sculpted them into stars and galaxies. In [...] this chapter, we will see how, by a sort of social gravity, cities and states were sculpted from scattered communities of farmers. As farming populations gathered in larger and denser communities, interactions between different groups increased and the social pressure rose until, in a striking parallel with star formation, new structures suddenly appeared, together with a new level of complexity.
>
> (Christian [2004] 2011, p. 245)

This passage illustrates just how Christian aims to make the vastly different timescales of cosmology and of human history commensurate with each other: much like in the fractal geometry of the Mandelbrot set, there are recursive processes at work which produce similar patterns at every scale.

Such fractal, self-similar structures allow for a smooth transition between timescales, because the same formal principles apply at all levels. This makes it possible to telescope different timescales into each other without the irritating scale effects that occur when we try to replicate a structure across different quantitative or spatial scales (see Ch. 10: Scales I). In Big History, the pattern that recurs across all scales is the gradual increase in complexity, the figure of a self-replicating, ever-ramifying order which resists the pull of entropy, whether on a cosmic, a biological or, finally, a social level. It manifests itself as much in the birth of stars over millions of years as it does in the formation of social structures over hundreds or thousands of years. Fractal patterns translate the macroscopic into the microscopic world, natural timescales into human ones. Big History thus proposes to overcome the epistemic split between nature and culture—but on the basis of an unabashedly teleological narrative: Christian's cosmos is one in which everything leads up to 'us'—if not to us as human beings, then at least to ever-more complex ordered states.

But the deep time the Anthropocene invites us to consider is not only the past. It also projects a deep future which explodes the temporal horizon of all established forms of prognostication and planning. As climate historian David Archer writes: 'Our fossil fuel deposits, 100 million years old, could be gone in a few centuries, leaving climate impacts that will last for hundreds of millennia. The lifetime of fossil fuel CO_2 in the atmosphere is a few centuries, plus 25% that lasts essentially forever' (2009, p. 11). By burning fossil fuels, humans are not only frittering away the legacy of 100 million years in the geological equivalent of an all-night binge. They are also hurling themselves into a vertiginously deep future of unstable climate. This entails a radical mismatch between the brief time horizons of political decision-making and the barely longer timescales implied in many forms of managing the future, such as the precautionary principle or the idea of sustainability, on the one hand, and the unimaginably long-lasting consequences of climate change, on the other. For Chakrabarty, the abyss that separates the temporality of climate change from the temporalities underlying modern forms of time-management points to the fundamental difficulty of getting an epistemic and political grip on the deep future of the Anthropocene (2014, pp. 4–9). This difficulty is also reflected in the various attempts to reduce the idea of humans as a geological *force* into the categories and timescales of political *power* (Chakrabarty 2018). Mediating between geological and human timescales is one of the fundamental challenges of the Anthropocene.

If a future is so distant as to be unfathomable, we often fall back on narratives which enable us to examine the present from the perspective of an imagined future (Horn [2014] 2018). By positing a particular, determinate future, such narratives also enable a clearer picture of their own historical moment to emerge. In the prologue of his popular introduction to the Anthropocene as a geological concept, *The Earth After Us* (2008), Jan Zalasiewicz does precisely that: he imagines a team of extra-terrestrial archaeologists visiting our planet 100 million years into the future. Zalasiewicz imagines a stratigraphic perspective on our present and thereby lays open the heuristic fiction that stands at the center of the notion of the Anthropocene as a geological epoch. To speak of the present as the Anthropocene is to look at it *in retrospect*, as it were, from the vantage point of an imagined future in which the present will have become nothing but a thin layer in the rock.

The vast timescales of the Anthropocene also have significant biopolitical implications; they call into question the various ways in which contemporary society seeks to anticipate and manage the future. In most cases, such attempts remain focused on our figurative 'children' or 'grandchildren'—members of the human species to whom we are genealogically related and whose lifetime overlaps with our own. Donna Haraway has argued that in the face of the Anthropocene, this way of conceiving of our ethical obligations is much too constrained. Drawing on anthropological scholarship which emphasizes the flexibility of the concept of 'kinship', she argues that we should rework our understanding of kinship so that it would no longer be limited to blood relations, but also include very distant forms of human life, as well as members of other biological species (Haraway 2016; see also Ch. 8: Biopolitics). A politics and an ethics that would be commensurate with the challenges of a deep future cannot only be oriented towards the welfare of our closest biological relatives in the next few generations, but must open itself to radical alterity. In this effort, the deep history of our species is of indispensable value, because it gives us a sense of human life long before, and perhaps after, civilization.

If the remote future appears increasingly incalculable, so does the immediate future. The more we understand about the nature of the complex systems we inhabit, the more we are forced to recognize the radical opacity of the dynamics that govern them. As a highly complex, self-organizing system, the Earth is marked by synergistic effects and tipping points, that is, moments when quantitative change tips the system into a qualitatively new state (Gladwell 2000). Rockström's outline of a 'safe operating space' for humanity is designed to ensure that we stay clear of such tipping points. But it is in the nature of highly complex systems that it is very difficult to anticipate them in advance. That such systems are self-regulating does not preclude that they can reach a point of saturation or a critical mass (as a chemist or a physicist would put it, respectively), precipitating a phase of radical instability before the system converges on a new equilibrium. In everyday language, we call this 'catastrophe'.

What we can already anticipate is that the future, just like the deep past, will be marked by tipping points and episodes of sudden, profound change. Clive Hamilton therefore suggests that we give up the gradualist and uniformitarian mindset that has shaped geology—and not only geology—since the days of Lyell. Instead, we should adopt a world-view closer to that of Lyell's intellectual antagonist Georges Cuvier, who conceived of the Earth's history in terms of a series of cataclysmic transformations:

> The Anthropocene is [...] not a continuation of the past but a step change in the biogeological history of the Earth. The previous step change, out of the Pleistocene and into the Holocene, saw a 5°C change in global average temperature and a 120-m change in sea levels. Geologically speaking, the Anthropocene event, occurring over an extremely short period, has been a very abrupt regime shift, *closer to an instance of catastrophism than uniformitarianism.*
>
> (Hamilton 2016, p. 100, emphasis in the original)

Here, the geology of the Anthropocene becomes a history of catastrophes—and is, for precisely that reason, eminently political. It might not be the recurrence of a single fractal pattern of ever-increasing complexity as Big History suggests by making human and geological timescales commensurate. It is rather a history of repeating episodes of radical upheaval and transformation. Viewed in the larger context of the Earth's history, the appearance of the human species, and especially the massive transformations wrought by the Great Acceleration, resemble the kind of abrupt change caused by huge volcanic eruptions or meteorite impacts. Zalasiewicz makes this point with inimitable succinctness: 'We are the meteor' (Zalasiewicz *et al.* 2017).

EH

References

Archer, D., 2009. *The Long Thaw. How Humans Are Changing the Next 100,000 Years of Earth's Climate.* Princeton: Princeton University Press.

Assmann, A., [2013] 2019. *Is time out of joint? On the rise and fall of the modern time regime.* Trans. S. Clift. Ithaca: Cornell University Press.

Beer, G., 2000. *Darwin's Plots. Evolutionary narrative in Darwin, George Eliot and nineteenth-century fiction.* 2nd ed. Cambridge: Cambridge University Press.

Blumenberg, H., [1966] 1983. *The Legitimacy of the Modern Age.* Trans. R.M. Wallace. 7th ed. Cambridge: MIT Press.

Bonneuil, C., and Fressoz, J.-B., 2016. *The Shock of the Anthropocene: The Earth, History and Us.* Trans. D. Fernbach. London and New York: Verso.

Chakrabarty, D., 2009. The Climate of History. Four Theses. *Critical Inquiry*, 35(2), 197–222.

Chakrabarty, D., 2014. Climate and Capital: On Conjoined Histories. *Critical Inquiry*, 41(1), 1–23.

Chakrabarty, D., 18–19 February2015. *The Human Condition in the Anthropocene, The Tanner Lectures in Human Values* [online]. New Haven: Yale University. Available from: https://tannerlectures.utah.edu/Chakrabarty%20manuscript.pdf [Accessed 14 April 2019].

Chakrabarty, D., 2018. Anthropocene Time. *History and Theory*, 57(1), 5–32.

Childe, V.G., 1941. *Man Makes Himself*. London: Watts.

Christian, D., 2010. The Return of Universal History. *History and Theory*, 49(4), 6–27.

Christian, D., [2004] 2011. *Maps of Time. An Introduction to Big History*. 2nd ed. Berkeley: University of California Press.

Clark, T., 2015. *Ecocriticism at the Edge. The Anthropocene as a Threshold Concept*. London and New York: Bloomsbury.

Gladwell, M., 2000. *The Tipping Point. How little things can make a big difference*. Boston: Little, Brown.

Hamilton, C., 2016. The Anthropocene as rupture. *The Anthropocene Review*, 3(2), 93–106.

Harari, Y.N., [2011] 2014. *Sapiens. A Brief History of Humankind*. Trans. Y.N. Harari, J. Purcell and H. Watzmann. London: Harvill Secker.

Haraway, D., 2016. *Staying with the Trouble: Making Kin in the Chthulucene*. Durham and London: Duke University Press.

Horn, E., [2014] 2018. *The Future as Catastrophe. Imagining Disaster in the Modern Age*. Trans. V. Pakis. New York: Columbia University Press.

Horn, E., 2017. Jenseits der Kindeskinder: Nachhaltigkeit im Anthropozän. *Merkur* [online], 71(814), 5–17. Available from: www.merkur-zeitschrift.de/2017/02/23/jenseits-der-kindeskinder-nachhaltigkeit-im-anthropozaen/ [Accessed 8 January 2019].

Johns-Putra, A., 2019. *Climate Change and the Contemporary Novel*. Cambridge: Cambridge University Press.

Koselleck, R., 2004. 'Space of Experience' and 'Horizon of Expectation': Two Historical Categories [1979]. In: R. Koselleck. *Futures Past. On the Semantics of Historical Time*. Trans. K. Tribe. New York: Columbia University Press, 255–275.

Lyell, C., [1830–1833] 1997. *Principles of Geology*. London: Penguin Classics.

Michelet, J., 2013. Introduction to world history (1831). Trans. F. Kimmich. In: J. Michelet. *On History*. Trans. F. Kimmich, L. Gossman and E.K. Kaplan. Cambridge: Open Book Publishers, 23–118.

Nixon, R., 2011. *Slow violence and the environmentalism of the poor*. Cambridge: Harvard University Press.

Nordblad, J., 2017. Time for politics: How a conceptual history of forests can help us politicize the long term. *European Journal of Social Theory*, 20(1), 164–182.

Scott, J.C., 2017. *Against the grain. A deep history of the earliest states*. New Haven: Yale University Press.

Shryrock, A., and Smail, D.L., 2011. Introduction. In: A. Shryrock, D.L. Smail and T.K. Earle, eds. *Deep History. The Architecture of Past and Present*. Berkeley: University of California Press, 16–49.

Smith, B.D., 1995. *The Emergence of Agriculture*. New York: Sci Am Library.

Spier, F., 1998. *Big History: Was die Geschichte im Innersten zusammenhält*. Darmstadt: Wissenschaftliche Buchgesellschaft.

Stager, C., 2011. *Deep Future. The next 100,000 years of life on Earth*. New York: Thomas Dunne Books.

Veland, S., and Lynch, A.H., 2016. Scaling the Anthropocene: How the stories we tell matter. *Geoforum*, 72, 1–5.

Zalasiewicz, J., 2008. *The Earth After Us. What legacy will humans leave in the rocks?* Oxford: Oxford University Press.

Zalasiewicz, J., *et al.*, 2017. *We are the Meteor. Interview in* WNYC [online]. Available from: www.wnyc.org/story/we-are-meteor/ [Accessed 8 January 2019].

12 Conclusion

How Western is the Anthropocene?

To think the Anthropocene is to think along fault lines, in terms of tensions and contradictions. Our guiding assumption in this book is that this is especially true for the humanities. Their bailiwick are traditions that are specific to particular languages and cultures, and historical epochs which rarely span more than a century. The Anthropocene challenges the humanities to place their knowledge and their methods in relation to the super-sized image of the planet which Earth system science and other scientific disciplines have drawn. They are thus compelled to think of the whole, but they must not lose sight of the parts. In rising to this challenge, we invariably run the risk of mistaking our own perspective, shaped as it is by biographical accidents and particular interests, for an objective 'view from nowhere' (Nagel 1986). There is no panacea for this problem. This makes it all the more important that we reflect on the position from which we see what we see, so that others may have an easier time to see the things that we don't.

This book is the result of extensive dialogues with many colleagues from Europe and North America, Asia and Australia, with literary scholars and historians, geographers and geologists. But the bulk of it was written in Asia: in Bangkok, on Bali and Taiwan. Looking at the wildly proliferating discourse on the Anthropocene from this vantage point, we are struck above all by one thing: despite its claims to universality, Anthropocene talk remains largely a Western phenomenon. In Thailand, Indonesia or Taiwan, no magazine covers were devoted to the Anthropocene, no exhibitions, TV specials, or bestselling books. Much the same appears to be true for most other countries in Asia. If the term even comes up, it is almost exclusively in a scholarly context (with reference to China: Weigelin-Schwiedrzik 2018, p. 19).

At the same time, the importance of this world region for the Anthropocene can hardly be overstated. The principal reason why all the curves of the Great Acceleration are still pointing relentlessly upwards (except, one might add, that for population) is the mind-blowing economic dynamism of this region. Since the 1980s, about 2 billion people have joined the 'global middle class', and the Organisation for Economic Co-operation and Development (OECD) anticipates that another 2 billion will follow over the next decade—the vast majority of them in Asia. Around the middle of the century, it is calculated that 80% of this global middle class will live in Asia (Kharas 2017, p. 11). Modern consumer capitalism may have originated in the Western industrial nations, but anyone who spends a day in Seoul or Shanghai, Taipei or Singapore will realize that the West is no longer calling the shots when it comes to the more or less glamorous squandering of money and natural resources. How the Anthropocene plays out will to a large extent depend on what form middle-class consumption patterns take in Asia. Any talk of how 'we' should comport ourselves in the face of the Anthropocene that doesn't take into account the outsized role Asia will play in it is pointless.

It is important to emphasize that the lack of resonance of the Anthropocene concept in Asia does not seem to reflect a general lack of interest in global ecological problems. Climate change, plastic waste in the oceans, and the loss of biodiversity are important topics of public debate, even though they are often overshadowed by local environmental issues such as air and water pollution. And yet, the reframing of all these issues in terms of the Anthropocene doesn't seem to hold the obvious fascination that it does for many Western intellectuals. This raises the question of whether there is something about the concept that is particularly attuned to 'Western' ways of thinking.

Amitav Ghosh offers a possible answer to this question. Like Bruno Latour, Ghosh understands the Anthropocene as the historical moment when the Western conception of modernity as open-ended progress collides with the finitude of the Earth. In the West, the vast discrepancy between living conditions in the industrial nations and the (post-)colonial periphery was usually interpreted as reflecting different degrees of progress—implying that the rest of the world would in due time catch up with the West. Intellectuals from the periphery, however, understood from very early on that the project of modernization was to a significant degree based on exploitation and expropriation. They also realized that the promise of progress and prosperity for *all* people could not possibly be realized. Ghosh quotes a speech by Mahatma Gandhi from 1928 which reads like an anticipation of the Neomalthusian fears which would grip the West two decades later: 'God forbid that India should ever take to industrialism after the manner of the West. If an entire nation of 300 millions [sic] took to similar economic exploitation, it would strip the world bare like locusts' (cited in Ghosh 2016, p. 111). The sheer number of people in Asia reveals the universalism of modernity as a sham. In the West, the Anthropocene comes as a shock because it disrupts the historical horizon of expectation. Asia shares neither the Western horizon of expectation nor its space of experience. For that reason, the Anthropocene is not experienced as a radical break.

Ghosh concludes that people in Asia are more sensitive to ecological limits than Westerners (ibid., pp. 111f.). If one considers the uncompromising fervor with which countries such as South Korea, Taiwan, the People's

Republic of China or India have plunged into the project of modernity over the past few decades, however, this seems more than doubtful. But it is surely true that many Asian societies have a longer and more tangled experience with the transformation of their natural environments. Wet-rice farming, which has been of essential importance for many Asian civilizations for millennia, changes ecological processes much more profoundly than the traditional forms of agriculture which prevailed in Europe, at a level comparable to 'modern mono-cropped fields' (Morrison 2018, n.p.). The archaeologist Kathleen D. Morrison has pointed out that current models of the Earth system frequently underestimate the global effects of agriculture because they use Europe as their benchmark. A greater familiarity with the environmental history of Asia, Morrison argues, will make it clear that 'anthropogenic change actually has a longer, more complex, or more variable trajectory than is generally assumed' (ibid.). In a similar vein, Mark Hudson proposes that the region provides a wealth of 'case studies of long-term strategies for sustaining diversity, memory, and crisis response within Anthropocene social-ecological systems' (2014, p. 955).

It is not surprising, then, that Chinese scientists tend to favor Ruddiman's hypothesis of an early Anthropocene, beginning with sedentism and the transition to agriculture (Weigelin-Schwiedrzik 2018, pp. 19f.). The historian Mark Elvin has shown that China began to transform its natural environment at a grand scale long before the advent of Western modernity. The early development of states with a highly efficient administrative apparatus enabled gigantic infrastructure projects such as the Grand Canal which linked the Yangtze and the Yellow River in the north of the country, over a length of almost 1,800 kilometers. This facilitated a much more intensive, but also more destructive use of ecological resources than in Europe. Daoism and Buddhism, whose wisdom is often touted as offering the key to a more 'harmonious' relationship to nature, did very little to slow deforestation and species loss (Elvin 2004, p. 471). Already by the thirteenth century, China had developed a system of cultivation which, thanks to irrigation pumps and high-yield strains of rice, was able to feed twice as many people per acre of farmland as the most advanced forms of agriculture in Europe (Krausmann et al. 2008, p. 642). At the end of the eighteenth century, China's population numbered 300 million, twice as much as all of Western and Central Europe combined. But this also meant that the country was operating at the limits of its ecological carrying capacity. In contrast to the European nations, it could rely neither on fossil fuels nor on imports from the New World to overcome this bottleneck. While the Industrial Revolution was taking off at the far end of the Eurasian landmass, China descended into chaos. During the period of civil strife around the middle of the nineteenth century, which was accompanied by epidemics and severe famine, roughly 20% of the population died, about 100 million people (Lee and Zhang 2013, p. 295), while the Qing emperors were repeatedly humiliated by European military interventions.

In the nineteenth century, China, India, and many other Asian countries were the great losers of modernization. Against this historical backdrop, the message that modernity is done for—at the very moment when Asia is finally catching up with the West!—obviously holds very little appeal. China's effort to recover its accustomed position at the center of the political world order is a particularly poignant example of how the geopolitical struggle for power impacts the Earth system. If the Great Acceleration was driven by the Cold War, we are currently living through a new phase of geopolitical rivalry between the old and new industrial nations, between Asia and 'the West'—with equally devastating ecological consequences. Not only the development in China itself, but above all the 'Belt and Road' project, which is supposed to link the country with Europe and Africa and to foster economic exchange with its Asian neighbors (Tracy et al. 2017), is a replay of the gigantic investments in freeways, airports and hydroelectric dams through which the rivals of the Cold War sought to buttress their economic and political power.

Once again, this development entails the enclosure and destruction of common pool resources that support local subsistence economies. This was a characteristic feature of the development that led us into the Anthropocene, and it remains in full swing—not only in Asia, but also Latin America and especially in Africa, which presently holds about 60% or the world's uncultivated arable land (Hecht 2018). The chief difference today is that the investors luring local governments with the promise of jobs and foreign currency no longer come only from the old industrial nations, but just as often from China, South Korea, or India (Pearce 2012). In countries such as Indonesia, Kenya, or Brazil, the destruction of tropical forests is accelerating. They are replaced by soybean, sugar cane or palm oil plantations, the products of which flow into the wealthy metropolitan centers. The loss of these forests is a catastrophe not only for the local populations, because the soils quickly degrade and become worthless. It is also of global consequence: tropical forests are among the most biodiverse ecosystems in the world, and they are one of the largest sinks in the global carbon cycle. The amount of carbon dioxide entering the atmosphere as a result of deforestation exceeds the sum of all emissions from combustion engines (Scheer and Moss 2019). Over the past few years, forest fires in Indonesia, often deliberately set in order to open up the land for economic development, have produced more carbon dioxide than fossil fuel use in the entire European Union (Huijnen et al. 2016).

These examples make it clear that if we wish to get a handle on the Anthropocene, it is useless to tally up historical debts. The old industrial nations of Europe and North America may have started the recent transformation of the Earth system, but they are no longer in the driver's seat. Today, the Asian nations are as much a part of the problem—and they must be a part of the solution, if there is to be one. In this regard, too, it is worthwhile to take a closing look at China. Since the turn of the millennium, the ideal of an 'ecological civilization' (*shengtai wenming* 生态文明) has come to play an increasingly prominent role in the political agenda of the Chinese Communist Party (Heurtebise and Gaffric 2017). In his address to the 19th national congress of the party, Xi Jinping listed 'harmony between human and nature' among the 14 goals to which the government ought to devote itself over the next five years (Xi 2017). These are not just empty words. The party understands very well that the devastating ecological consequences of rapid economic development have the potential to undo not only the country's newly won prosperity, but also its own political legitimacy. More than any other country in the world, China has sought to replace gross domestic product (GDP) as a measure of economic well-being with a so-called 'green GDP'—a form of accounting which would factor in ecological costs. The technical hurdles of putting such a system into practice are considerable, and thus far it has only been implemented at the local level. However, there is a good chance that it will eventually be introduced nationally and become part of the criteria for the evaluation of party cadres. If this were to happen, China would set a global standard for ecologically sound economic policy (Weigelin-Schwiedrzik 2018).

For many people in the West, such a development would come as a shock, because it would put into question the conviction, widely shared in the West, that only a democratic, emancipatory politics will be able to meet the challenges of the Anthropocene (e.g. Bonneuil and Fressoz 2016, Purdy 2015). By contrast, the path that China seems to have chosen might best be described as a radical and authoritarian form of ecomodernism, and it is not unlikely that many Asian countries will follow its lead. Urban planners in the region envision 'smart cities' in which the consumer behavior of city dwellers is closely monitored. If the 'green GDP' became official policy, the data thus collected would play a key role: 'Green GDP accounting needs to include data on how individuals use rare resources such as water and energy, treat their waste and take care of their health by eating what they are supposed to eat, sticking to their daily sport activities and refraining from [...] drinking and smoking' (Weigelin-Schwiedrzik 2018, p. 34). In combination with a social credit system, such as the Chinese government has been experimenting with over the past few years, this could give rise to a comprehensive system of biopolitical control which completely dissolves the boundary between the private and the public sphere.

Whether such a system would actually be able to get the ecological problems of the Anthropocene under control is an open question. From a Western standpoint, it certainly represents a terrifying vision—but that is something we also like to say about climate change, even as we comfort ourselves that we are helping to save the Earth by lugging our groceries home in a cotton tote bag. Given the glaring inability of liberal democracies to limit consumption to a level that is 'compatible with the permanence of genuine human life', as Hans Jonas ([1979] 1984, p. 11) once put it, the West would be well-advised to tone down the moral outrage. If humanity is to have a desirable future, we must not only change our habits of consumption, but our economic, political and legal systems, our infrastructures, our pedagogy, our art, and our everyday lives. These paths into the future have yet to be paved, and they surely will follow many different routes. The 1992 United Nations Framework Convention on Climate Change expressed this insight in a formula that leaves little room for improvement. It holds not only for climate change, but for all the challenges of the Anthropocene: the preservation of the Earth system is a task for which humanity bears 'common but differentiated responsibilities' (United Nations 1992).

HB

References

Bonneuil, C., and Fressoz, J.-B., 2016. *The Shock of the Anthropocene. The Earth, History and Us.* London and New York: Verso.

Elvin, M., 2004. *The Retreat of the Elephants. An Environmental History of China.* New Haven: Yale University Press.

Ghosh, A., 2016. *The Great Derangement. Climate Change and the Unthinkable.* Chicago and London: The University of Chicago Press.

Hecht, G., 2018. The African Anthropocene. *Aeon* [online], 7 February. Available from: https://aeon.co/essays/if-we-talk-about-hurting-our-planet-who-exactly-is-the-we. [Accessed 24 April 2019].

Heurtebise, J.-Y., and Gaffric, G., 2017. Éco-Orientalisme et 'civilisation écologique': entre mythologie académique et construction politique. In: J.-P. Maréchal, ed. *La Chine face au mur de l'environnement?* Paris: CNRS Editions, 175–194.

Hudson, M.J., 2014. Placing Asia in the Anthropocene: Histories, Vulnerabilities, Responses. *The Journal of Asian Studies*, 73(4), 941–962.

Huijnen, V., et al., 2016. Fire Carbon Emissions Over Maritime Southeast Asia in 2015 Largest Since 1997. *Scientific Reports* [online], 6(26886), no pages. Available from: www.nature.com/articles/srep26886 [Accessed 12 March 1019].

Jonas, H., [1979] 1984. *The Imperative of Responsibility: In Search of an Ethics for the Technological Age.* Trans. J. Jonas and D. Herr. Chicago: Chicago University Press.

Kharas, H., 2017. The Unprecedented Expansion of the Global Middle-Class. An Update. *Brookings Global Economy and Development Working Paper* [online], 100. Available from: www.brookings.edu/wp-content/uploads/2017/02/global_20170228_global-middle-class.pdf [Accessed 14 February 2019].

Krausmann, F., et al., 2008. The Global Sociometabolic Transition: Past and Present Metabolic Profiles and Their Future Trajectories. *Journal of Industrial Ecology*, 12(5–6), 637–656.

Lee, H.F., and Zhang, D.D., 2013. A Tale of Two Population Crises in Recent Chinese History. *Climatic Change*, 116(2), 285–308.

Morrison, K.D., 2018. Provincializing the Anthropocene: Eurocentrism in the Earth System. In: G. Cederlöf and M. Rangarajan, eds. *At Nature's Edge. The Global Present and Long-term History.* New Delhi: Oxford University Press. Kindle.

Nagel, T., 1986. *The View From Nowhere.* Oxford: Oxford University Press.

Pearce, F., 2012. *The Land Grabbers. The New Fight Over Who Owns the Earth.* Boston: Beacon Press.

Purdy, J., 2015. *After Nature. A Politics for the Anthropocene.* Cambridge: Harvard University Press.

Scheer, R., and Moss, D., 2019. Deforestation and Its Extreme Effect on Global Warming. *Scientific American* [online]. Available from: www.scientificamerican.com/article/deforestation-and-global-warming/ [Accessed 12 March 2019].

Tracy, E.F., *et al.*, 2017. China's New Eurasian Ambitions. The Environmental Risks of the Silk Road Economic Belt. *Eurasian Geography and Economics*, 58(1), 56–88.

United Nations, 1992. *United Nations Framework Convention of Climate Change* [online]. Available from: https://unfccc.int/resource/docs/convkp/conveng.pdf [Accessed 14 March 2019].

Weigelin-Schwiedrzik, S., 2018. Doing Things With Numbers: Chinese Approaches to the Anthropocene. *International Communication of Chinese Culture*, 5(1), 17–37.

Xi, J., 2017. *Report at the 19th CPC National Congress* [online]. Available from: www.xinhuanet.com/english/special/2017-11/03/c_136725942.htm [Accessed 12 March 2019].

Index